Between Science and Economics

ISSN: 2051-6304

Series Editor: Frank Witte *(University College London, UK)*

The series *Between Science and Economics* aims at providing a mix of undergraduate and graduate textbooks, research monographs and essay and paper collections to serve as a library and resource for teachers, students, graduate students and experts studying fields in which economic and science issues and problems come together. The thrust of the series is to demonstrate that the contributing disciplines can benefit from learning from one another as well as contributing to the resolution of multi- and interdisciplinary questions. This involves the economic principles at work in science and technology as well as the roots of economic processes in biological, chemical and physical fundamentals in nature. It also encompasses the problems associated with complexity, order-to-disorder transitions, uncertainty, deterministic chaos and geometric principles faced by economics as well as many of the natural sciences.

Published

Vol. 1 *Blockchain Economics: Implications of Distributed Ledgers*
Markets, Communications Networks, and Algorithmic Reality
edited by Melanie Swan, Jason Potts, Soichiro Takagi,
Frank Witte and Paolo Tasca

Blockchain Economics: Implications of Distributed Ledgers

Markets, Communications Networks, and Algorithmic Reality

Between **Science** and **Economics** – Vol. 1

Blockchain Economics: Implications of Distributed Ledgers

Markets, Communications Networks, and Algorithmic Reality

Editors

Melanie Swan
Purdue University, USA

Jason Potts
RMIT University, Australia

Soichiro Takagi
International University of Japan, Japan

Frank Witte
University College London, UK

Paolo Tasca
University College London, UK

World Scientific

NEW JERSEY • LONDON • SINGAPORE • BEIJING • SHANGHAI • HONG KONG • TAIPEI • CHENNAI • TOKYO

Published by

World Scientific Publishing Europe Ltd.

57 Shelton Street, Covent Garden, London WC2H 9HE

Head office: 5 Toh Tuck Link, Singapore 596224

USA office: 27 Warren Street, Suite 401-402, Hackensack, NJ 07601

Library of Congress Cataloging-in-Publication Data
Names: Swan, Melanie, editor.
Title: Blockchain economics : implications of distributed ledgers--markets, communications networks, and algorithmic reality / by editor: Melanie Swan (Purdue University, USA) [and four others].
Description: New Jersey : World Scientific, [2018] | Series: Between science and economics ; volume 1
Identifiers: LCCN 2018039260 | ISBN 9781786346384 (hc : alk. paper)
Subjects: LCSH: Finance--Technological innovations. | Blockchains (Databases)--Economic aspects. | Electronic funds transfers.
Classification: LCC HG173 .B574 2018 | DDC 330.0285/574--dc23
LC record available at https://lccn.loc.gov/2018039260

British Library Cataloguing-in-Publication Data
A catalogue record for this book is available from the British Library.

For any available supplementary material, please visit
https://www.worldscientific.com/worldscibooks/10.1142/Q0190#t=suppl

Desk Editors: Bindu Bhaskar/Jennifer Brough/Shi Ying Koe

Typeset by Stallion Press
Email: enquiries@stallionpress.com

Printed in Singapore

About the Editors

Jason Potts has a PhD from Lincoln University in New Zealand on theoretical foundations of evolutionary and complexity economics. He is Professor of Economics in the School of Economics, Finance and Marketing at RMIT University, and Director of the Blockchain Innovation Hub, established in 2017 as the first social science research institute on Blockchain in the world. Dr Potts is a Fellow of the Academy of Social Sciences of Australia and is one of Australia's top economists, specializing in economic growth, innovation and institutions, as well as the theory of economic evolution and complexity. His work has been applied to the economics of creative industries, intellectual property and cities, and common pool resources. He received the Australian Research Council's Future Fellowship, and won the International Joseph A. Schumpeter Prize. He has written five books and published over 80 articles on these themes, and is a regular media commentator. He is currently the Vice President of the International Joseph A. Schumpeter Society, an Adjunct Fellow at the Institute of Public Affairs, editor of the *Cambridge Elements* series on Evolutionary Economics, and editor of the *Journal of Institutional Economics*.

Melanie Swan is the Founder of the Institute for Blockchain Studies, a Technology Theorist in the Philosophy Department at Purdue University, and a Singularity University faculty member. Her education includes an MBA in Finance from Wharton at the University of Pennsylvania, an MA in Philosophy from the New School in New York, NY, an MA in Contemporary Continental Philosophy from Kingston University London and Université Paris 8, and a BA in French and Economics from

Georgetown University. Her primary research interests are Blockchain Economics and Blockchain Network Theory. In pure research, Melanie applies quantitative methods from mathematics, physics, complexity science, and machine learning to blockchains. In applied research, she focuses on payment channels, debt, net-settled capital, risk, integrated business ledgers, and blockchain health economics. Regarding social organization, she has proposed the "Smart City Cryptopolis and Blockchain Enlightenment," a social theory of dignity for a multi-species society of human, algorithm, and machine. In applied economics, she has formulated *algorithmic trust*, a network mechanism that moderates credit availability and facilitates blockchain markets to Nash equilibria more quickly than classical markets. Advanced conceptual research focuses on BCI cloudminds, the Brain as a DAC, the biocryptoeconomy, and blocktime (the native time domain of blockchains).

Soichiro Takagi is Executive Research Fellow and the General Manager of Research Division at the Center for Global Communications (GLOCOM) at the International University of Japan. He is the director of the Blockchain Economic Research Lab at GLOCOM and also a Visiting Associate Professor at The University of Tokyo. He also served as an Asia Program Fellow at Harvard Kennedy School, etc. His major field is information economics, focusing on the relationship between information technology and the economy. He has examined a variety of topics including offshore outsourcing, cloud computing, open data, sharing economy, digital currency, and blockchain. He has authored many books and articles, including *Blockchain Economics* (in Japanese) and *Reweaving the Economy: How IT Affects the Borders of Country and Organization* (University of Tokyo Press). He received a PhD in Information Studies from The University of Tokyo.

Paolo Tasca is a Digital Economist specializing in P2P financial systems. An advisor on blockchain technologies for international organizations such as the EU Parliament and the United Nations, Paolo is the founder and Executive Director of the Centre for Blockchain Technologies at University College London (UCL CBT). Previously, he was Lead Economist on digital currencies and P2P financial systems at the Deutsche

Bundesbank in Frankfurt. Paolo is also co-author of the bestseller *FINTECH Book*, co-editor of the book *Banking Beyond Banks and Money*, Associate Editor of the *Journal of Risk Finance* since 2016, and Guest Editor of the *Journal of Digital Banking* since 2017. He is author of various scientific papers about blockchain published by prestigious international scientific journals. Dr Tasca holds an MA in Politics and Economics *summa cum laude* from the University of Padua and an MSc in Economics and Finance from Ca' Foscari, Venice. He did his PhD studies in Business between Ca' Foscari, Venice and ETH, Zürich. Other recent appointments include being a Permanent Member of ISO TC 307 committee on standardization of blockchain systems (ISO), Member of the DLT/1 technical committee at the British Standards Institution (BSI), Adjunct Fellow at Griffith University Law Futures Centre, Honorary Professor at Sogang University Blockchain Research Centre, and Honorary Research Associate at University of Cape Town Financial Innovation Lab.

Frank Witte completed an MSc in Theoretical Astrophysics (1992) at Utrecht University in the Netherlands and received his PhD in Theoretical Physics (1995) from the University of Heidelberg. As an Assistant and Associate Professor, he taught theoretical physics at Utrecht University and University College Utrecht (1997–2010) and published on diverse topics such a phase-transitions in non-equilibrium field theories, bound-states of fermions under gravitational interactions, and the foundations of quantum game theory. As his research interests shifted toward the application of physics-inspired methods and concepts in economics; he accepted a position in the Department of Economics of University College London where he is working today. He teaches Economics of Science, with a forthcoming textbook to be published by World Scientific, and Environmental Economics as well as Computational Methods for Economists. Frank has spent extended academic visits, including teaching and research, at St. John's College, Cambridge (UK), the Quantum Optics & Laser Science group at Imperial College London and as International Fellow of Grinnell College (US).

About the Contributors

Dr Darcy W.E. Allen is a Postdoctoral Research Fellow in the Blockchain Innovation Hub at RMIT University in Melbourne and an Adjunct Fellow at the Institute of Public Affairs. He is an institutional economist focusing on entrepreneurial discovery of opportunities for new technologies. His current research focuses on the economics and political economy of blockchain technology as a form of new economic infrastructure. Dr Allen's scholarly contributions have appeared in a wide range of journals, books, and conference proceedings including the *International Journal of the Commons*, the *Journal of Peer Production,* and *New Perspectives on Political Economy.* He has appeared as an expert witness to provide evidence before a number of state and federal Australian parliamentary inquiries; his commentary has been featured widely across the print and the electronic media, and he is the former editor of Australia's longest running quarterly magazine on politics and culture. His PhD dissertation in economics, examining the economics of the development of new technologies, was passed outright at RMIT University in 2017.

Chris Berg is a Senior Research Fellow at the RMIT Blockchain Innovation Hub, an Adjunct Fellow with the Institute of Public Affairs, and an Academic Fellow with the Australian Taxpayers' Alliance. Dr Berg is the author of six books including *The Libertarian Alternative.* He is one of Australia's most prominent voices for free markets and individual rights. He is a widely published commentator on blockchains, cryptocurrencies, privacy, and civil liberties. He has been a regular newspaper columnist, is a frequent media commentator on television and radio, and appears regularly throughout the electronic press. He holds a

PhD in Economics from RMIT University, which was awarded in 2016, and a Bachelor's degree in History and Political Science from the University of Melbourne. His scholarly contributions on areas such as Australian history, economic methodology, regulation, and technological change civil liberties have appeared in journals such as *Australian Journal of Political Science*, *Econ Journal Watch*, *Ledger*, and *Trends in Anaesthesia and Critical Care*. With Sinclair Davidson and Jason Potts, he is developing the field of institutional cryptoeconomics, which studies the consequences of distributed ledger technology for firms, markets, and governments.

Sinclair Davidson is Professor of Institutional Economics in the School of Economics, Finance and Marketing at RMIT University; an Associate with the RMIT Blockchain Innovation Hub; an Adjunct Research Fellow at the Institute of Public Affairs; and an Academic Fellow at the Australian Taxpayers' Alliance. He is a member of the Centre for Independent Studies Council of Academic Advisers. Sinclair has published in academic journals such as the *European Journal of Political Economy*, *Journal of Economic Behavior and Organization*, *Economic Affairs*, and *The Cato Journal*. He is a regular contributor to public debate. His opinion pieces have been published in *The Age*, *The Australian*, *Australian Financial Review*, *The Conversation*, *Daily Telegraph*, *Sydney Morning Herald*, and *Wall Street Journal Asia*. He blogs at Catallaxy Files and tweets as @SincDavidson.

Renato P. dos Santos is a Researcher on blockchain technologies and Graduate Professor at the Lutheran University of Brazil. He is a member of the British Blockchain Association, holds a DSc (Physics) degree and did his postdoctoral work in Artificial Intelligence, and he also did his specializations in data science and blockchain technologies. He is also the author of more than 100 scientific papers about the philosophy of cryptocurrencies, data science in STEM education, second life in STEM education, web 2.0 technologies, ethnoscience, physics teaching, artificial intelligence and computer algebra in physics, and quantum field theory in prestigious scientific periodicals and events around the world. He is a Reviewer and Editor of prestigious scientific periodicals and events around the world and has developed systems for second life, Forex market, qualitative physics, and computer algebra.

Olga Feldmeier is the CEO of SMART VALOR, a Swiss-based blockchain start-up building a decentralized marketplace for tokenized alternative investments. Olga has extensive experience working in the banking and financial services sector for global brands such as Barclays Capital, UBS Wealth Management, and Boston Consulting Group, where she focused on strategy projects at financial institutions such as Deutsche Bank, Unicredit, and Commerzbank. Prior to founding SMART VALOR, Olga held the position of Commercial Managing Partner at the prominent Silicon Valley Bitcoin startup Xapo. Olga is a founding member of Switzerland's Crypto Valley community and is the producer of the ICO Summit — the first global conference focusing on blockchain crowdfunding in Switzerland. She is also a mentor at the largest European accelerator program, Kickstart Accelerator, and regularly delivers talks at conferences and universities on the regulation of blockchain industry, the tokenization of assets, and the disruption of the banking industry.

John Hargrave is the Publisher of *Bitcoin Market Journal*, (www.bitcoinmarketjournal.com), the leading investor website for bitcoin, altcoins, and new token offerings. He leads a team of 75 analysts, journalists, and researchers who have evaluated over 1,500 new token projects, developing best practices for driving value for both token creators and investors. He is also the CEO of Media Shower (www.mediashower.com), the leading blockchain media company. In his paper "How blockchain will decentralize the media", he lays out a new vision for media companies, based on the principles of radical decentralization and citizen ownership. He and his team are actively building media shower into that model media company. Hargrave is also the author of four books, including *Blockchain for Everyone* (Simon & Schuster/Gallery Books, 2019), the first book to explain blockchain technology to the non-technical reader. Hargrave received his MBA from Babson College and frequently writes and speaks about blockchain all over the world, building global confidence.

John B. Hooks is a Distributed Ledger (Blockchain) Technologist and Venture Capital/Private Equity Advisor and Council Member in the Technology and Telecommunications Practice of the Gerson Lehrman Group (GLG), and an Advisory Board Member to several emerging Blockchain, and Big Data/IoT and AI companies. Currently, Mr. Hooks is the Chairman, President, and CEO of Spectramesh, Inc. Spectramesh combines wireless advances and microelectronics with the emerging technology of blockchain in a core mesh router capable of communicating across a mixed spectrum of wireless TCP/IP, Bluetooth, and IoT spectra — a first for router devices. He is also the Chief Data Engineer and AI Business Development Executive at AmmbrTech US. Mr. Hooks holds a certificate in Private Equity and Corporate Governance from the Harvard Graduate School of Business, and an MBA, Financial Management degree from the Lubin School of Business, Pace University. He was also a doctoral candidate at New York University and held concurrent appointments to the faculty of the University of Bridgeport and Pace University. John Hooks has held several securities licenses including Series 7, 63, 65, and 66 while he was an advisor with UBS Private Wealth.

Dr Alex Kayal obtained his PhD from the Interactive Intelligence section of the Intelligent Systems Department, Delft University of Technology in the Netherlands, and his Masters from the Royal Institute of Technology (KTH) in Sweden. His PhD thesis focused on synthesizing and evaluating social commitment models for location sharing in the family life, grounded in user requirements, with the aim of better supporting (and understanding) human norms and values. He currently works as a Data Scientist for Exact, a Dutch business software provider, where he focuses on leveraging artificial intelligence, machine learning, and blockchain to streamline and automate manual business processes.

Rumy Narayan is a doctoral candidate at the School of Management, University of Vaasa, Finland. Her research focuses on sustainability networks, innovation systems, and sociotechnical transitions. Prior to her doctoral studies, she has been a Business Journalist, an Information Analyst, and Sustainability Consultant and Manager. In these roles, she has worked with companies like Walmart and Tetra Pak, and organizations like Environmental Protection Encouragement Agency (EPEA), a scientific research consultancy working with the Cradle-to-Cradle design concept. She has also been part of developing a certificate program on Corporate Social Responsibility (CSR) for the Indian Institute of Corporate Affairs (IICA).

Mikayla Novak is a Postdoctoral Research Fellow with the RMIT Blockchain Innovation Hub, RMIT University (Melbourne, Australia). An academically trained economist, Mikayla Novak attained a First Class Honours degree at The University of Queensland (Brisbane, Australia) and was awarded a doctorate at RMIT University. Prior to her appointment at RMIT University, Novak had worked for public sector agencies in Australia and New Zealand as well as for industry associations and non-profit think tanks. Her research specialties include institutional cryptoeconomics, public finance and public sector economics, regulation and regulatory governance, economic sociology, public choice, and institutional economics. The academic writing of Mikayla Novak includes contributions toward an understanding of economic and social dimensions of inequality, evolutionary dimensions of cultural and social change, and the political economy of blockchain technology. Novak has been a prolific contributor to public policy debates, having written over 240 opinion articles as well as research papers and peer-review publications. Mikayla Novak is the author of *Inequality: An Entangled Political Economy Perspective* (Palgrave Macmillan).

Dr Judith Redi obtained her PhD from the University of Genoa (Italy) in 2010, with a thesis on learning machines for objective image quality assessment, final result of a project on visual quality in displays funded by Philips research. After receiving the award for the best ICT thesis from University of Genoa, she moved to Eurecom (France) for a postdoc on Digital Image Forensics and 3D face recognition. In October 2010, she became an Assistant Professor at the Multimedia Computing group of Delft University of Technology, Faculty of Electrical Engineering, Mathematics and Computer Science (EEMCS). At TU Delft, she worked on image and video understanding toward the maximization of the Quality of (multimedia) Experiences. This is a highly multidisciplinary field that connects visual perception, cognitive science and engineering, machine learning, and computer vision. In 2015, she also became a Faculty fellow at the Benelux Center for Advanced Studies of IBM, where she contributed to the implementation of the Inclusive Enterprise vision. In February 2016, she became a part-time researcher at the Distributed and Interactive Systems group of CWI. Finally, convinced that we need more girls in the field, as a DEWIS (Delft Women in Science) ambassador in EEMCS, she works to promote activities to support gender diversity and women networking within her faculty. Since July 2017, she has been a Principal Data Scientist at Exact Business Software in the Netherlands.

Erich C.G. Schnoeckel has been infected by the Blockchain virus some 5 years ago and started researching the effect of the technology in different industries since. Erich has been responsible for the Blockchain projects at Exact Software and now acts as an independent Consultant and Advisor at 3Thin.gs Blockchain from where he advises several companies and government institutions on the use of technology. Erich is also one of the founders of Dint.io from where ICO's ratings are used to pool and syndicate investments into these ICOs. Erich regularly speaks at conferences on Health, Fintech, and Supply Chain solutions with a particular interest on building consortia and optimizing value chains with their business processes and also shares that knowledge during lectures at schools in the Netherlands, Belgium, and the UK. Erich holds a degree in Modern Japanese Studies and Economics from Erasmus University Rotterdam.

Navroop Sahdev is a Fellow at MIT Connection Science and holds a host of leadership roles in the DLT space, both as a practitioner as well as a researcher. An economist by training, Navroop is currently building a FinTech company that seeks to leverage blockchain technology. She is also a Research Associate at the Centre for Blockchain Technologies (CBT) at University College London and holds three Masters' degrees in IP Management, Economics of Innovation, and Applied Economics. A United Nations Youth Delegate for 2017, Navroop recently co-authored Hyperledger's Blockchain for Business online course. She speaks regularly at FinTech and blockchain conferences, and currently serves on the advisory board of a host of blockchain companies across various industries. Previously, she has worked at Harvard University and the United Nations Environment Programme. Her research interests are focused on distributed ledger technologies, game theory, networks theory, and complex systems science.

Arisa Siong is an Economist by training and trade. She honed her economic cynicism at London School of Economics where she obtained a BSc and MSc in Economics (Distinction) and subsequently has worked as an economic consultant for over a decade. She has advised on regulatory, competition, policy formulation, and market design issues in a range of industries including ICT, media, and financial services. Arisa currently works for the Infocomm and Media Development Authority of Singapore with a focus on digital economy issues. She has written her chapter in a personal capacity. Her view is that new technologies will fundamentally alter how market decisions are made, e.g. blockchain (autonomous), AI (automatic), and IoT and robotics (machine executed), and in doing so create new market constructs and signals (tokens and data). This will present a need for new economic frameworks and analytical tools to examine new market dynamics. There will also be an increasing need to look at the interplay between law, economics, technology, and public policy — the economic scholarship will benefit from collaborating with the legal, business, and tech communities in examining regulatory, governance, and policy issues in the digital world.

Annika Tidström is a Professor at the School of Management, University of Vaasa, Finland. Her research interests are related to business networks, industrial relationships, coopetition, tensions, and strategy-as-practice. She has published several articles in journals such as *Industrial Marketing Management*, *Journal of Business and Industrial Marketing*, *Journal of Purchasing and Supply Management*, and *Scandinavian Journal of Management*. Professor Tidström is an active member of the international coopetition research community, and she is also involved in the Industrial Marketing and Purchasing (IMP) group.

Horst Treiblmaier is a Professor in International Management at MODUL University Vienna, Austria. He received a PhD in Management Information Systems in 2001 from the Vienna University of Economics and Business in Austria and worked as a Visiting Professor at Purdue University, University of California, Los Angeles (UCLA), University of British Columbia (UBC), University of Technology in Sydney (UTS), and the Kazakhstan Institute of Management, Economics and Strategic Research (KIMEP). He has more than 15 years of experience as a researcher and consultant and has worked on projects with Microsoft, Google, and the United Nations Industrial Development Organization (UNIDO). His research interests include the economic and business implications of blockchain, cryptoeconomics, methodological and epistemological problems of social science research, and gamification. Currently, he serves on the board of the "City of Blockchain", an Austrian association promoting the blockchain and cryptographic technologies. His research has appeared in journals such as *Information Systems Journal*, *Structural Equation Modeling*, The *DATA BASE for Advances in Information Systems, Communications of the Association for Information Systems*, *Information & Management*, *Journal of Electronic Commerce Research*, *Journal of Global Information Management*, *Schmalenbach Business Review*, and *Wirtschaftsinformatik (Business & Information Systems Engineering)*.

Uwe J. Umlauff is a Serial Entrepreneur, Portfolio Investor, leisure-time Database Coder, and not to forget Director of Steinbeis Transfer Institute Innovation & Business Creation in Munich, an institute of the Steinbeis University Berlin with a focus on entrepreneurship, start-up innovations, and the convergence of technologies such as blockchain, artificial intelligence, cyber sec, virtual and augmented reality, and industrial Internet of things. Steinbeis International Network is a technology transfer company under the umbrella of a foundation based in Stuttgart, Germany, with more than 1,000 research and tech transfer centers in 60+ countries. Uwe has more than 25 years of work experience in founding, consulting, financing, and internationalizing companies, mainly in CEE and in media, real estate, and IT business. He is an author of several books and articles on entrepreneurship and business administration. Moreover, he is the Co-Founder and Chairman of the City of Blockchain, a joint initiative of more than 60 public, corporate, non-governmental, and private partners in Vienna, Austria and beyond, with a view to promote distributed ledger technologies mainly in the context of smart city agendas. Uwe holds a Master's degree in business administration and information systems.

Jingwen Yao is a User Experience Designer and Researcher who has an interest in designing for positive social impacts and improving livelihoods in underdeveloped regions. With an educational background in Industrial Design (MSc from Delft University of Technology), she is specialized in adopting Human-Centered Design Methodologies to different requests and circumstances. Be it by diving into local communities' lives in rural Uganda and Tanzania for designing a frugal medical thermometer and a honey processing system or traveling all around The Netherlands to interview financiers and entrepreneurs for investigating the possibilities of financing SMEs with blockchain technologies. In the past 10 years, Jingwen, who originally comes from Beijing, has worked on and studied various topics such as Social Innovations, Social Entrepreneurship, Sustainable Design, Blockchain, and Accounting Business in more than 5 countries across Asia, Europe, and Africa. Currently, she is based in The Netherlands, working at Exact Business Software as a User Experience Designer, while preparing for her one-year travel plan, where she wants to explore more social design opportunities and sustainable living styles.

Contents

Introduction

Blockchain Economics: Implications of Distributed Ledgers
Markets, communications networks, and algorithmic reality

> "A society's wealth is its productive capacity, not its specie capital reserves"
> —John Stuart Mill (*Principles of Political Economy*, 1848)

Abstract

Blockchain is emerging as one of the key enabling technologies of the 21st century. Blockchain Economics is the discipline that articulates and analyzes the new economic models that are developing with the implementation of distributed ledgers, and which serve to underline blockchain technology's potential as an institutional technology (to evolve traditional institutions). Some of the distinguishing features of the Blockchain Economics paradigm are open platform business models, cryptotoken money supplies, and Initial Coin Offerings (ICOs) as a new and official form of financing. This book addresses the themes of Economic Theory and Market Structure, Open Network Innovation, Behavioral Economics, Financial Theory and Complexity Science, Policy, Regulation, and Incentives, and Income Inequality and Economic Inclusion. Ideas are synthesized from computer science, network theory, complexity, policy, economics, cognitive psychology, and behavioral economics. The potential impact of this work is providing a foundational understanding and theoretical framework for Blockchain Economics as a novel and potentially transformative discipline.

1.1 Introduction

Taking Mill's maxim seriously (also supported by David Hume (1748) and Adam Smith (1776)[a]), the challenge at hand is using blockchain technology to continue to expand the productive capacity of society. This means the productive capacity to solve contemporary problems such as debt, technological unemployment, resource scarcity, and poverty. It also means the capacity to approach future-class endeavors such as energy efficiency, space settlement, predictive mechanisms of disease, and producing and consuming not only material goods but intangible quality-of-life goods such as liberty, dignity, autonomy, and choice.

Blockchain Economics is the discipline that articulates and analyzes the economic models that are emerging with the implementation of distributed ledgers. Some of the distinguishing features of the Blockchain Economics paradigm are open platform business models, cryptotoken money supplies for value transfer and community participation, and Initial Coin Offerings (ICOs) as a new and official form of financing. Blockchains are positioned as an institutional technology [Davidson *et al.*, 2018]. This makes sense in that although the current mode of storing money is in banks, the approaching future could include a shift toward storing money and assets in networks. Political and economic interactions involve sensitive and private information such as identity confirmation, monetary transfer, paperwork signing, and legal and regulatory compliance, and thus traditionally institutions have been the means for fulfilling these interactions, however this could be offloaded to blockchain networks. Trustless cryptographic validation could be the transfer mechanism as opposed to human-administered institutions, in a "de-organization" or "de-institutionalization" of trust [Takagi, 2017].

Economics more generally is the study of the production, distribution, and consumption of goods and services. Decision making by groups and individuals plays a crucial role because wants are bigger than resources (there is always scarcity and opportunity cost). Three eras of economics,

---

[a] David Hume (1748) "Of Interest," in *Essays Moral and Political*; Adam Smith (1776) *Wealth of Nations.*

investigating supply and demand, and resource discovery and propagation, might be identified. Classical Economics addresses material goods, Network Economics focuses on digital goods, and Blockchain Economics concerns cryptographic assets, smart contracts, and new entities such as DApps (decentralized applications). Technology adoption is proceeding quickly in the blockchain sector. IDC estimates global spending on blockchain solutions to more than double in 2018 to $2.1 billion, and reach $9.2 billion in 2021 [Hebblethwaite, 2018]. The World Economic Forum estimates that 10% of global GDP will be stored in blockchains by 2027 [WEF, 2015]. The use of open source software has allowed the blockchain community to develop more quickly and collaboratively than might have been possible otherwise. The beneficial effects of open source software in market expansion have been documented [Lerner and Tirole, 2005; von Krogh *et al.*, 2012]. Given the blockchain sector's growth, it is timely to theorize about the economic models that are in development, and aim at providing a level guide through the exuberance toward genuine value creation.

Technically, a blockchain is a type of distributed ledger technology in which confirmed and validated batches of transactions are held in blocks, and the blocks are linked (chained) in a tamper-resistant append-only chain which starts with a genesis block and in which each block contains a hash of the prior block in the chain [Tasca and Tessone, 2017]. Conceptually, blockchain technology is software, an Internet protocol for transferring money and other items of value such as property, contracts, and identity credentials with cryptographic proof as opposed to via institutional intermediaries such as a bank or government [Swan and de Filippi, 2017].

Digital money is a new and more sophisticated kind of Internet protocol-based traffic. As such, it requires special functionality. To ensure that money is only spent once (preventing the double-spending problem), it is necessary to have an always-on apparatus on the Internet checking in real-time whenever a transaction is submitted to confirm that the owner controls this particular money or asset, and is only transferring it once, to another party, in a valid and authenticated transaction. Having a vast, automated, Internet-based system for confirming and transferring value on demand means that the current methods for conducting value transfer, human-based intermediaries such as banks and governments, could be superseded.

Economic principles have always been used in blockchain design. The cryptosecurity is based on earlier computing structures to deter spam. Hashcash, the Proof of Work algorithm used by Bitcoin, was initially proposed in 1997 as a mechanism to prevent Internet abuse by making it too expensive [Back, 2002]. Likewise, in Bitcoin, miners must demonstrate the proof of doing work, bearing the actual cost to compute an NP-hard (difficult) problem to prove that they are not malicious agents.

1.1.1 *Public and private blockchains*

There are two kinds of blockchains, public and private. Public blockchains are open such that anyone can download a wallet and start conducting transactions. Transactions are pseudonymous (using a 32-character address) on most public blockchains such as Bitcoin and Litecoin, or confidential (sender and receiver address and the amount transferred are masked) if using Monero or Zcash. Public blockchains are *trustless*, meaning that transactions are executed using "cryptographic proof instead of trust" [Nakamoto, 2008]. Users only need to trust the software, not human intermediaries or counterparties.

On the other hand, *private blockchains* are enterprise blockchains operated by business or government entities in which users are known and credentialed for specific kinds of read and write access. Examples include Hyperledger, Ethereum Quorum, Corda, and Symbiont. Public blockchains are *trusted* in that users may still need to know and trust counterparties, and understand how consensus operates on the network to validate and confirm transactions. Each enterprise blockchain platform conducts the consensus process with slightly different mechanisms (for example, Ripple's validators, Hyperledger's endorsement policies, Corda's notaries, and Ethereum Quorum's raft consensus).

Blockchain properties could spur the development of new classes of applications in both enterprise and consumer markets. For organizations, blockchain is a next-generation enterprise information technology that allows a new level of re-engineering, shared business processes and integrated ledgers, and secure automation (the automation, and legal and financial tracking of arbitrarily-many items). For consumers, some of the important blockchain properties are data privacy and payments. One premise is that individuals would be willing to share more information if it were kept private and remunerated. This could lead to a new tier of applications running as an overlay to social networks, unlocking additional consumer value. The idea is extending "likes" to validated (i.e. not fake) opinions, recommendations, and referrals, supported by micropayments, for example, in the areas of personal finance, health, and jobs.

1.1.2 *Blockchain economic literature*

The Bitcoin and Ethereum white papers constitute some of the first writing on the blockchain concept. Once networks are in place, digital cash becomes a straightforward idea. There had been several previously attempted projects following Chaum's proposal of a blind signature system for untraceable payments [Chaum, 1982]. However, Nakamoto finally proposed a viable solution to the double-spending problem (instances of money should only be spent once) in "Bitcoin: A Peer-to-Peer Electronic Cash System" [Nakamoto, 2008]. Ethereum further extends the concept of blockchain beyond simple cryptocurrencies for monetary payments to the idea of "decentralized applications that add an economic layer to computation network" [Buterin, 2014].

One of the first books to appear on the topic of Blockchain Economics is Swan's *Blockchain: Blueprint for a New Economy* [2015]. This book articulates three potential developmental phases. Blockchain 1.0 comprises real-time payments and monetary transactions. Blockchain 2.0 considers more complex financial arrangements enacted over time with smart contracts such as mortgages and insurance products. Blockchain 3.0 contemplates future-class applications enabled by blockchains as a new form of global computational infrastructure such as automated fleet management, big health data, and asynchronous space communication.

In 2016, Narayanan *et al.* provide a technical overview of cryptocurrencies in *Bitcoin and cryptocurrency technologies: A comprehensive introduction.* Several books appeared in 2017. To mention a few specifically related to Blockchain Economics, one is Morabito's *Business Innovation Through Blockchain: The B3 Perspective*. This book describes blockchain in a readily accessible way for business managers with a wide range of potential applications. Kariappa's *The Blockchain*

Alternative: Rethinking Macroeconomic Policy and Economic Theory highlights blockchain in the bigger context of financial technology and suggests the application of complexity methods. Chuen *et al.*'s *Handbook of Blockchain, Digital Finance, and Inclusion* addresses sustainability, financial inclusion, and regulation. A valuation model for cryptographic assets is proposed by Burniske and Tatar in *Cryptoassets: The Innovative Investor's Guide to Bitcoin and Beyond.* These references provide an excellent introduction to the field. The current book attempts to build on this foundation with an interdisciplinary approach to crystallize the Blockchain Economics paradigm in a comprehensive theoretical manner.

1.2 Blockchain Economics: Analysis Methods and Themes

It is precisely at the moment of the emergence of a new field such as Blockchain Economics that it is important to apply a variety of analysis methods to understand the field and its implications. The current volume thus includes a variety of scientific analysis models ranging from quantitative methods to social theorizing to articulate the emerging Blockchain Economics paradigm. Table 1 illustrates the classical to contemporary shift in the traditional research analysis models in different fields related to Blockchain Economics, several of which are explored in this book.

Table 1. Classical to Contemporary Expansion of Research Analysis Models in Several Fields.

	Economics	**Econophysics**	**Statistics**	**Artificial Intelligence**	**Network Science/ Graph Theory**	**Neuroscience**
Classical	Equilibrium	Schrödinger Equation	Gaussian Distributions (normal)	Expert Systems	Global System Properties	Signaling cascade
Contemporary	Complexity	Path Integrals	Mandelbrot Distributions (fat-tailed)	Deep Learning	Scale-free Small-world	Neural field models

In pure economic theory, there has been a move away from the unrealistic laboratory-like conditions of equilibrium models in favor of the recognition that economics may be better studied as a domain of complexity [Potts, 2000; König and Battiston, 2009; Arthur, 2013]. There is starting to be a wider application of physics models to economics, markets, and finance, extending a narrow use of the Schrödinger Equation in the Black Scholes option pricing model [Romero *et al.*, 2014], to path integrals and other methods in the emerging fields of econophysics and quantum finance [Witte, 2003]. In statistics, event distributions have been found to be non-normally distributed and have fat-tails, meaning that outlier events, both positive and negative, occur more frequently than may have been thought [Mandelbrot and Hudson, 2006; Taleb, 2007].

In artificial intelligence, the conceptual paradigm has shifted from the encoding of all knowledge in expert systems to running straightforward algorithms over very-large data corpora, currently in the form of deep learning neural nets [Halevy *et al.*, 2009; LeCun *et al.*, 2015]. Network science has likewise advanced, from a focus on identifying the global properties of systems in a top-down and bottom-up approach to instead the observation of scale-free (power law) [Barabasi and Albert, 1999], and small-world (only a small number of hops to reach other nodes in a graph) [Watts and Strogatz, 1998] phenomena. Neuroscience too is indicative of a shift to more sophisticated analysis paradigms, for example from simple signaling cascades to neural field theory [McCulloch and Pitts, 1943; Cowan, 2006]. For the current project, the point is to take advantage of evolving research paradigms in related fields to apply innovative tools and methods to the analysis and articulation of Blockchain Economics.

1.2.1 *Quantum computing*

Quantum computing could influence the Blockchain Economy in several ways. First, although quantum cryptography might be able to break the current cryptography used by blockchains (mainly SHA-256), blockchains might likely upgrade to quantum cryptography as methods become available, and there could be quantum-secured blockchains [Kiktenko *et al.*, 2018]. Second, since quantum cryptography would only be adding a quantum layer to the standard blockchain protocol, next-generation projects might instantiate the blockchain itself with quantum computation. One proposal is to create a blockchain using quantum particles that are entangled in time (encoding the blockchain into a temporal GHZ (Greenberger-Horne-Zeilinger) state of photons) [Rajan and Visser, 2018]. Data would be encoded on a quantum particle, which would store the history of all its predecessors in a way that could not be hacked without destroying it.

Third, quantum computing is based on the physics of information, and also the related field of quantum game theory. Quantum game theory extends classical game theory and features the quantum entanglement of initial states, and the superposition of strategies to be used on the initial states. Quantum blockchains might be used to test experimental or simulated evidence to support theories proposed in quantum game theory. For example, the 'quantum aspects' of quantum game theory models could be interpreted as describing novel aspects of the preferences of the agents engaged in these decision-making processes [Witte, 2002]. In contrast with classical models, a non-commutative nature of pay-off operators may be deduced. Quantum game theory could allow for repeated gambling game-strategies that generate time-correlated pay-offs for the quantum players [Witte, 2005]. Different forms of equilibria might be available in blockchain-based game theoretic models.

1.3 Chapter Overview

This book presents a variety of chapters that address the themes of Economic Theory and Market Structure, Open Network Innovation, Social Science and Behavioral Economics, Financial Theory and Complexity Science, Policy, Regulation, and Incentives, and Income Inequality and Economic Inclusion, as outlined in Table 2.

Table 2. List of Chapters and Economic Themes.

Focus and Chapter Title		Topic	Economic Themes
Part 1: Economic Theory and Market Structure			
1	Swan: Blockchain Economic Theory: Digital Asset Contracting Reduces Debt and Risk	Causal model of new forms of financial interaction enabled by blockchain-registered digital assets	Economic theory, digital assets, payment channels, debt, systemic risk, net settlement, real-time balance sheets, enterprise blockchains
2	Takagi: Does Blockchain "Decentralize" Everything?: An Insight from Organizational Economics	Impact of decentralization on organizational economics	Decentralization, organizational economics, coordination models, the firm, economic behavioral incentives, agent decision-making
3	Siong: The Blockchain Antidote to Monopolization	Monopoly and competitive dynamics in blockchain networks and digital platforms	Policy, regulation, competition, monopoly, collusion, network effects, platform economics, incentives, values
Part 2: Blockchain Economic Open Network Innovation			
4	Kayal *et al.*: Financing Small & Medium Enterprises with Blockchain: An Exploratory Research of Stakeholders' Attitudes	Small-to-medium enterprise (SME) blockchain-based credit history and financing	Small-to-medium enterprise (SME), financing, credit, factoring, collateralized finance, inventories, blockchain adoption, blockchain awareness and attitudes
5	Narayan and Tidström: Blockchains for Accelerating Open Innovation Systems for Sustainability Transitions	Open innovation platforms for sustainable economic production and consumption	Sustainability, production, consumption, open innovation, platform economics, peer production, global networks, resource scarcity, values-based business models

(*Continued*)

Table 2. (*Continued*)

Focus and Chapter Title		Topic	Economic Themes
Part 3: Social Science and Behavioral Economics			
6	Treiblmaier and Umlauff: Blockchain and the Future of Work: A Self-Determination Theory Approach	Self-determination theory to frame future-of-work attitudes toward blockchain technology	Future of work, social theory, human needs, incentives, intrinsic and extrinsic motivation, technological unemployment
7	Hargrave *et al.*: How Value is Created in Tokenized Assets	Building investor confidence in Initial Coin Offerings (ICOs)	Cryptotokens, digital assets, evaluation, investor confidence, ICOs, behavioral economics, frameworks
Part 4: Financial Theory and Complexity Science			
8	Dos Santos: Consensus Algorithms: A Matter of Complexity?	Complexity analysis of blockchain consensus algorithms	Complexity, consensus algorithms, systemic risk, chaoticity, flash crashes, Crutchfield's statistical complexity, proof of work, proof of stake
9	Swan: Blockchain Theory of Programmable Risk: Black Swan Smart Contracts	Risk reduction through user-selected level of risk programmed into smart contracts	Risk, options, probability, statistics, black swan financial theory, insurance, smart contracts
Part 5: Policy, Regulation, and Incentives			
10	Allen: Entrepreneurial Exit: Developing the Cryptoeconomy	Blockchain-based property enforcement allows entrepreneurs to *cryptosecede* from the traditional economy	Entrepreneurship, regulation, competition, institutions, policy, decentralization, legal regime, authority, sovereignty
11	Berg *et al.*: Towards Crypto-friendly Public Policy	Crypto-friendly public policy for government modernization and competitive advantage	Regulation, policy, institutions, government services, institutional economics, competitive advantage, public goods

(*Continued*)

Table 2. (*Continued*)

	Focus and Chapter Title	Topic	Economic Themes
Part 6: Income Inequality and Economic Inclusion			
12	Novak: The Implications of Blockchain for Income Inequality	Positive and negative impact of blockchain technology on income inequality	Income inequality, policy, power asymmetries, distributional economics, externalities, technological unemployment
13	Hooks: The Mesh Economy: How Blockchain and Alternative Networks can Bridge the Digital Divide and Facilitate Economic Inclusion	Mesh networks combined with blockchain for Internet access and financial services resulting in economic empowerment	Inclusion, inequality, underserved markets, network theory, digital divide, communications networks, empowerment, mesh networks, alternative communications networks (ACNs)

1.4 Chapter Summaries

1.4.1 *Economic theory and market structure*

Swan proposes a Blockchain Economic Theory of Digital Asset Contracting as an explanatory model of the Blockchain Economy. The premise is that blockchain-registered digital assets enable new kinds of contracting (smart contracts) and new forms of money (cryptotokens), which in turn produce new structures of financial interaction such as payment channels, ICOs, real-time balance sheets, and enterprise blockchains. Distributed ledger structures might be applied to structural economic challenges such as debt, systemic risk, technological job outsourcing, healthcare cost-outcome disconnects, and financial inclusion. A key innovation is Payment Channels, which enable the use of capital on a net rather than a gross basis, and thus might lead to restructuring debt burdens. Other structures such as Real-time Balance Sheets and Black Swan Smart Contracts might provide firms and regulators with greater financial control and risk management capacity.

Takagi provides a nuanced contemplation of organizational economics in the context of decentralization and the corresponding incentives for management and workers. In the traditional organizational model, there are motivations for both management and workers to participate in the firm. Managers reap the benefits of scale economies and reduced opportunism (not having to take undue risk by being confident that other opportunities will be forthcoming). Workers benefit from smoother income streams than if they are independent contractors or entrepreneurs and also from efficient decision-making (individuals need not be involved in every decision). Now, however, with the possibility of decentralizing organizations with blockchain technology, the incentive structure could be different. One point is that there may be less decentralization in blockchain models than is thought. Further, although management incentives may be improved with blockchain technology's ability to automate tasks, worker incentives may be foregone, in the sense that the traditional benefits of participating in a firm (smoother income streams and efficient decision-making) may not be present to workers in blockchain models.

Siong argues that regulators should be taking a more prominent role to lead the thinking, dialogue, and regulatory stance on blockchain to alleviate uncertainty and ensure competitive markets. This is important given the new economic challenges presented by the blockchain domain such as circular markets, dynamic token signals, and the potential for collusion in private blockchains. Digital platforms and network effects lead to large-scale projects (such as Facebook and Bitcoin) which seem to constitute monopolies (outsized market power) in some ways but not in others. With the sprawling reach of these transnational network platforms, forward-looking government regulators might take up the challenge of revising the definitions of monopoly and competition for the digital network era.

1.4.2 *Blockchain economic open network innovation*

Kayal *et al.* posit that financing for small-to-medium enterprises (SMEs) might be more readily available if instantiated through blockchain-based mechanisms such as invoice factoring and collateralized inventory finance. A study interviewing seven stakeholders (financiers, accountants, and SMEs) was conducted. The results were that stakeholders thought that the key benefit of blockchains for SME financing would be having a detailed, comprehensive, and trustworthy credit history instantiated in blockchains. This could be helpful in preventing fraud, and in minimizing the administrative costs of providing credit. Blockchains might substantially improve the financing opportunities available to SMEs.

Narayan and Tidström argue that current systems of production and consumption are unsustainable (citing climate change, inequality, environmental degradation, and resource scarcity), and that new forms of organizing are needed. A theory of blockchain innovation and sustainability is developed from three lines of research: open innovation networks, sustainability transitions, and technology adoption. Blockchains provide the possibility of using open innovation networks to develop and transition to models that are more sustainable. A novel model is proposed as an example, having a sustainable materials index and an IPFS-type network[b] (i.e. an always-on, resilient, globally-distributed resource) in the form of an open innovation platform for those wanting to work with sustainable materials. In this heightened form of crowdsourced eMarketplace, smart contracts could be used to coordinate obligations and remuneration between employers and workers, and enact values-based economic activity, in this case, supporting the affinity of using sustainable materials.

1.4.3 *Social science and behavioral economics*

Treiblmaier and Umlauff examine the future of work. A social theoretic framework based on self-determination theory is presented to articulate the potential impact of blockchain technology. Self-determination theory extends Maslow's hierarchy of needs by focusing on three key extrinsic motivations that a successful future of work program would do well to contain, the ability for individuals to realize autonomy, competence, and social relatedness. Twenty-four qualitative interviews were conducted, which elicited a range of positive and negative responses to the potential impact of blockchain technology on the future of work, specifically in the areas of industry, work life, and private life. This chapter surfaces some of the deeper social themes concerning anxiety and the lack of clear pathways

---

[b] IPFS: Interplanetary File System.

ahead for the future of work and the role of technology, of which blockchain-based systems is one example.

Hargrave *et al.* address the problem of distinguishing between promising bona fide Initial Coin Offerings (ICOs) and those that are not worthwhile or are outright fraud. Drawing from behavioral economics and cognitive psychology, the authors propose a new instrument, the Framework for Token Confidence, as a checklist that potential investors could use to analyze and develop confidence in a cryptotoken offering. The framework is based on the Timmons Model of Entrepreneurship and Kahneman's *Thinking Fast and Slow*. Investors might use the structured framework (5-category, 20-element) to subjectively assess the business problem, proposed solution, addressable market size, team, and token mechanics of an ICO. The general concept is using a structured criteria-based framework to develop confidence in a new economic domain.

1.4.4 *Financial theory and complexity science*

Dos Santos points out that although economics has been recognized as a domain of complexity, econophysics methods such as complexity theory and chaos theory have not yet been widely applied to the blockchain context. The chapter investigates blockchain consensus algorithms with Crutchfield's Statistical Complexity. This is a measure of Shannon entropy and the randomness of order in a system. The formula is used to compute complexity on a scale between 0 and 1; 0 is low complexity, as found in a fair coin toss; and 1 is high complexity (chaoticity), as found in the movement of a double pendulum. Dos Santos finds that proof-of-work (PoW) consensus algorithms have low complexity as compared with proof-of-stake (PoS) consensus algorithms, and therefore may lead to lower systemic risk and less chaoticity. The implication is that PoW (even if resource intensive) not only provides a cryptosecure system, but also one with low complexity, a desirable attribute in a computational financial system. This work could be helpful in consensus algorithm design, understanding risk in blockchain systems, and assessing emergent chaotic market behavior such as programmatically-induced flash crashes.

Swan proposes a Blockchain Theory of Programmable Risk that can be implemented with Black Swan Smart Contracts. The theory is developed from the two perspectives of risk theorizing in philosophy, social science, and finance; and black swan financial theory (risk distributions are fat-tailed (Mandelbrotian), not normal (Gaussian)). Event distributions can be formulated as s-curves with convex, linear, and concave segments, such that a desired level of risk may be selected (convexity equates to lower risk). Black Swan Smart Contracts could instantiate s-curve event distributions such that risk could be more effectively managed by users selecting low-medium-high risk as a standard contract parameter. Potential applications of Black Swan Smart Contracts include Insurance as a Digital Service, eBays for Money, Information Markets, and Autonomous Risk Management as a Smart Network property.

1.4.5 *Policy, regulation, and incentives*

Allen discusses how blockchain technology enables entrepreneurs to develop new decentralized governance structures to coordinate human interaction and exchange. The implication is that blockchains enable market participants to *cryptosecede* from traditional political-economic systems (laws, courts) through new forms of property rights protection and enforcement. The analysis draws on institutional economics and development economics, drawing parallels between territorial economic development and the cryptoeconomy to explain collaboration between blockchain entrepreneurs within governance structures such as hackathons and conferences. One challenge blockchain entrepreneurs may face is launching a private economy in the face of complementary protective institutional activities. However, the collaborative governance structures already arising in the blockchain economy are evidence of the entrepreneurial success of the self-governed economic development of the cryptoeconomy.

Berg *et al.* posit that distributed ledgers are institutional technologies that pose complex regulatory and public policy challenges, both internal and external to jurisdictional domains. The chapter applies an institutional theory of regulation to assess how blockchains affect relative institutional costs and guide public policy choices. Having a crypto-friendly public policy toward blockchain technology is suggested as a productive policy stance for governments to sort out the relevant challenges as the cryptoeconomy develops, and as a source of competitive advantage on the international stage. Policy-makers should be cognizant that blockchain applications may interact with existing regulatory frameworks and thus provide new regulatory challenges. Blockchains might be adopted by governments to improve the efficiency of public service delivery, for both government-provided services and to manage privately-provided public goods. Applications such as property rights and identity management are considered.

1.4.6 *Income inequality and economic inclusion*

Novak discusses the implications of blockchain technology for income inequality, a complex and emergent (rather than a simple and static) phenomenon. Blockchain technology might both ameliorate and exacerbate the distribution of income within society. There could be a positive impact as a result of reducing power asymmetries held by intermediaries, but also a negative effect from job displacement to technology and in favor of specialists. So far, there is some evidence of wealth concentration amongst cryptoeconomy participants. The durability of such effects is unclear, given that the Blockchain Economy is in the formative stages of development, subject to energetic attention, early adoption, and use-discovery processes. It is difficult to make concrete assessments as to whether any short-term income inequality effects will persist over the longer term. However, policy-makers would do well to emphasize the equality effects of blockchain by insisting on an open and permissionless environment for blockchain participation.

Hooks proposes that alternative deployment networks such as mesh networks combined with blockchain technology could address underserved populations and spur economic development by providing access to Internet connectivity and financial services. The premise is that mesh networking and blockchain technologies could reshape the telecommunications industry by bringing the promise of economic empowerment to areas currently not served or underserved by traditional solutions. An example of one such (non-blockchain) Alternative Community Network (ACN) is considered as a demonstration case.

Guifi.net has contributed to building the largest worldwide community network, with an annual turnover of millions of euros and the creation of dozens of direct jobs. The implementation of blockchain-enabled mesh networks could help to provide services, and to produce data sets to characterize the key parameters of the deployment and operation of these alternative infrastructures to extend their reach. This could economically empower those who do not have Internet connectivity and access to financial services.

1.5 Limitations

This book is necessarily limited and has not explored all topics related to Blockchain Economics. One omission is a detailed look at quantitative valuation methods for cryptographic assets. So far, the proposed solutions have primarily emphasized MV=PQ [Burniske, 2017; Lannquist, 2018]. However, MV=PQ is more of an arithmetic computation than a valuation model that indicates the drivers of growth. In MV=PQ, PxQ is GDP, the price (P) times the quantity (Q) of goods and services produced and sold in the economy. The Money Supply (M) has to turn over a certain number of times (V, the velocity of turnover) to accommodate the GDP activity. Traditionally, governments use MV=PQ to calculate how much money needs to be in supply to support and manage the economy. However, cryptotoken money supplies are fixed, so the calculation makes less sense. In the cryptotoken use case, the valuation assumption is that if the economy of a cryptotoken increases, so too will the cryptotoken's value. True, but obvious, and MV=PQ does not show the levers of value creation. It is easy to compute that an increasing GDP divided by the outstanding money supply leads to an increase in token value, but the key point for valuation is identifying the drivers of GDP growth.

A more robust model for identifying the underlying drivers of growth in a cryptoeconomy could be extending network valuation models based on the number of subscribers (users) and average revenue per user (ARPU). This could provide better insight into the different customer segments using the open platform cryptoeconomy to contribute and earn tokens, access resources, and otherwise participate. New metrics of cryptoeconomy participant stickiness could be developed. The point is that quantitative valuation methods may be in the early phases of development and it could take time to understand valuation drivers and metrics in emerging cryptoeconomy communities.

Also absent is the detailed application of economic principles in blockchain design from the computer science perspective. For example, Rizun uses supply and demand curves to evaluate transaction selection by Bitcoin miners [Rizun, 2015]. Specifically, the incentive for a rational Bitcoin miner (a mining software client) would be to select transactions from the node's mempool (memory pool of unconfirmed transactions) at the point where supply and demand curves meet. The curves are the block space supply curve (the size specification of the block, if any) and the mempool demand curve (the demand for transaction processing).

Setting transactions fees is another computational problem to which economic principles might be applied. Deep learning algorithms have been proposed for such optimization problems, to set cryptocurrency transaction fees, and to time the transaction submission [Al-Shehabi, 2018]. Just as economics is becoming a layer in computation networks with blockchain technology, so too deep learning algorithms could be another layer in the stack. A related project has sketched an idea for blockchain-based eMarketplaces for successful deep learning algorithms [Kurtulmus and Daniel, 2018].

Social risks are also not considered such as the increasing dependence on technology and the lack of offsetting risk mitigation strategies. Risk reduction efforts could address both technical and social concerns. Technically, having a response to large-scale network disruption, for example resulting from a natural or malicious electromagnetic pulse (EMP) is necessary. Socially, expecting a backlash from an overly technologized experience of reality ("algorithmic reality"), and having different potential responses and support resources would be helpful.

1.6 Conclusion

This book develops the discipline of Blockchain Economics in the thematic areas of Economic Theory and Market Structure, Open Network

Innovation, Social Science and Behavioral Economics, Financial Theory and Complexity Science, Policy, Regulation, and Incentives, and Income Inequality and Economic Inclusion. The implication of blockchain technology is that the only sectors that have not yet been fully re-engineered for the Internet era, financial services, and legal and governance services, can now be digitized and updated. Blockchains are emerging as an institutional technology, and as such, an economic consequence of widespread blockchain adoption could be that the corporate and governmental structure of society could shift to one that is computationally-based and thus has a diminished need for human-operated brick-and-mortar institutions.

The measure of blockchain's success could depend on the extent to which Mill's challenge is implemented, expanding the productive capacity of society with distributed ledgers. From a social perspective, the greater impact of blockchain technology could be reformulating models of social organization [Swan, 2018a]. As an institutional technology, distributed ledgers could have a significant potential impact in reconfiguring the patterns of social, financial, legal, and political interaction. Privacy could the first skirmish (possibly transitioning to an economy of widespread confidential transactions). Social maturity lags technological innovation, and a lengthy power struggle could ensue if societies attempt to evolve toward flatter more equitable models of organization. A period of *cryptoenlightenment* could arrive, in which individuals finally think freely of the dictates of authority, as Kant encouraged in the Renaissance Enlightenment [Kant, 1784].

From a communications network perspective, blockchain technology represents a break-through functionality that could be a watershed moment. The nature of communications networks is being transformed from simple conveyance to complex conveyance. Whereas all previous network activity from mainframes to mobile phones comprises information transfer on simple networks, the new era of network activity is transferring value on smart networks. Blockchains are the first example of an intelligent conveyance mechanism, automatically switching value-laden content on Internet networks. Increasing orders of magnitude of complexity might be coordinated with smart networks, for example adding intelligence as a smart network layer with deep learning algorithms to the nascent blockchain economic layer [Swan, 2018b]. Fostering future societies comprised of human, algorithm, and machine is a challenge to which blockchain smart networks might be deployed to enforce a productive quality of life and flourishing.

References

Al-Shehabi, A. (2018). Bitcoin Transaction Fee Estimation Using Mempool State and Linear Perceptron Machine Learning Algorithm. SJSU Master's Projects. 638. pp. 1-65.

Arthur, W.B. (2013). Complexity economics: a different framework for economic thought. In *Complexity and the Economy*. (2014). Arthur. Oxford, UK: Oxford University Press.

Back, A. (2002). Hashcash - A Denial of Service Counter-Measure. http://www.hashcash.org/papers/hashcash.pdf.

Barabasi, A.L. and Albert, R. (1999). Emergence of scaling in random networks. *Science*. 286(5439): 509-12.

Bheemaiah, K. (2017). *The Blockchain Alternative: Rethinking Macroeconomic Policy and Economic Theory*. New York, NY: Apress.

Burniske, C. (2017). Cryptoasset Valuations. https://medium.com/@cburniske/cryptoasset-valuations-ac83479ffca7.

Burniske, C. and Tatar, J. (2017). *Cryptoassets: The Innovative Investor's Guide to Bitcoin and Beyond.* New York: McGraw-Hill Education.

Buterin, V. (2014). A Next-Generation Smart Contract and Decentralized Application Platform. Ethereum Whitepaper. Retrieved from www.fintech.academy/wp-content/uploads/2016/06/EthereumWhitePaper.pdf.

Chaum, D. (1982). Blind signatures for untraceable payments. Santa Barbara, CA: Department of Computer Science, University of California.

Chuen, D.L.K. and Deng, R. (Eds.) (2018). *Handbook of Blockchain, Digital Finance, and Inclusion*. Cambridge, MA: Academic Press.

Cowan, J. (2006). Statistical Mechanics of the Neocortex. *The Science Network*.

Davidson, S., de Filippi, P., and Potts, J. (2018). Blockchains and the Economics institutions of capitalism. *Journal of Institutional Economics*. 1-20.

Halevy, A., Norvig, P., and Pereira, F. (2009). The Unreasonable Effectiveness of Data. *IEEE Intelligent Systems*. 24(2): 8-12.

Hebblethwaite, C. (2018). IDC: Global blockchain spending to hit $9.2 billion in 2021. *The Block*.

Kant, I. (1784). Answering the Question: "What Is Enlightenment?" *Berlin Monthly*. F. Gedike and J.E. Biester (Eds.). Dec. 1784.

Kiktenko, E.O., Pozhar, N.O., Anufriev, M.N., Trushechkin, A.S., Yunusov, R.R. Kurochkin, Y.V., Lvovsky, A.I., and Fedorov, A.K.. (2018). Quantum-secured blockchain. https://arxiv.org/pdf/1705.09258.pdf.

König, M.D., and Battiston S. (2009). From Graph Theory to Models of Economic Networks. A Tutorial. In: Naimzada A.K., Stefani S., and Torriero A. (Eds.). *Networks, Topology and Dynamics. Lecture Notes in Economics and Mathematical Systems*. 613. Heidelberg, DE: Springer.

Kurtulmus, A.B. and Daniel, K. (2018). Trustless Machine Learning Contracts; Evaluating and Exchanging Machine Learning Models on the Ethereum Blockchain. arXiv:1802.10185v1 [cs.CR] 27 Feb 2018. pp. 2-11.

Lannquist, A. (2018). Today's Crypto Asset Valuation Frameworks. *Medium*.

LeCun, Y., Bengio, Y., and Hinton, G. (2015). Deep Learning. *Nature*. 521: 436-444.

Lerner, J. and Tirole, J. (2005). The Economics of Technology Sharing: Open Source and Beyond. *Journal of Economic Perspectives*. 19(2): 99-120.

Mandelbrot, B. and Hudson, R.I. (2006). *The Misbehavior of Markets: A Fractal View of Financial Turbulence*. New York, NY: Basic Books.

Morabito, V. (2017). *Business Innovation Through Blockchain: The B3 Perspective*. Cham, CH: Springer.

McCulloch, W.S. and Pitts, W.H. (1943). A Logical Calculus of the Ideas Immanent in Nervous Activity. *Bulletin of Mathematical Biophysics*. 5: 115-133.

Mill, J.S. (2006). *Principles of Political Economy*. Indianapolis, IN: Liberty Fund, Inc.

Narayanan, A., Bonneau, J., Felten, E., Miller, A., and Goldfeder, S. (2016). *Bitcoin and Cryptocurrency Technologies: A Comprehensive Introduction*. Princeton University Press.

Nakamoto, S. (2008). Bitcoin: A Peer-to-Peer Electronic Cash System. Bitcoin.org. Retrieved from https://bitcoin.org/bitcoin.pdf.

Potts, J. (2000). *The New Evolutionary Microeconomics: Complexity, Competence and Adaptive Behaviour*. Cheltenham, UK: Edward Elgar.

Rajan, D. and Visser, M. (2018). Quantum Blockchain using entanglement in time. https://arxiv.org/abs/1804.05979.

Rizun, P.R. (2015). A Transaction Fee Market Exists Without a Block Size Limit. https://www.bitcoinunlimited.info/resources/feemarket.pdf.

Romero, J.M., Lavana, U., and Miranda, E.M. (2014). Schrödinger group and quantum finance. *International Journal of Pure and Applied Mathematics*. 90(3): 287-296.

Swan, M. (2015). *Blockchain: Blueprint for a New Economy*. Sebastopol, CA: O'Reilly Media.

———. (2018a). Blockchain Enlightenment and Smart City Cryptopolis. *CryBlock 2018*. ACM. June 15, 2018, Munich, Germany.

———. (2018b). Blockchain for Business: Next-Generation Enterprise Artificial Intelligence Systems. In *Advances in Computers*. Vol. 111. Blockchain Technology: Platforms, Tools and Use Cases. Published: 1st September 2018. Serial Volume. Raj, P. and Deka, G.C. (Eds.). London, UK: Elsevier.

Swan, M. and de Filippi, P. (2017). Introduction, In Toward a Philosophy of Blockchain. Swan, M. and de Filippi, P. (Eds.). *Metaphilosophy*. New York: Wiley & Sons. 48(5):603-19.

Takagi, S. (2017). Blockchain and Organizations: A Consideration from "De-organization" of Trust (in Japanese). Chijo. Vol. 121. pp.8-16.

Taleb, N.N. (2007). *The Black Swan: The Impact of the Highly Improbable*. New York, NY: Random House.

Tasca, P. and Tessone, C. (2017). Taxonomy of Blockchain Technologies. Principles of Identification and Classification (March 31, 2018). Available at SSRN: https://ssrn.com/abstract=2977811.

von Krogh, G., Haefliger, S., Spaeth, S., and Wallin, M.W. (2012). Carrots and Rainbows: Motivation and Social Practice in Open Source Software Development. *MIS Quarterly*. 36(2): 649-676.

Watts, D.J. and Strogatz, S.H. (1998). Collective dynamics of 'small-world' networks. *Nature*. 393: 440-42.

Witte, F.M.C. (2002). On pay-off induced quantum games. arXiv quant-ph/0208171.

———. (2003). Book Review: Path Integrals in Quantum Mechanics, Statistics, Polymer Physics and Financial Markets. *Journal of Statistical Physics*. 111(1/2): 497-499.

———. (2005). Quantum 2-player gambling and correlated pay-off. *Physica Scripta*. 71(2): 229.

World Economic Forum. (2015). Deep Shift: Technology Tipping Points and Societal Impact. *Survey Report*.

Part 1

Economic Theory and Market Structure

Chapter 1

Blockchain Economic Theory: Digital Asset Contracting Reduces Debt and Risk

Melanie Swan

Purdue University, USA

Abstract

Disparate aspects of the emerging Blockchain Economics paradigm have been discussed, particularly cryptotokens and Initial Coin Offerings (ICOs), however, a comprehensive picture of the greater economic transformation unfolding with blockchain technology has not yet been articulated. This chapter proposes a Blockchain Economic Theory of Digital Asset Contracting as an explanatory model. The central argument is that blockchain-registered digital assets can be transacted instantaneously and pledged in new ways. This advance is leading to new modes of contracting (smart contracts) and new forms of money (cryptotokens), which in turn facilitate new structures of financial interaction. Distributed ledgers and blockchain-based structures might be applied to structural economic problems such as debt, systemic risk, technological job outsourcing, entitlements overhang, healthcare cost-outcome disconnects, and financial inclusion. A key innovation is Payment Channels, which enable the use of capital on a net rather than a gross basis, which might eventually lead to a restructuring of debt burdens.

1.1 Introduction

While not a panacea, one litmus test for blockchain technology could be the extent to which it might be used to address structural economic problems. Existing challenges include debt, systemic risk, an orderly transition to the automation economy (technological job outsourcing [Swan, 2017a]), entitlements overhang, a disconnect between healthcare costs and outcomes, and financial inclusion. Table 1 enumerates outstanding economic challenges and potential solutions using blockchain technology. This chapter discusses the challenges and solutions in the form of a causal model.

Table 1. Economic Challenges and Potential Blockchain-based Solutions.

	Economic Challenge	**Blockchain-based Solution**
1	Debt	Net Settlement • Payment Channels • Securities as a Service
2	Systemic Risk	Programmable Risk • Real-time Balance Sheets • Black Swan Smart Contracts
3	Automation Economy	Future of Work • Maslow Self-development Smart Contracts • Shared ownership in automated means of production
4	Entitlements Overhang	Smart Contract Futures (Inflation-protected) • Contractual link of current earnings to future payout • Securities as a Service
5	Healthcare Outcomes	Blockchain Health Economics • Global Healthcare Equivalency Units (quantified outcome tracking) • Digital ID, smart contract consent, interoperable data
6	Financial Inclusion	eWallet Banking Serivces • Officially-recognized Digital ID Credentials • Open Source Credit Bureaus

1.2 Blockchain Economic Theory: Digital Asset Contracting

A Blockchain Economic Theory of Digital Asset Contracting is proposed. The theory presents the distinguishing features of the emerging Blockchain Economics paradigm in the form of a causal model to explain the relationships between the elements (Figure 1). The premise is that blockchain-registered digital assets lead to new modes of contracting and new forms of money, which facilitate new structures of financial interaction. Framed more formally, the hypothesis is that the dependent variable (structures of financial interaction), is influenced by the independent variable (blockchain-registered digital assets), and further affected by the moderating variables (modes of contracting and forms of money).

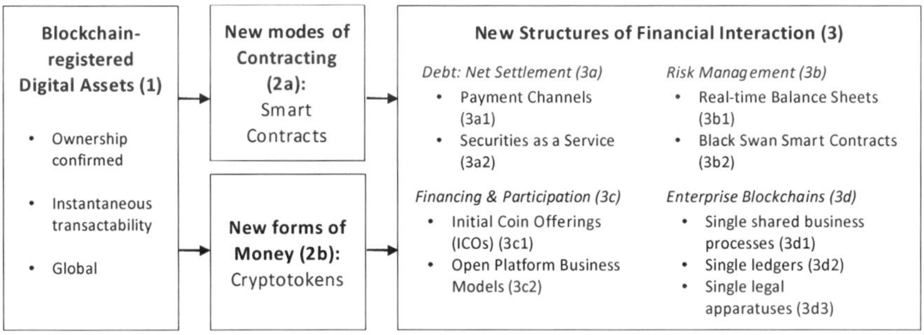

Figure 1. Blockchain economic theory of digital asset contracting.

Outlining the model in detail, blockchain-registered digital assets (1) have the novel functionality that asset ownership is already confirmed, which means that they can be transacted instantaneously, on a global basis. Digitally-registered assets can therefore be pledged in new ways which leads to new modes of contractual relationships between parties (smart contracts) (2a) and new forms of money (cryptotokens) (2b). New modes of contracting and new forms of money facilitate new structures of financial interaction (3). Regarding debt (3a), there is the possibility that capital might be engaged on a net rather than a gross basis with vehicles such as Payment Channels (3a1) and Securities as a Service (3a2). Risk management (3b) could be enhanced with Real-time Balance Sheets (3b1) and programmable risk Black Swan Smart Contracts (3b2). Cryptotokens lead to new modes of financing and participation (3c) such as Initial Coin Offerings (ICOs) (3c1) and participative Open Platform Business Models (3c2). Enterprise Blockchains (3d) configure the possibility of single shared business processes, ledgers, and legal apparatuses (3d1-3). Decentralized methods of contracting and economic orchestration are an extension of digital models more generally. Already with the widespread implementation of the Internet, regulators realized the evolutionary implications of digital network technologies for central banking, including global settlement, and a much smaller institutional footprint and control apparatus for monetary transfer [King, 1999; Ize *et al.*, 1999].

1.3 Blockchain-Registered Digital Assets (1)

Distributed ledgers mean that assets (both physical and digital) can be registered to blockchains for confirmation, control, and transfer. Enforcement mechanisms for connecting physical assets to electronic transfer are non-trivial [Dupont, 2017; Nelson, 2017], but not discussed here. For economic theory, the point is that blockchain-registered digital assets have a heightened mode of exchange. Assets exist in a state of readiness for transfer with the ownership of the asset and the identity of the owner pre-confirmed. Blockchain-based assets should be understood as having the property of being instantaneously transferable, including per digital contractual arrangements. A variety of digitally-enabled and automated transfer mechanisms are made possible. The network-confirmed ownership is the salient mechanism for how parties who do not know each other can nevertheless become contractually obligated. A bank or lawyer is not needed as an intermediary; the network software instantiates the contractual relationship for the peer-to-peer transaction. The principles of the instantaneous digital transferability of assets and the real-time confirmability of identity credentials enable new modes of contracting between parties (2a) and new forms of money (2b).

1.4 New Modes of Contracting: Smart Contracts (2a)

To be legally binding, a contract typically has four elements: two or more parties to the contract, financial consideration, and terms. A *smart contract* is a contract registered to a blockchain, including for some portion of its execution to be automated [Swan, 2015]. For example, the interest rate on a floating-rate mortgage is reset on a monthly basis. Resets are orchestrated digitally at present, and could be further automated with greater transparency with blockchain-based lookup processes using *oracles* (independent data providers). The interest rate reset might be a standard smart contract process calculating the rate as Libor + 150 basis points (1.5%). Blockchain technology might start to be used to coordinate both the initial asset registration and transfer process, as well as the ongoing execution of financial contracts. The implication is that the economy could become increasingly digitally operated. Electronic signatures and digital contracts are legally binding in many geographical domains, enforced in the U.S. through the E-Sign Act (2000) [Stern, 2001] and globally with the UN's Model Law on Electronic Commerce [1996]. The future incarnation of digital contracts could be blockchain-based smart contracts.

1.5 New Forms of Money: Cryptotokens (2b)

Cryptotokens constitute a new kind of money. Conceptually, cryptotokens are "money +" in that they confer the usual functions of money plus additional community participation features. The three tradition functions of money are serving as a medium of exchange, a store of value, and a unit of account. Cryptotokens are a new form of digital money, which have these standard aspects together with additional functions. Definitionally, *cryptotokens* represent a particular fungible and tradable asset that is found on a blockchain ledger [Investopedia, 2018a]. *Digital tokenization* is the process of creating cryptotokens by turning an asset, right, or good (digital or physical) into a tradable unit, and instantiating the asset on a blockchain for its exchange. Cryptotokens are a more complicated and feature-rich form of money that is also a tool for enabling participants to undertake more actions within an economic community, in particular, to earn money, access resources, and vote on decisions.

Cryptotokens could inaugurate a new phase for how individuals expect to interact with Internet-based communities. In blockchain communities, the expectation may be to have both economic and governance participation. The Ethereum project District0x is an example of such a community. A key incentive for users to join a crypto community could be that there is economic participation in terms of an accounting system that tracks and rewards contributions, and a voice in community governance through voting, decision-making, and the ability to propose and discuss initiatives. Rewards for contributions could include earning royalties whenever user-created content is used (e.g. software code, music, art). Community members could likewise pay to access community resources (e.g. content, file storage).

Table 2. User Participation Expectations in Internet-based Communities.

Information Internet 1990-2005	**Social Internet (Web 2.0)** 2005-Present	**Token Internet** 2017-Present
Static information	Engage with dynamic content: like, share, comment, mash-up	Meaningful participation in the economic community: earn money, access resources, vote on decisions

Table 2 considers the evolution of user expectations when engaging with web communities. Initially, websites presented static information, and there was no possibility of interaction. Then, with the social web, users started expecting to be able to “like,” comment, share, and interact with dynamic content and other community members [O’Reilly, 2005]. Now in a third phase, what it means to be a token project is to engender the notion of a participative economic community. Tokens are a means of providing remuneration to those who participate in the community and add value. A greater vesting of responsibility and intensity of community participation is enabled, literally allowing members to “put their money where their mouth is" (i.e. contribute economic resources to areas of concern). This is precisely the greater economic and political self-definition that Kant calls for in *What is Enlightenment?* [1794]. Blockchains enable us to rethink who we are as subjects, configuring the sensibility of the *cryptocitizen* as one who thinks freely from the dictates of authority [Swan, 2018b].

1.6 New Structures of Financial Interaction (3)

1.6.1 *Debt: Net Engagement of Capital (3a)*

Traditionally, capital has been engaged at the gross, not the net level. *Net settlement* is a settlement system between parties in which transactions are accumulated and offset against each other, with only the net difference transferred. Most national and international banking and payments systems, however, operate on a real-time gross settlement (RTGS) basis. Significant financial operations also engage capital at the gross level, for example fundraising. A municipality building a bridge borrows the whole amount needed in an Industrial Development Bond (IDB) (Figure 2). However, with digitally-registered blockchain assets, new kinds of arrangements might be possible to engage capital on a net basis [Swan, 2017b]. The economic question is to what extent public sector activity might be instantiated in distributed ledgers. The public sector currently comprises 15% of OECD economies federally [Baddock *et al.*, 2015], plus 14.2% at the state level in the U.S. [Frohlich and Kent, 2015]. Overly large public sectors have been shown to hamper growth [Olson, 1999].

Smart contracts might be employed to address the time lag between current and future cash flows such that capital could be pledged and transferred in smaller more regular payments. In the bridge example, smart contracts could match expected tax receipts with cost outlays for the bridge construction. In principle, a bond offering might not be necessary with directed tax receipts. Smart contracts could transfer weekly tax receipts from constituents to contractor construction expenses. In a more efficient system, real-time finance could be a possibility. Blockchain-based contractual structures might enable capital to be utilized more effectively. One benefit could be offering an alternative to the monolithic structure of debt, a problem affecting sovereign states [Zumbrun, 2017; Frewen, 2010], institutions [Choudhry *et al.*, 2014], and individuals [Sweet *et al.*, 2013] alike.

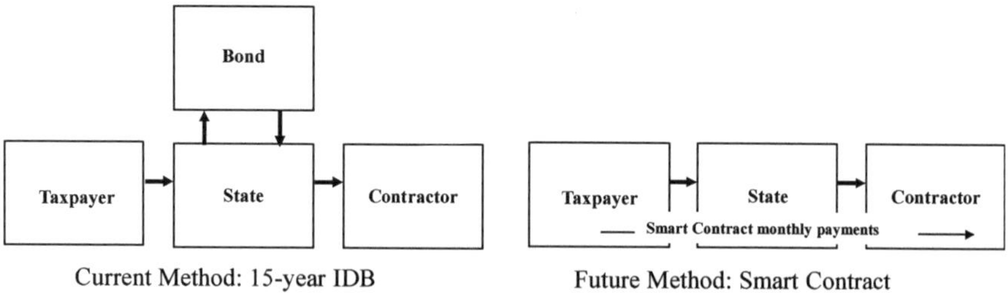

Figure 2. Structure of municipal finance: bonds could become smart contract pledges.

Net settlement is not a new concept. Before central banking, there was an historical precedent for net settlement amongst parties and free banking systems (meaning a plurality of banks each issuing their own notes). Societies with more equitable distributions of power were more likely to have net-settled systems. Notable examples include Canada (1800-1935), Sweden (1831-1902), and the Fukien province in China (1644-1911) [Selgin, 1988, pp. 7-15]. White describes English and Scottish free banking (1716-1845), particularly in the linen industry, where trust and a diversity of IOU instruments played a role in financing remote trade in the Scottish Highlands [1996]. Smith argues that net-cleared financial systems are less risky because self-preservation is more prominent [1990, pp. 178-184].[a] Banks having reciprocal claims on each other may instill greater financial responsibility than centralized methods. Selgin proposes a theory of free banking, suggesting that money supplies are more stable and resilient when there is competitive note issuance [1988]. Despite the historical precedent of net clearing, many countries were forced to adopt a central banking system in wartimes. The central banking model is prevalent today, however distributed ledgers might enable a return to net settlement, including net clearing models facilitated by central authorities [DTCC, 2017]. A preference for the benefits of net clearing can be seen in

[a] A specific balance sheet example of net-cleared note issuance is provided [Smith, 1990, pp. 197-200].

securities industry implementations of blockchain technology [Guo and Liang, 2016; Mainelli and Milne, 2016; FINRA, 2017].

The market benefits of net settlement and the possibility of digitized value transfer on blockchain networks suggest that a greater portion of the economy might be net-settled rather than gross-settled. The economic gains could be more effective capital utilization by restructuring debt into smaller borrowed amounts and obviating the need for fallow pools of capital. For example, PricewaterhouseCoopers [2015] estimates that $3.9 trillion of otherwise unused working capital is committed in global supply chains. Similarly, Ripple claims that $5 trillion in capital is stored unproductively in local bank accounts around the world to fund the conduct of international business [2017]. These fallow capital pools might be remedied by blockchain-based real-time net settlement.

1.6.1.1 *Payment Channels (3a1)*

One important new form of financial relationship that has emerged in the blockchain economy is the payment channel. A *payment channel* is a three-step financial contract between parties. First, one party deposits an escrow balance with another party, together with a request for a refund for the full amount, which the other party signs as an acknowledgement. The deposit does not become live (is not broadcast to the blockchain network) until the receiving party signs the refund. Thus, both parties (who may not know each other) are protected. Either party can end the payment channel at any time, and the then-current balance is refunded. Second, during the specified period (e.g. an hour, day, or month), the first party consumes a resource against the escrow balance (e.g. watches video minutes or drinks a daily coffee), or the second party performs work for the first party against the escrow balance (e.g. programmer hours worked against a contract). At each activity update, a new refund transaction is signed by both parties acknowledging the elapsed activity against the escrow deposit (e.g. each hour of work, or each coffee consumed). Third, at the end of the period, the payment channel is closed, with the latest refund transaction between the parties broadcast to the network.

Payment channels engage capital on a net basis in that only the opening deposit transaction and ending net transaction are broadcast to the network, not each intermediary transaction. This could facilitate blockchain scalability since only the net activity is posted to the long-term record. Both parties are protected since they are contractually obligated the whole time, and any party can close the contract at any time, triggering the latest signed refund to be broadcast to the network. The net settlement aspect becomes more prominent in two-way payment channels, such as roommates sharing expenses, local neighborhood economies, and small business networks [Swan, 2018c]. Payment channels could be used at any level of economic activity for individuals, businesses, and municipalities for the net engagement of capital [Swan, 2018e].

1.6.1.2 *Securities as a Service (3a2)*

The contractual pledging of assets in distributed ledgers could enable new modes of ownership such that it is no longer necessary to own the whole asset or amount. Fractional ownership can be executed easily with blockchain-based models. The sharing economy has demonstrated that the consumable benefits of an asset can be rented on demand. Streaming music and video services have supplanted CD and DVD ownership, and Uber and Airbnb have obviated the need to own cars and homes. Theoretically, there is no reason why this could not also be the case with securities. *Securities as Service* is a model that grants access to the consumable benefits of the asset (cash flows and price appreciation) without having to own the underlying asset [Swan, 2016]. At present, it is still necessary to own the underlying assets, securities, to provide for one's retirement. Instead, there could be smart contracts (implemented slowly over time to engender sufficient trust and proven results) that deliver the consumable benefit of owning securities without having to own the underlying securities. These kinds of choices are available to sophisticated investors (e.g. invest in the capital appreciation tranche in a securitized offering), but the principles could be more widely applied to provide these kinds of benefits to a broader audience. The potential impact is freeing capital for more productive uses and reducing uncertainty about future cash flows. Entitlement overhangs (governments unable to meet future obligations to retired workers) might be addressed by instantiating pension systems with Securities as a Service smart contracts to guarantee future cash flows.

1.6.2 *Risk Management (3b)*

1.6.2.1 *Real-time Balance Sheets (3b1)*

Blockchain-registered digital assets enable the possibility of new mechanisms of financial control and risk management such as real-time balance sheets for organizations [Swan, 2018a]. Private views of real-time balance sheets could be shared with regulators to better manage bank capital requirements and systemic risk (the risk of large-scale failure in financial systems [Rimkus, 2016]). The consolidated effect of off-balance sheet liabilities could become more transparent. More importantly, the need for off-balance sheet liabilities could disappear as there is more trust and less risk in financial systems with real-time asset valuation, immediate transactability, and greater visibility into counterparty obligations [Swan, 2018d]. There could be greater predictive management of systemic risk. Regulators could have better access to data to model the intensity and effects of financial institution interdependence to protect against contagion (the impact of one institution's failing on the overall market). Since blockchain-based data may be more readily available, data science methods such as deep learning algorithms might be applied to the understanding of risk. For example, the risk posed by programmatic or high-frequency trading (HFT) is unclear. HFT has doubled since the 2008 financial crash, and comprises 55% of the volume in U.S. equity markets [Miller and Shorter, 2016]. HFT is implicated in flash crashes, a recent phenomenon in financial markets in which there are extremely rapid price declines caused by automated trading [Kirilenko *et al.*, 2014].

1.6.2.2 *Black Swan Smart Contracts (3b2)*

Distributed ledgers could be implemented to facilitate both *monetary economics*, monetary transfer in the present moment, and *financial economics*, the more complicated financial instruments related to transfer in future periods such as mortgages. In finance, options are a standard instrument used to manage risk in future time periods. Options give the holder the right to buy (call) or sell (put) an asset at a certain price at a future date. Smart contracts have the same functionality of financial options: the possible right to buy or sell an asset at a certain price at a certain date. However, smart contracts might be used to control a wider variety of assets, not only financial assets. The degree of risk could be a user-selected parameter of any smart contract. The most basic choices could be low-medium-high risk. Just as users do not need to have a legal background to pick a Creative Commons license for a YouTube Video from standard drop-down choices (e.g. Attribution, ShareAlike, NonCommercial), likewise users would not need to have financial expertise in order to select the desired level of risk for a smart contract. Thus, *programmable risk* could become a standard smart contract feature.

In Black Swan financial theory, risk is mapped in the form of an s-curve [Taleb, 2007]. The risk curve is s-shaped: convex (a bowl facing upward) at the start, then linear, then concave (a bowl facing downward). Engaging with a phenomenon at the convex portion of the risk curve may be preferable because there is protection against downside risk. Big data analytics indicates that the s-curves which characterize financial risk may have a wider application, particularly in the healthcare domain. Risk curves are used in disease treatment to find the optimal amount of drug dosage for patients that is not too little to have an effect and is not so great as to produce harm [Davis and Svendsgaard, 1990].

S-curve risk quantification can be combined with insurance methods to generate Black Swan Smart Contracts. It is straightforward to measure the cost of risk for large-scale known phenomena. For example, in the insurance market, the percent of car crashes and the cost of repair for any postal code is known. These kinds of metrics could be used to price the cost of insurance in a smart contract. Insurance for any known and quantified situation might be automatically included as an option in any smart contract, similar to the way flight insurance is offered as an option with online airline ticket purchases. Black Swan Smart Contracts allow the user to programmatically select the amount of risk in the smart contract.

1.6.3 *Financing and Participation (3c)*

1.6.3.1 *Initial Coin Offerings (ICOs) (3c1)*

Initial Coin Offerings (ICOs) have emerged as a novel and official form of financing in Blockchain Economics. Whereas Initial Public Offerings (IPOs) sell investors access to a company's equity, ICOs sell access to a cryptotoken money supply connected to a specific project. Definitionally, an ICO is a means by which funds are raised for a new cryptocurrency venture by selling a percentage of the cryptocurrency to early backers of the project [Investopedia, 2018b]. In the U.S., after crowdfunding (a donation-type investment for product pre-purchase) became legal in 2016 [Puutio, 2016], there was a boom of ICOs under the auspices of crowdfunding until, due to their securities-like properties, the SEC started regulating ICOs as such in July 2017 [SEC, 2017]. China has banned ICOs, but the precedent is that many other countries treat ICOs as securities that must comply with local regulatory laws [Reese, 2017].

Already in June 2017, it was reported that blockchain entrepreneurs had raised more through ICOs than traditional VC funding ($327 million as compared with $295 million) [Sunnarborg, 2017]. As of February 2018, it was cited that cumulatively, ICOs had raised $8.84 billion [Coindesk, 2018], as VCs and other investors now invest in cryptotoken projects through ICOs. On one hand, *regulated* ICOs are the official financing vehicle of the blockchain economy. On the other hand, ICOs have a tainted reputation. Commentators and former regulators alike note that perhaps 99% of *unregulated* ICOs may end up worthless, if not completely fraudulent [Suberg, 2017; Poppernov, 2017]. It should be noted that even regulated ICOs are still quite risky due to the uncertain future prospects of projects, and because best practices have not yet arisen as to standard expectations regarding how funds are to be used and recirculated to token holders. (In the future all of this might be stipulated by smart contract with standardized Creative Commons-type selections, for example Automatic Profit Sharing to Token Holders.)

ICOs are an advance in that they offer an even more direct interest in a project than was possible previously. In a sense, ICOs are a capital budgeting mechanism because they offer project-level investment. The progression is that in IPOs, access to equity ownership in a firm is pre-sold to investors before being available to the general market. In crowdfunding (e.g. via Kickstarter and Indiegogo), access to a company's product is pre-sold. In ICOs, access to the platform and local economy is pre-sold with the participation token. The next phase could be using blockchain models to surface and pre-commit customer demand for a project. Blockchain-based pre-contracts could attest to customer demand for a potential product or service. Financing might be obtained on the basis of securitized customer demand.

ICOs are emblematic of the blockchain economic principle of tighter linkage between the sources and uses of capital, and the contributions and rewards of economic community participants. A closer connection between supply and demand (the supply of capital and the demand for products and services) can be seen in the owner-user model of ICOs because owners are users. ICOs are an example of *platform cooperativism* [Scholz, 2016] in that token offerings facilitate the ownership of assets by their users (although investor-only owners also participate). The incentive to invest in a token offering is that a token holder can use the platform, and also realize any capital appreciation benefits that accrue if the platform's user community grows.

1.6.3.2 *Open Platform Business Models (3c2)*

A cryptotoken-based system for monetary transfer enables open platform business models for large-scale global participation. Not only is the underlying blockchain software often available as APIs and open source code that can be modified, but the business models too are open, in the sense of operating on open platforms (open to any user to develop an application on the platform). The traditional Internet-based business model is closed proprietary platforms such as Netflix, Facebook, and Instagram. The idea is to establish a proprietary database and network, with the goal of maximizing users, content generation, and revenue [Manigart and Wright, 2013]. Users can contribute content but not applications on closed platforms. Instead, the blockchain model is open platforms, in which the goal is maximizing user participation, value creation, and rewards to participants, so that the overall economy grows and all participants can benefit. An intermediary point between closed proprietary platforms (Netflix) and open platforms (Ethereum) is App Stores (e.g. Apple, Android, and Windows), in which user-contributed applications can be merchandized to consumers and revenue is shared between the platform and the developer.

In digital economies (whether open or closed platform), *network effects* occur in that network platforms have increasing returns to scale as more users are added [Eisenmann *et al.*, 2006]. Network effects are described mathematically by Metcalfe's Law, as the value of a network being proportional to the square of the number of connected users [Shapiro and Varian, 1999]. Economists argue that networks lead to natural monopolies due to the network effect that the overall value delivered to users increases if everyone uses the same network instead of having competing networks. Therefore, inefficiencies arise due to the market power of Internet giants such as Google, Amazon, and Facebook, because they can impose rent-seeking (exploitative) behavior [Catalini and Gans, 2018]. Market power inefficiencies allow one-way network effects to accrue to proprietary platform owners, particularly as enforced through the system of private property ownership. Instead, blockchain models allow two-way network effects to accrue to all community participants, because the platforms are not singularly owned [Barrera, 2018].

Given the shared ownership model in blockchain projects, rent-seeking tokens (those merely earning a pass-through fee) have been criticized as compared with value-creation tokens (those which reward contribution). Two-way network effects (which benefit all parties, not just the platform owner) are characteristic of the sharing economy generally, and the blockchain economy specifically [Brynjolfsson and McAfee, 2017]. One indication of how two-way network effects operate in the blockchain economy is through bootstrapping. This is the value created by the compressed time-to-market of entrepreneurs being able to deploy new token projects on an already-existing network without having to bootstrap (create) their own network. Since Ethereum is an open platform for decentralized applications (DApps), a new token project can ostensibly reach the entire installed base of Ethereum wallets [Anacrypt, 2017]. Unlike the App Store example, the platform hosting the application (Ethereum) does not take a fee, but does charge for computation resources in the form of *gas*. Further, Ethereum is an ecosystem model such that any holder of the platform's native token, Ether, experiences appreciation in value as more users and applications start using the platform.

There is social empowerment through the economic decision-making and ownership dimensions of token projects. *Platform cooperativism* is the idea of digital platforms being owned as co-operatives [Scholz, 2016]. Digital platform co-operatives are a proactive alternative to resisting economic monopolies and other mechanisms of hierarchical control and exploitation. Further, user-owned means of production not only resist hierarchical control, but also decrease income inequality [Piketty, 2013], improve social equity [Wilkinson and Pickett, 2011], and could foster an orderly transition to the automation economy (jobs outsourced to technology) [Swan, 2017a].

1.6.4 *Enterprise Blockchains (3d)*

Business blockchains could enable substantial improvements in efficiency. Ultimately, there could be just one instance of the shared business processes, accounting ledger, and legal apparatus, wherein each party in the value chain engages with separate read-write views [Swan, 2018a]. Implementing single shared business processes could take time as sufficient trust and accustomation to blockchain processes would be necessary. However, efficiency savings could propel adoption as separate record-keeping no longer makes sense in an era of digital services and blockchain-based asset pledging and transfer. It is expensive for firms to reconcile transactions across private ledgers [Iansiti and Lakhani, 2017], when the cost of basic operations such as invoice processing might be decreased by as much as 80% in blockchain networks [IBM, 2017].

Not only might single shared business processes, ledgers, and legal apparatuses be enabled among firms in a value chain, but firms might also run payment channel-type accounts with one other instead of having traditional vendor credit relationships. In the Blockchain Economy, digitized assets imply that value transfer can be immediate. Every asset is always available online for transfer at any time. Since assets are stored digitally, they can be escrowed and collateralized, which means that parties can more easily run an on-demand credit account with one another.

The 30-60-90 day vendor terms that must be approved piecemeal for trading partners now could become obsolete as parties start to run payment channel accounts with one another protected by digital collateral, smart contracts, and automatic payment transfer.

1.7 Risks, Limitations, and Future Outlook

This analysis is limited by many factors, in particular a necessarily speculative outlook given the early phase of development of the blockchain sector. Some of the most prominent risks facing the industry include technology scalability, political regulation, and consumer adoption. Blockchain technology is challenging to understand both conceptually and technically, and the steep learning curve could produce costly failures as it is implemented. It may be too early to propose a model linking elements that could continue to evolve considerably from their current form.

1.8 Conclusion

This chapter provides a comprehensive overview of the distinct and emergent Blockchain Economics paradigm and proposes a causal model of the relationships between elements. The central argument is that blockchain-registered digital assets can be transacted instantaneously and pledged in new ways. This advance is leading to new modes of contracting (smart contracts) and new forms of money (cryptotokens), which in turn facilitate new structures of financial interaction.

The practical impact of this work is that tools and structures are proposed which might be implemented to overcome contemporary economic challenges. Distributed ledgers and blockchain-based structures might be applied to structural economic problems such as debt, systemic risk, technological job outsourcing, entitlements overhang, healthcare cost-outcome disconnects, and financial inclusion. A key innovation is Payment Channels, which enable the use of capital on a net rather than a gross basis, and thus might lead to a restructuring of debt burdens. Other structures such as Real-time Balance Sheets and Black Swan Smart

Contracts might provide firms and regulators with greater financial control and risk management capacity.

The theoretical impact of this work is two-fold. First, foundational economic theorizing is proposed which includes a shift to engaging capital on a net rather than a gross basis, the ability to quantize and select risk parameters, and the possibility of increasing efficiency through single-shared business processes and real-time valuation mechanisms. Second, a novel explanatory model is articulated, a Blockchain Economic Theory of Digital Asset Contracting. The gap bridged is that although specific aspects of the emerging Blockchain Economics paradigm have been discussed, a comprehensive picture of the causal interaction of elements has not yet been proposed. This model could serve as a structure for understanding developments as the Blockchain Economy continues to unfold, and lead to improved decision-making in the context of policy-making, corporate investment, consumer adoption, and entrepreneurial innovation.

References

Anacrypt. (2017). How to add a New Token to MyEtherWallet.com. *Steemit*.

Baddock, E., Lang, P., and Srivastava, V. (2015). Size of the Public Sector. *World Bank*.

Barrera, C. (2018). The Blockchain Effect: Network Effects without Market Power Costs. *Medium*.

Brynjolfsson, E. and McAfee, A. (2017). *Machine, Platform, Crowd: Harnessing Our Digital Future*. New York: W. W. Norton & Company.

Catalini, C. and Gans, J. S. (2017). Some Simple Economics of the Blockchain. Rotman School of Management Working Paper No. 2874598. MIT Sloan Research Paper No. 5191-16.

Choudhry, T., Jayasekera, R., and Kling, G. (Eds.) (2014). The impact of the Global Financial Crisis on Banks, Financial Markets and Institutions in Europe. *Journal of International Money and Finance*. 49(B): 191-492.

Coindesk. (2018). ICO Tracker. https://www.coindesk.com/ico-tracker/.

Davis, J. M. and Svendsgaard, D. J. (1990). U-shaped dose–response curves: their occurrence and implications for risk assessment. *J Toxicol Environ Health*. 30: 71-83.

DTCC. (2017). DTCC Selects IBM, AXONI and R3 to Develop DTCC's Distributed Ledger Solution for Derivatives Processing. Press Release.

Dupont, Q. (2017). Blockchain Identities: Notational Technologies for Control and Management of Abstracted Entities. *Metaphilosophy*. 48(5): 634-653.

Eisenmann, T. R., Parker, G. O., and Van Alstyne, M. W. (2006). How to Launch Your Digital Platform: Strategies for Two-Sided Markets. *Harvard Business Review*.

FINRA. (2017). Distributed Ledger Technology: Implications of Blockchain for the Securities Industry. https://www.finra.org/sites/default/files/FINRA_Blockchain_Report.pdf.

Frewen, J. (2010). Debt Burden Cripples Poorer Nations. *Worldpress*.

Frohlich, T. C. and Kent, A. (2015). States with the most government workers. *24/7 Wall St*.

Guo, Y. and Liang, C. (2016). Blockchain application and outlook in the banking industry. *Financial Innovation*. pp. 2-24.

Iansiti, M. and Lakhani, K. R. (2017). The Truth About Blockchain. *Harvard Business Review*.

IBM. (2017). Boosting financial intelligence with cognitive computing. *Economia*.

Investopedia. (2018a). Crypto Token. https://www.investopedia.com/terms/c/crypto-token.asp

———. (2018b). Initial Coin Offering (ICO). https://www.investopedia.com/terms/i/initial-coin-offering-ico.asp.

Ize, A., Kovanen, A., and Henckel, T. (1999). Central Banking Without Central Bank Money. *IMF Working Paper*. WP/99/92.

Kant, I. (1784). Answering the Question: What Is Enlightenment? Berlin Monthly, F. Gedike and J. E. Biester (Eds.). Dec. 1784.

King, M. (1999). Challenges for monetary policy: new and old. *Bank of England Quarterly Bulletin*. (39): 397-415.

Kirilenko, A., Kyle, A. S., Samadi, M., and Tuzun, T. (2014). The Flash Crash: The Impact of High Frequency Trading on an Electronic Market. *U.S. CFTC*.

Mainelli, M. and Milne, A. (2016). The impact and potential of blockchain on securities transaction lifecycle). *SWIFT Institute*. Working Paper No. 2015-007.

Manigart, S. and Wright, M. (2013). Venture Capital Investors and Portfolio Firms. *Foundations and Trends in Entrepreneurship*. 9(4-5): 365-570.

Miller, R. S. and Shorter, G. (2016). High Frequency Trading: Overview of Recent Developments. *U.S. Congressional Research Service*. 7-5700. R44443. https://fas.org/sgp/crs/misc/R44443.pdf.

Nelson, J. S. *et al.* (2017). Sweetbridge White Paper. Available at: https://sweetbridge.com/public/docs/Sweetbridge-Whitepaper.pdf

Olson, M. (1999). *Power and Prosperity: Outgrowing Communist and Capitalist Dictatorships*. New York, NY: Basic Books.

O'Reilly, T. (2005). What Is Web 2.0: Design Patterns and Business Models for the Next Generation of Software. O'Reilly Media.

Piketty, T. (2013). *Capital in the Twenty-First Century*. Harvard University Press.

Poppernov, N. (2017). Initial Coin Offerings Horrify a Former S.E.C. Regulator. *New York Times*.

PricewaterhouseCoopers. (2015). Bridging the Gap 2015 Annual Global Working Capital Survey.

Puutio, T. A. (2016). Equity crowdfunding is now legal, but don't expect anything to change just yet. *Tech Crunch*.

Reese, F. (2017). ICO Regulations by Country. *Bitcoin Market Journal*.

Rimkus, R. (2016). Systemic Risk: Definition and Application. *CFA Institute*.

Ripple. (2017). Company press release. https://ripple.com/ripple_press/ripples-blockchain-network-now-100-strong/.

Scholz, T. (2016). Platform Cooperativism. Challenging the Corporate Sharing Economy. New York: Rosa Luxemburg Stiftung.

SEC. (2017). SEC Issues Investigative Report Concluding DAO Tokens, a Digital Asset, Were Securities. United States Securities and Exchange Commission (US SEC), Press Release, July 25, 2017. https://www.sec.gov/news/press-release/2017-131

Selgin, G. (1988). *The Theory of Free Banking: Money Supply Under Competitive Note Issue*. London: Rowman & Littlefield.

Shapiro, C. and Varian, H. R. (1999). *Information Rules*. Cambridge: Harvard Business Press.

Smith, V. C. (1990). *The Rationale of Central Banking: And the Free Banking Alternative*. University Park IL: Liberty Fund.

Stern, J. E. (2001). The Electronic Signatures in Global and National Commerce Act. *Berkeley Technology Law Journal*. 16(1): 391-414.

Sunnarborg, A. (2017). ICO Investments Pass VC Funding in Blockchain Market First. *Coindesk*.

Suberg, W. (2017). Andreas Antonopoulos, *Cointelegraph*.

Sweet, E., Nandi, A., Adam, E., and McDade, T. (2013). The High Price of Debt: Household financial debt and its impact on mental and physical health. *Soc Sci Med*. 91: 94-100.

Swan, M. (2015). *Blockchain: Blueprint for a New Economy*. Sebastopol, CA: O'Reilly Media.

———. (2016). Decentralized Finance: Blockchains, Prediction, and Valuation. The Economist - Finance Disrupted, New York, NY, October 13, 2016. http://www.financedisrupted.com/melanie-swan/.

———. (2017a). Is Technological Unemployment Real? Abundance Economics. In *Surviving the Machine Age: Intelligent Technology and the Transformation of Human Work*. James Hughes and Kevin LaGrandeur (Eds.). London: Palgrave Macmillan. pp.19-33.

———. (2017b). Anticipating the Economic Benefits of Blockchain. *Technology Innovation Management Review*. 7(10): 6-13.

———. (2018a). Blockchain Economics: 'Ripple for ERP' integrated blockchain supply chain ledgers. *European Financial Review*. Feb-Mar: 24-7.

———. (2018b). Blockchain Enlightenment and Smart City Cryptopolis. *CryBlock 2018*. ACM. June 15, 2018, Munich, Germany.

———. (2018c). Blockchain Economics: Tackle Debt and Systemic Risk. Virginia Tech Inaugural Blockchain Symposium. April 20, 2018. https://www.slideshare.net/lablogga/blockchain-economics-tackle-debt-and-systemic-risk.

———. (2018d, In review). Blockchain Economic Networks: Economic Network Theory of Systemic Risk and Blockchain Technology. In *Implications of Blockchain*. H. Treiblmaier and R. Beck (Eds.). Palgrave Macmillan.

———. (2018e). Blockchain Economics: Tackle Debt and Systemic Risk. Virginia Tech Blockchain Symposium. April 20, 2018. Available at: https://www.slideshare.net/lablogga/blockchain-economics-tackle-debt-and-systemic-risk.

Taleb, N. N. (2007). *The Black Swan: The Impact of the Highly Improbable*. New York, NY: Random House.

U.N. Commission on International Trade Law (UNCITRAL) (1996, 1998). UNCITRAL Model Law on Electronic Commerce Guide to Enactment. https://www.uncitral.org/pdf/english/texts/electcom/05-89450_Ebook.pdf

White, L. H. (1996). *Free Banking in Britain: Theory, Experience and Debate 1800-1845*. London: Institute of Economic Affairs.

Wilkinson, R. and Pickett, K. (2011). *The Spirit Level: Why Greater Equality Makes Societies Stronger*. London, UK: Bloomsbury Press.

Zumbrun, J. (2017). Just Four Large Countries Have a Higher Debt Burden Than the U.S. *Wall Street Journal*.

Chapter 2

Does Blockchain "Decentralize" Everything?: An Insight from Organizational Economics

Soichiro Takagi

GLOCOM, International University of Japan, Japan

Abstract

There have been increasing expectations that blockchain technology would decentralize organizations in a wider range of services such as sharing economy, public ledgers, and electricity. On the other hand, decentralization is facing difficult challenges such as seen in the split of Bitcoin and the growing expectation on permissioned ledgers. This chapter aims to shed light on the economic mechanisms behind blockchain-enabled decentralization from the viewpoint of organizational economics. An analysis is provided with an in-depth case study of the Bitcoin ecosystem. Results reveal that blockchain technology decentralizes organizations by reducing uncertainty through codifying tasks and also by reducing the risk of opportunism through the governance by distributed participants, while those decentralization applies only to a fraction of the whole ecosystem. Additionally, decentralization sacrifices workers' incentives such as income risk aversion and efficient decision-making. Therefore, the extent of blockchain-enabled decentralization is determined by the trade-offs between efficiency through tasks marketization and workers' incentives.

1.1 Envisioned decentralized organizations

One of the reasons blockchain is attracting attention as one of the most disruptive technologies that would deeply impact society and the economy is its potential to eliminate the need for an organizational structure with a central authority. The success of Bitcoin, with more than 8 years of stable operations, suggests that providing a medium of exchange service can be conducted by a network of anonymous participants rather than organized central banks. Nakamoto [2018] describes it as "a system for electronic transactions without relying on trust." The attempt to enable economic transactions without central authority seems to have succeeded.

The idea that the essential impact of blockchain is to enable information management and service provision without relying on the trust provided by a central entity has been widely accepted. Swan [2015] describes blockchain as "the architecture for a new system of decentralized trustless transaction" [Swan, 2015, p. x], and Tapscott and Tapscott [2016, p. 5] stated that blockchain "ensured the integrity of the data exchanged among these billions of devices without going through a trusted third party." Campbell-Verduyn [2018] described how the application of blockchain would disintermediate the roles of key centralized actors, and Takagi [2017b, p. 12] suggested that blockchain's impact is the "de-organization" of trust.

Since then, there have been increasing expectations that blockchain, the fundamental technology that enabled Bitcoin, would decentralize organizations in a wider range of services. In fact, blockchain's continuous development and smart contract function as seen in Ethereum, has made it possible for anonymous and distributed computers to provide a wider range of services, not only cryptocurrencies. Based on the expectations of such transformative innovation on organizational structures, an amount of visions, attempts, and trials have been provided to establish the concept of DAO (Decentralized Autonomous Organizations). Such efforts can be observed in Arcade City (a decentralized ride sharing), Colony (a decentralized crowdsourcing), Storj (a decentralized cloud storage), and Blockstack (a decentralized Internet data management).

However, despite its increasing popularity, Bitcoin itself is facing difficult challenges with its efficient functionality, which is caused by its decentralized organizational structure. For example, in order to coordinate the miners' work, an excessive amount of electricity is consumed in the mining process. On the other hand, the split of Bitcoin into Bitcoin (BTC) and Bitcoin Cash (BCH) that happened in August 2017 suggested the difficulty of collective decision-making without a central authority.

In addition, with the increasing expectations of large enterprises to utilize blockchain technology as a new computing architecture, there has been a strong temptation to use the technology in a closed and secure environment as a "permissioned" ledger. This trend is driven by the current businesses' needs, which require compliance with regulations such as the audit and control over customer data and sufficient performance such as the transactions throughput. As a result, the use of decentralized technology by centralized organizations has rapidly increased in the past few years. Therefore, the original idea of blockchain technology, which is to enable service provision without central authority, is meeting critical challenges that questions whether decentralized organizations have a fundamental advantage over the incumbent organizational structure with central authorities.

In this regard, there are several significant studies on Bitcoin's and blockchain-enabled services' governance structure. For example, De Filippi and Loveluck [2016] described in detail the Bitcoin community's governance structure from a political economy's perspective and suggested that the community is controlled by a rather small number of core developers. Hsieh *et al.*'s [2018] analysis, based on a corporate governance's perspective, examined if decentralization is valued by investors. Surprisingly, they found out that a cryptocurrency operated by a centralized management team is more valued by investors. Oermann and Töllner [2015] examine the Bitcoin community's governance structure particularly around Bitcoin Foundation and the developers and suggest that its architecture is not so transparent as an open source project. On the other hand, Musiani *et al.* [2018] analyzed the decision-making process of the "fork," the split of source code that governs the functionality of Bitcoin, which happened in March 2013, and found power asymmetry among actors. Gencer *et al.* [2018] assessed the decentralization of the network of Bitcoin and Ethereum from technological perspective.

Generally speaking, these prior studies describe Bitcoin's governance structure of its development, implementation, and operations based on the political economy and an anthropologic view, and also technological perspectives. On the other hand, the comparison between decentralized organizations and those with central authority can be deeply analyzed through cumulative studies on "markets or hierarchies" in organizational economics. Therefore, this chapter aims to shed light on the economic mechanisms behind the blockchain-enabled decentralization from the viewpoint of organizational economics. More specifically, this chapter tries to answer the following questions: 1) how blockchain technology "decentralizes" organizations from an organizational economics' perspective, 2) whether decentralized organizations have fundamental advantages over incumbent organizations with centralized authority, and 3) whether it is possible to decentralize everything using blockchain.

1.2 Framework to assess the decentralization of organizations

In order to assess how Blockchain is affecting organizational structure, this section reviews the organizations' traditional analyses from an economic point of view and discusses the points that should be taken into consideration to assess how blockchain technology affects organizational structure.

1.2.1 *The definition of an organization*

As a starting point for a discussion, it would be meaningful to clarify the definition of an "organization" as discussed in this chapter. In the broadest meaning, any coordinated activities among individuals can be considered to be carried out through organizations [Barnard, 1938; Milgrom and Roberts, 1992]. Based on this meaning, any wide range of coordination, such as a country, a capitalistic economic system, or even a market, can be identified as an organization (D_0 in Figure 1).

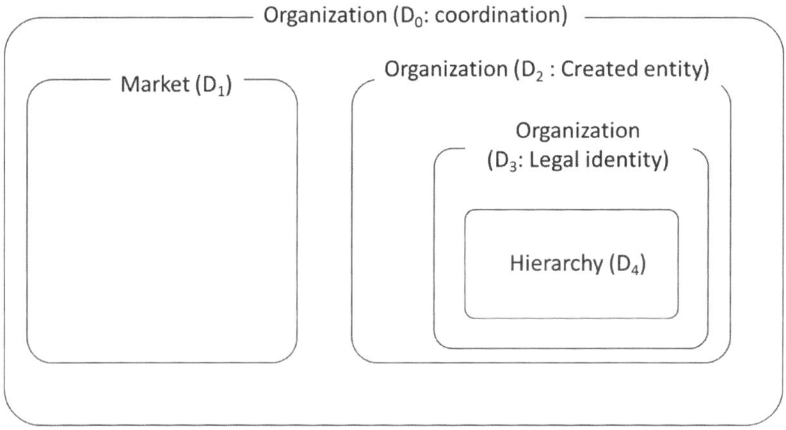

Figure 1. Category of organizations.

For a more practical definition, Milgrom and Roberts [1992] introduce two layers of organizations. The first layer defines economic organizations as "[...] created entities within and through which people interact to reach individual and collective economic goals" (p. 20, D_2 in Figure 1). In this broad definition, any economic activity involving people's interactions with some economic goal should be included in the definition of an organization. As Adam Smith [1776] showed, by coordinating the activities of entities with different skill sets and by performing economic transactions among them, all counterparts are better off by achieving a larger output as a group.

In a narrower definition, organizations are characterized by being an independent legal identity, which enables them to enter binding contracts [Milgrom and Roberts, 1992, p. 20, D_3 in Figure 1]. The existence of a legal identity suggests that this entity has some obligations and rights against outside entities, and these obligations and rights are distributed to individuals inside the organization. In one case, this distribution is conducted through the nexus of contracts [Alchian and Demsetz, 1972], such as employment contracts, which are characterized by hierarchical and authoritative control. However, the distribution does not necessarily involve employment contracts in cases of industrial groups, non-profit organizations, foundations, etc. Market, that is characterized by voluntary bargaining [Milgrom and Roberts, 1992], is also shown as D_1 in Figure 1.

As a result, organizations are categorized into four modes based on the degree of centralization. The degree of decentralization is evaluated based on how strongly the individuals' activities are coordinated. The scale of decentralization is shown in Figure 2.

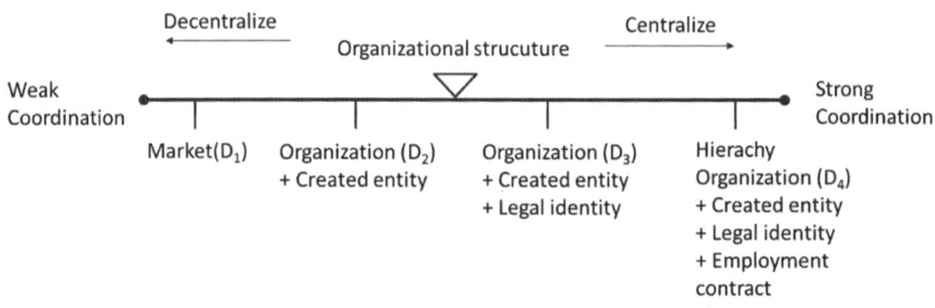

Figure 2. The scale of decentralization.

1.2.2 *Transaction cost economics*

The factors that affect the organizational structure are categorized into two forces. The first is the decision on "make or buy" from management's perspective. Milgrom and Roberts [1992] characterize a market by "voluntary bargaining" and a hierarchy by "strict lines of authority" (p. 20) and the economic reasoning for the two forms has been studied based on transaction cost economics.

Ronald Coase opines that the tasks in an organization are conducted within the organization when it is less costly to do so than carrying out the transactions through the market [Coase, 1988]. Transaction costs include various costs incurred to conduct transactions in the market, such as finding partners and making and enforcing contracts. Oliver E. Williamson developed Coase's theory by introducing two important human factors behind transaction costs: opportunism and bounded rationality [Williamson, 1975]. Williamson showed that the market fails when these two human factors are combined with environmental conditions: bounded rationality with uncertainty and opportunism with small numbers exchange relations.

Williamson [1975, p. 9] states "If [...] it is very costly or impossible to identify future contingencies and specify, *ex ante*, appropriate adaptations thereto, long-term contracts may be supplanted by internal organization." On the other hand, opportunism is caused by *Ex Ante Small Numbers* [Williamson, 1975, p. 48]. Simply put, a first contract winner acquires specific assets such as know-how and better understanding of the contract, and this asset helps the seller win future contracts. Where a buyer cannot switch the supplier because of the specific assets that are acquired by the first contractor, a *hold-up* problem arises. Williamson [1975] suggests that such a situation can be mitigated by conducting the activity in-house, because internal audits and hierarchical order can reduce information asymmetry and opportunism. Usually the coordination of work in the hierarchical organizations is backed up by employment contracts, which ensure payroll in exchange for requiring employees to follow the orders of the higher-position person.

The dichotomy of a market or a hierarchy is already integrated in the definition of organizations as seen in Figures 1 and 2. The market characterized by voluntary bargaining is placed outside of the organization D_2 (created entity). On the other hand, a hierarchy (D_4) is considered one of the tools to coordinate activities strongly within the organizations in legal entity D_3.[1]

Market and hierarchy are considered as extreme cases in the intensity of coordinating individual tasks (Figure 2). In practice, a wide range of varieties between markets and hierarchies have been provided such as subcontracting, supply-chain systems, distribution channels, franchising, partnerships, alliances, and these forms have been extensively studied as

---

[1] It is also possible to have hierarchical structure in the organizations without legal identity such as in hobby groups. However, this chapter considers hierarchy to be used primarily in organizations with legal identity following on the discussion of organizational economics.

an organizational hybrid form [Ménard, 2004; Makadok and Coff, 2009]. Williamson [1991] modeled the hybrid governance structure as having an intermediate level of five internal attributes: incentive intensity, administrative controls, adaption of autonomy, adoption of cooperation, and contract law.

1.2.3 *Workers' incentives*

Transaction costs do not fully explain the decision between a market or a hierarchy [Tadelis and Williamson, 2013]. Basically, it explains the firms' boundaries from management's perspective, but workers have different reasons to work in hierarchical organizations rather than to work as freelancers or individual contractors. Incentives to work in organizations could be various, but the major reasons are income risk aversion, decision-making efficiency, and collective reputation [Milgrom and Roberts, 1992]. Among them, the reputation effect is based on the assumption that firms last longer than a person's lifetime and attain greater reputation based on a long-term track record. However, blockchain-based services are quite new and this assumption usually does not apply. Therefore, only the former two factors are taken into consideration.

One of the reasons to work in an organization is to avoid risks. Even if the person has competitive skills, there is no guarantee that the need for his skills will continue to be high in the market. The workers also bear the risk that they cannot provide the services for various reasons. If the worker transacts his or her skills in the market directly, they are exposed to those risks. Therefore, in order to hedge such risks, they choose to use employment contracts. Employment contracts ensure stable payroll in exchange for the requirement to follow the employer's orders [Simon, 1951, Milgrom and Roberts, 1992]. In fact, Dillon and Stanton [2017] statistically compared paid workers' and entrepreneurs' incomes and showed that paid workers' income distribution concentrates around the middle-income range. Entrepreneurs' incomes can be higher, although the median and average entrepreneurs' incomes are lower than those of paid workers.

Hierarchical organizations also achieve efficient decision-making. When a group needs to make a strategic decision to respond to a change in technology or the environment, it takes long time to achieve a consensus. On the other hand, authoritative allocation is a key characteristics of organizations for an efficient decision-making [Arrow, 1974], and the firms also function as a conflict resolution mechanisms [March, 1962]. If the group delegates the right to make a decision to someone who is better at the task, all counterparties can reach an efficient decision as a collective group [Milgrom and Roberts, 1992]. Distributed decision-making also poses the risk of less efficient decisions caused by intertemporal compromise and contradictions between collective and individual tasks [Garicano and Rayo, 2016]. In this way, there is an advantage for workers to be a part of a hierarchical organization to achieve efficient collective decision-making. Whether blockchain technology can decentralize organizations is also affected by such mechanisms in which workers choose to be a part of hierarchical organizations.

In summary, how blockchain technology is able to affect organizational structure is shown in Figure 3. On one hand, its affect is through the change in transaction costs from managements' perspective. On the other hand, it affects through workers' incentives, such as risk aversion and efficient decision-making. Whether blockchain-enabled decentralization is advantageous compared to a centralized hierarchy is determined by how blockchain can affect these factors.

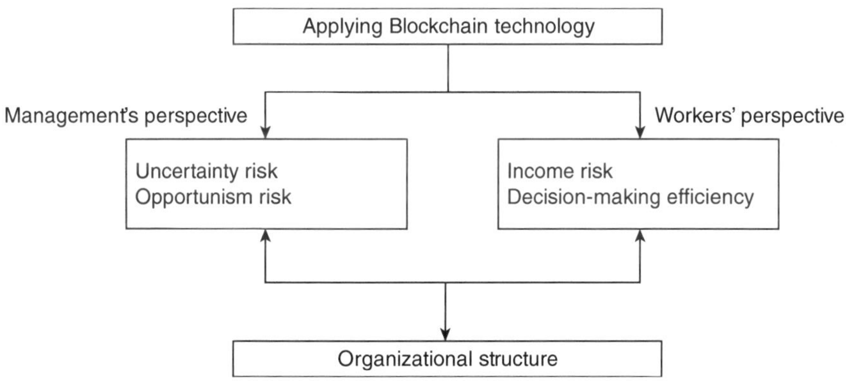

Figure 3. Factors affecting organizational structure.

1.3 Case study: Bitcoin's organizational institution

This section examines how blockchain technology is actually affecting organizational structure using the case of Bitcoin. The services provided by Bitcoin, in a narrower term, generally correspond to those of central banks. Blockchain creates currency as a means of exchange, controls its supply, and settles payments. In fact, if the service includes the whole payment ecosystem, it is conducted through a mixture of decentralized platforms and centralized entities such as exchanges and wallet providers. This issue of mixture is separately mentioned in the conclusion section.

Bitcoin has no public face and no actual institution that can represent it [De Filippi and Loveluck, 2016]. While this fact does symbolize its decentralized characteristics, there are several institutional arrangements designed to pursue its collective goals. These institutional arrangements are often perceived as twofold. One is the consensus mechanisms to maintain the ledgers' integrity through a "proof-of-work" algorithm, and the other is the community of developers who contribute to the development and maintenance of the Bitcoin core software [De Filippi and Loveluck, 2016]. The present study divides the first into two functions: consensus building on the ledgers' integrity, and voting mechanism decision-making on the software functions. As a result, the governance institutions are threefold: *competitive mining for ledger integrity*, *community of Bitcoin developers*, and *miners' voting for decision-making*.

1.3.1 *Competitive mining for ledger integrity*

The first governance institution is designed to manage the ledgers' integrity. An incumbent institution, such as a central bank, usually owns large-scale centralized computers to manage currency issuance and inter-bank settlements, and also guarantee the integrity of information as an organizations that is represented by executives. On the other hand, Bitcoin depends on distributed and unspecified computers, which share the data in the Bitcoin blockchain, and settlement is conducted without central computers or executives. In order to address the risk of different ledger versions coexisting in unspecified and distributed computers, a consensus mechanism is necessary to confirm which is the right version. Bitcoin blockchain adopts a "proof-of-work" algorithm that allows the computer with the best computing power to become the fastest one to create a new block and to add a new block to the latest blockchain. The newly created block is evaluated by other miners and when the other miners accept it as the newest block in their blockchain, the creator of the block acquires the mining reward.

When two or more new blocks coexist in the global blockchain, the miners choose which block should be the valid one. As the course of these choices repeats several times, one of the different versions becomes the longest, and this longest version is considered as the valid blockchain [Antonopoulos, 2015]. The "trustless" nature of blockchain is applied to the ledgers' integrity management, but is also referred to as "distributed trust" rather than "trustless" [Mallard *et al.*, 2014]. This distributed process actually depends on the *competition* among the miners' computing power in terms of creating "candidate" blocks and on the *voting* process by other mining peers with respect to the "determination" on the valid block.

1.3.2 *The Bitcoin developers community*

The second governance institution is the community of developers who contribute to create, test, and maintain the code that defines Bitcoin's functions. Historically, Bitcoin's governance institutions have changed over time. In the early stage, a bitcoin.org website was registered by the initial leaders, including Satoshi Nakamoto, but later the responsibility of maintaining the site was distributed to more developers to prevent a specific person from gaining full control over the Bitcoin project. Between 2011 to 2013, this site was used for releasing new code versions[2].

Bitcoin Foundation was established in 2012 to "standardize, protect and promote the use of Bitcoin cryptographic money for the benefit of users worldwide."[3] However, it failed to play a central role to coordinate Bitcoin's development and rather focused on promotional and lobbying activities. Bitcoin Foundation faced a few upheavals such as the cash flow

---

[2] *Source*: Bitcoin.org https://bitcoin.org/en/about-us.

[3] *Source*: https://en.wikipedia.org/wiki/Bitcoin_Foundation.

shortage, the dissolution crisis, and the resignation of key persons [De Filippi and Loverluck 2017, Wikipedia[4]], and its central role was transferred to the Bitcoin Core community.

"Bitcoin Core" has two meanings. The first one is Bitcoin's reference implementation, which originates from Satoshi Nakamoto's work.[5] The Bitcoin Core source code is hosted in GitHub and its compiled software is used by "nodes," including miners. The source code defines the aspects of Bitcoin's various functions, such as currency issuance, consensus mechanisms, and peer-to-peer communications. In this sense, the code represents the rules on which all stakeholders coordinate their tasks and services as a foundation of trust.

Bitcoin Core also refers to the open source project for Bitcoin's community of developers. In its official expression, the design of the community is quite open. "The Bitcoin Core project operates an open contributor model where anyone is welcome to contribute towards development in the form of peer review, testing and patches" and "there is no particular concept of "Core developers" in the sense of privileged people."[6] In fact, anyone can propose a revision of the codes in the form of "pull requests" that will be assessed by a reviewer who is not specifically appointed by any authority. However, its contribution guideline[7] clearly admits the need for "some hierarchy for practical purpose" and more hierarchical structure is employed with the decision of how to apply those updates. Bitcoin Core employs "maintainers" who are responsible for merging update requests and a "lead maintainer" who is responsible for the newest version releases, the appointment of maintainers, etc.[8] As a result, the software update decisions depend on a small number of highly-skilled developers [De Filippi and Loveluck, 2016]. Such a technocratic development organizational structure has gathered criticism. De Filippi and Loveluck [2016, p. 18] argue that "only

---

[4] *ibid.*

[5] *Source*: https://en.wikipedia.org/wiki/Bitcoin_Core.

[6] *Source*: Contribution guideline. https://github.com/bitcoin/bitcoin/blob/master/CONTRIBUTING.md as of April 11, 2018.

[7] *ibid.*

[8] *ibid.*

a small number of individuals (the core developers) have the power to decide which changes shall be incorporated into the main branch of the software" and this technocratic approach contradicts Bitcoin's "original concept." Musiani *et al.* [2018] point out that there are a number of micro-hierarchies among the developers.

Despite criticism of its technocratic and less decentralized structure, Bitcoin Core still maintains its structure without depending on a formal and legal relationship such as an employment or an outsourcing contract. The community is trying to allow anyone to participate in the development activities as well as preserve less efficiency in the decision-making. In fact, the decision-making efficiency is largely compromised, as seen in the next section.

1.3.3 *Miners' voting for decision-making*

Generally speaking, the developers community can propose improvements for a Bitcoin function and create the code, but the final implementation decision depends on the miners who operate the Bitcoin nodes. Technically, the ultimate decision is made by the fraction of newly created blocks that reflects the miners' hashing power. Therefore, this process resembles a weighted voting system based on the miners' computing resources.

The difficulty of decision-making has been a challenging issue in the Bitcoin ecosystem. There were several symbolic issues and one was exhibited in the Bitcoin XT implementation in 2015 [Musiani *et al.*, 2018]. Bitcoin XT was intended to improve its throughput by increasing the block size but failed to get a majority support by the miners. The issue also caused a severe conflict within the developers community on the direction and ideology of Bitcoin's decentralization. The Bitcoin XT proposal was abandoned and DeFilippi and Loveluck [2016] illustrated its process and consequences. The authors emphasized that this governance crisis was due to the contradiction between the Bitcoin network's decentralized nature and its highly centralized governance model, which relied on a small number of players.

A similar incident, but with different consequences, happened again in 2017. After a long discussion to solve Bitcoin's scalability challenge,[9]

---

[9] Bitcoin could process only 7 transactions per second, which was considered too small given the increasing demand for the currency as a means of remittance and payments.

three major solutions were proposed. The new functionality concept was proposed through the BIP (Bitcoin Improvement Proposal) document [Oermann and Töllner, 2015]. The first was BIP 91. It proposed a reduction in the transaction size by the "Segwit" method and also the increase in block size to 2MB. BIP 91 also proposed the "poll" method to assess how many miners would support the proposal. When more than 80% of the blocks signaled a support for Segwit during 2.5 days, any blocks onwards that did not support Segwit were considered invalid. These signals were embedded into blocks by the miners. This proposal was based on the miners' consensus reached at a face-to-face meeting in New York City,[10] subsequently called the "New York consensus."

The second proposal was BIP148, which includes Segwit but does not increase the blocks size. However, a more significant difference between BIP91 and BIP148 was that BIP148 does not require a voting consensus. Instead, BIP148 tries to automatically enact Segwit by ignoring blocks that do not support it. BIP 148 set the date for the proposal implementation to August 1, 2017. If this were implemented, Bitcoin would have split into those with Segwit and those without it. If BIP91 gained majority, BIP148 is dismissed, because Segwit is included in BIP91. The third proposal was Bitcoin Cash, which intends to expand the block size to 8MB. This proposal also tried to automatically enact the expansion of the block size on August 1, 2017. If this happens, Bitcoin would have also split into those which support the 8MB size and those against it.

As a matter of fact, there were enough signals in support of the first proposal BIP91 at the end of July, and BIP148 was dismissed. However, Bitcoin Cash was not affected by this decision and the split actually happened on August 1, 2017. Currently, both Bitcoin and Bitcoin Cash are in operation and both are traded against fiat currencies. Bitcoin's split is partly due to the lack of structural mechanisms to enforce a single solution

---

[10] For details, see https://medium.com/@DCGco/bitcoin-scaling-agreement-at-consensus-2017-133521fe9a77 and https://www.coindesk.com/coindesk-explainer-bitcoin-bip-91-implements-segwit-avoiding-split/.

on all members. Since then, Bitcoin's split continues and has resulted into 19 versions as of January 2018.[11]

Bitcoin's functionality improvement is considered and developed by voluntary developers in the Bitcoin's community. However, the decision rights are distributed in accordance with the miners' hashing power. This also shows the power asymmetry between the actors in the Bitcoin ecosystem [Musiani *et al.*, 2018].

1.4 Framework-based analysis

This section analyzes how Bitcoin's organizational institutions could affect the elements that define the organizational modes shown in Figure 3. The effects of *Uncertainty*, *Opportunism*, *Income risk aversion*, and *Efficient decision making* are examined one by one.

1.4.1 *Uncertainty*

If a task is not perfectly codified and holds some extent of uncertainty, the task would be conducted in hierarchical organizations. In Bitcoin's case, at least to maintain the ledgers' integrity, the nodes' tasks are perfectly clear and literally codified. This shifts the conducted task more into a market structure. As previously seen, the task of ledger management is distributed through a competitive mining process and conducted by the best player in the market. Oermann and Töllner [2015] suggest that among the four governance factors: code, state law, contracts, and social norms, three factors other than the code should not play an important role in Bitcoin as code-based arbitration mechanisms. The supply of Bitcoin is also perfectly codified in its protocol based on total supply and generation rate [Musiani *et al.*, 2018], resembling to the notion "Code is Law" [Lessig, 2000]. As a result, the coordination of the task is virtually the same as the spot transaction in the marketplace. However, the task codification is only applied to maintaining the ledgers' integrity, and, in fact, there are far more tasks which used to be conducted in central banks,

---

[11] *Source*: Fortune, http://fortune.com/2018/01/23/bitcoin-forking-splits/.

such as updating the systems design and governing financial ecosystem. Since these tasks are out of codification, they remain with great uncertainty.

1.4.2 *Opportunism*

If the task falls into *small-numbers exchange* and the competition in the market is largely inhibited, the task should be conducted in hierarchical organizations. In the cryptocurrency's context, opportunistic behavior implies manipulating the ledgers to pursue devious economic goals, increasing mining rewards against the rule, making the ledger slow or malfunctioning, and so on. In Bitcoin's case, this opportunistic behavior is prevented through the oversight performed by many other nodes. For example, newly created blocks are evaluated by other nodes, and only reviewed blocks are added to the blockchain. The observability is a key factor to prevent opportunism [Holmström, 1979].

In this sense, blockchain represents "distributed trust" [Mallard *et al.*, 2014]. However, when it comes to distributed trust, there is a critical condition to prevent opportunism in blockchain. It requires a sufficient number of nodes in the blockchain, and these nodes, or the entities that operate the nodes, should not cooperate with each other in a game theoretical context. As Narayanan *et al.* [2016] suggest, the possibility that 51% the hash power is taken over by a certain entity can ruin the confidence of the whole blockchain. However, as a result of competitive mining, the mining nodes distribution converges to quite a small number of players, as only five players (including the mining pools) comprise more than 50 percent of the hashing power [12], and Gervais [2014] suggested 6 major centralized mining pools were controlling more than 75% computing power in Bitcoin. If the blockchain ecosystem fails to maintain non-cooperative games by sufficient number of diverse players, it would become difficult to prevent opportunism. If blockchain fails to maintain a sufficient number and the diversity of nodes, the whole ecosystem should be managed by a hierarchical organization.

---

[12] *Source*: https://blockchain.info/pools.

1.4.3 *Income risk aversion*

From workers' perspective, if the work poses too much income instability, they would choose to work in a hierarchical organization to secure a stable payment [Knight, 1921]. As seen in Bitcoin's distribution of hashing power, the wealth distribution as represented by the mining rewards, could also become oligopolistic. In addition, because the nature of finding nonce by conducting the hash function is probabilistic, the income also fluctuates. This income structure is somewhat similar to that of entrepreneurs compared to paid workers as shown in Dillon and Stanton [2017]. Despite blockchain-enabled decentralized organizations, it does not necessarily ensure a more equitable distribution of wealth [Takagi, 2017a]. If miners want to avoid income fluctuations, they would choose to work in hierarchical organizations.

One of the representations of avoiding income instability is the mining pool, a cooperative mining service. Through the mining pool, the miners can share both the risks and profits among the members, but the whole service is controlled by a certain provider. Therefore, the mining pool is a counter-force against decentralization in the Bitcoin ecosystem. On the other hand, there are several measures to avoid excessive wealth concentration among the miners in terms of consensus algorithms, such as the proof of stakes and PBFT (Practical Byzantine Fault Tolerance). However, these measures are based on the idea of mitigating competition, and paradoxically require more coordination through central control.

1.4.4 *Efficient decision-making*

If the decision-making among voluntary participants is inefficient, hierarchical organizations can replace the community. In Bitcoin's case, the decision-making on the blocks' validity is conducted thorough a competitive mining process. It should be noted that Bitcoin mining consumes around 35-terawatt hours of electricity annually, which exceeds Denmark's annual electricity consumption.[13] The cost should be comparable to major central banks' operating costs. In this sense, cost

[13] *Source*: Digiconomist, https://digiconomist.net/bitcoin-energy-consumption.

should be evaluated to assess the efficiency of proof-of-work as the decision-making tool. On the other hand, as Nakamoto [2008] suggests, monetary policy and control, which is independent from national sovereignty, is one of Bitcoin's goals. Therefore, cost would not be the sole criteria to be considered.

On the other hand, residual items that require collective decisions are not efficiently solved by blockchain. A specific entity should hold the residual decision rights for efficiency [Milgrom and Roberts, 1998], and there are a number of items that cannot be perfectly codified in blockchain. The failure to achieve agreement on the scalability solution, as seen with Bitcoin XT, Bitcoin Cash, and the consecutive "forks," suggests that collective decision-making is quite difficult in a decentralized organization. If something harms the collective goals and performance as a group, the organization should be conducted in a hierarchical structure. As seen in the findings of Hsieh *et al.* [2018], cryptocurrencies with centralized management could be more valued by investors. If the collective economic goal is harmed by inefficient decision-making, the whole ecosystem would be tempted to be centralized.

1.5 Conclusion

To summarize, blockchain technology generally decentralizes organizations by reducing uncertainty through codifying tasks and also reducing the risk of opportunism through governance by distributed participants. The reduction in transaction costs shifts the organizational structure toward a more decentralized structure and realizes collective services through market mechanisms. However, this shift toward the market applies only to a limited fraction of a certain business ecosystem. Various residual tasks, such as system improvements and the reaction to unexpected incidents, are not considered, and these residuals are also difficult to be perfectly codified. On the other hand, decentralization sacrifices workers' incentives, such as income risk aversion and efficient decision-making. As a result, the degree of decentralization depends on how much of the sacrifice of workers' incentives is tolerable. Therefore, the extent of blockchain-enabled decentralization is determined by the trade-offs between efficiency through tasks marketization and workers' incentives.

These findings provide significant implications for blockchain's wider use. There are a number of visions and trials in the field, such as the sharing economy, public registry, electricity, which should be conducted through a DAO structure. However, its success as a decentralized organization depends on how well the task can be codified to reduce uncertainty. It is also important to have a sufficient number of actors to avoid opportunistic behavior. In addition, decentralization is in fact conducted through marketization by reducing uncertainty and it could lead to highly competitive mechanism coordination. In other words, a wider application of DAO can lead to a society with more freelancers and entrepreneurs where it would be difficult to have a stable income. These points should be taken into consideration in order to build a vision to apply blockchain to a wider range of services.

On the other hand, in the instance of Bitcoin, the monetary function is realized through a combination of bitcoin blockchain and exchanges and wallet providers. Bitcoin blockchain provides only a fraction of the whole ecosystem, while the exchanges and the wallet providers still offer services through centralized organizations. As seen in various security incidents in the exchanges, the growing mining pools, and the Initial Coin Offerings conducted by certain firms with authority, it should be noted that centralized elements still have been playing important roles in the blockchain ecosystem. It is also important to pay attention to the whole ecosystem when assessing if blockchain is able to decentralize everything.

References

Alchian, A. A. and Demsetz, H. (1972) Production, Information Costs, and Economic Organization. *The American Economic Review*. Vol. 62, No. 5. pp. 777-795.

Antonopoulos, A. M. (2015) *Mastering bitcoin.* O'Reilly.

Arrow, K. J. (1974) *The limits of organization.* W.W. Norton & Company.

Barnard, C. I. (1938) *The functions of the executive.* Harvard.

Campbell-Verduyn, Malcolm, (ed.) (2018) *Bitcoin and beyond: Cryptocurrencies, blockchains, and global governance.* Routledge.

Coase, R. H. (1988) *The firm, the market, and the law.* University of Chicago Press.

De Filippi, P. and Loveluck, B. (2016) The Invisible Politics of Bitcoin: Governance Crisis of a Decentralized Infrastructure. *Internet Policy Review.* Vol. 5, No. 4.

Dillon, E. W. and Stanton, C. T. (2017) Self-employment dynamics and the returns to entrepreneurship. *NBER Working Paper Series.* No. 23168.

Garicano, L. and Rayo, L. (2016) Why Organizations Fail: Models and Cases. *Journal of Economic Literature.* Vol. 54, No. 1. pp. 137-192.

Gencer, A. E., Basu, S., Eyal, I., van Renesse, R. and Sirer, E. G. (2018) Decentralization in Bitcoin and Ethereum Networks. *Financial Cryptography and Data Security.*

Gervais, A., Karame, G. O., Capkun, S. and Capkun, V. (2014) Is Bitcoin a Decentralized Currency? *IEEE Security and Privacy Magazine.* Vol. 12, No. 3. pp. 54-60.

Holmström, B. (1979) Moral Hazard and Observability. *The Bell Journal of Economics.* Vol. 10, No. 1. pp. 74-91.

Hsieh, Y., Vergne, J. and Wang, S. (2018) The internal and external governance of blockchain-based organizations: Evidence from cryptocurrencies. in, ed. Campbell-Verduyn M. *Bitcoin and Beyond: Cryptocurrencies, Blockchains, and Global Governance.* Routledge, pp. 48-68.

Knight, F. H. (1921) *Risk uncertainty and profit.* Martino Publishing.

Lessig, L. (2000) *Code: And other laws of cyberspace.* Basic Books.

Mallard, A., Méadel, C. and Musiani, F. (2014) The paradoxes of distributed trust: Peer-to-peer architecture and user confidence in Bitcoin. *Journal of Peer Production.* No. 4. pp.http://peerproduction.net/issues/issue-4-value-and-currency/peer-reviewed-articles/the-paradoxes-of-distributed-trust/.

March, J. G. (1962) The Business Firm as a Political Coalition. *The Journal of Politics.* Vol. 24, No. 4. pp. 662-678.

Ménard, C. (2004) The Economics of Hybrid Organizations. *Journal of Institutional and Theoretical Economics.* Vol. 160, pp. 345-376.

Milgrom, P. R. and Roberts, J. (1992) *Economics, organization and management.* Prentice-Hall International.

Musiani, F., Mallard, A. and Meadel, C. (2018) Governing what wasn't meant to be governed. in, *Bitcoin and Beyond: Cryptocurrencies, Blockchains, and Global Governance*. Campbell-Verduyn M (Ed.). Routledge, pp. 134-56.

Nakamoto, S. (2008) Bitcoin: A Peer-to-Peer Electronic Cash System.

Narayanan, A., Bonneau, J., Felten, E., Miller, A. and Goldfeder, S. (2016) *Bitcoin and cryptocurrency technologies: A comprehensive introduction.* Princeton University Press.

Simon, H. A. (1951) Formal Theory of the Employment Relationship. *Econometrica.* Vol. 19, No. 3. pp. 293-305.

Smith, A. (1776) *An inquiry into the nature and causes of the wealth of nations.* Createspace Independent Pub.

Swan, M. (2015) *Blockchain: Blueprint for a new economy.* O'Reilly.

Tadelis, S. and Williamson, O. E. (2013) Transaction cost economics. in, *Handbook of organizational economics*. Gibbons R. and Roberts J. (Eds.). Princeton University Press, pp. 159-92.

Takagi, S. (2017) Blockchain and Organizations: A Consideration from "De-organization" of Trust (in Japanese). *Chijo.* Vol. 121, pp. 8-16.

Takagi, S. (2017) *Blockchain economics: A new form of the economy by decentralization and automation* (in Japanese). Shoeisha.

Tapscott, D. and Tapscott, A. (2016) *Blockchain revolution: How the technology behind bitcoin is changing money, business, and the world.*

Williamson, O. E. (1991) Comparative Economic Organization: The Analysis of Discrete Structural Alternatives. *Administrative Science Quarterly.* Vol. 36, No. 2. pp. 269-296.

Williamson, O. E. (1975) *Markets and hierarchies, analysis and antitrust implications: A study in the economics of internal organization.* Free Press.

Chapter 3

The Blockchain Antidote to Monopolization

Arisa Siong

Independent Economist

Abstract

Blockchain enables a new way of interacting with one another, directly, without the need for large corporations providing trust at the cost of high prices or privacy. Rather trust is delegated to protocols executed in code. Code however, is not easily understood and abstracts from trust. This is exacerbated by a lack of regulatory clarity and endorsement as well as a questionable reputation caused by skepticism over the legitimacy of the technology for mainstream use. Regulatory certainty can help alleviate these concerns and ensure competitive markets. It is incumbent on regulators to understand new dynamics of competition in a blockchain world — in the new ways market power can develop in the protocol layer of blockchain networks; in circular market dynamics and the dynamic impact of token signals; and in potential to collude via private blockchains.

1.1 Introduction

Facebook, Amazon, Microsoft, Google and Apple (FAMGA) are amongst the largest companies globally in terms of market capitalization. One in three people on Earth use Facebook's platform (2.1bn users) [Facebook, 2018]. Google has over 90% share of general search [Statscounter, 2018]. Amazon's share price has increased by over 90,000% from launch [Morningstar, 2018], making it one of the most expensive stock in the S&P500 [Khan, 2017].

The sheer popularity of these platforms reflects the enormous value they have brought to users. Cohen *et al.* [2016] estimated that US consumers would lose US$18m in consumer surplus if Uber disappeared for a day. Brynjolfsson *et al.* [2018] estimated that if we had to, we would be willing to pay, on a yearly basis, around US$18k for search engines, US$8k for email, US$4k for digital maps, US$1k for video streaming services, US$800 for e-commerce, US$300 for social media, US$170 for music and US$160 for instant messaging. There is significant value associated with "free" services provided by digital giants.

Against this backdrop, there has been growing concerns globally over the accumulation of economic and political power in the hands of digital giants. Cambridge Analytica has shone the spotlight on data privacy and consumer protection. There have also been well reported concerns regarding the concentration of economic power in the hands of digital giants [The Economist, 2016], [Farahoor, 2017], [Gapper, 2017] and the consequent impact on economic efficiency, innovation, inequality [Shapiro, 2017] [Stiglitz, 2017] and productivity [MGI, 2018].

A consistent theme coming out of these analyses has been the need to update competition policy to deal with the modern realities of digital platform business models [Khan, 2017], including developing new frameworks and tools for competition assessments [Coyle, 2018]. Whilst modernizing competition policy is important, it will not be the panacea to digital giant woes. The scale benefits associated with digital platforms means it may be hard to intervene if a market has been monopolized. Ensuring accountability to users, market vibrancy and competitiveness are therefore equally important.

Blockchain has the potential to tackle some of these concerns by enabling decentralized alternatives to existing services provided by FAMGA. More than a David versus Goliath story, blockchain has the potential to enable self-sovereign identity and give users autonomy over the use of their personal data. Barrera [2018] refers to blockchain as providing the benefits of network effects but without the cost of market power. Section 1.2 discusses the value of blockchain and explores why despite its immense promise, blockchain has yet to make a dent on existing digital incumbents.

The current noises on adapting competition policy given the threats of digital giants would advocate that the promise of blockchain should not grant it immunity from regulatory scrutiny. Indeed, the gap between "too small to care" and "too large to ignore" may not be large as network effects snowball. Section 1.3 discusses what a monopoly might look like and highlight some challenges in applying competition law in a blockchain powered world. Finally, Section 1.4 concludes.

1.2 The challenge and challenges of blockchain

Blockchain at its core is simply a digital record of sorts, a database of transactions. Protocols for data entry are designed to make it prohibitively costly, for example, in terms of electricity spent on hashing or by staking one's reputation, to alter existing entries on a blockchain. The beauty of the system lies in that each participant is incentivized to act in his/her own interests but is rewarded only if he/she acts honestly, thereby securing the blockchain.

Blockchain technology allows for a central source of truth without the need for a central authority. Rather, trust in a central authority is shifted to trust in the protocols (and the incentives they create) and the code to execute these protocols. This allows for a new digital method of exchange, of agreement and of trade without the need for the establishments we rely on today for these functions. Blockchains may be public, where anyone can participate or private, where participation is controlled.

This section looks at the value of blockchain and the challenge it poses to existing digital incumbents then explores the challenges faced by blockchain and why it has yet to make a significant impact.

1.2.1 *The value of blockchain*

1.2.1.1 *Open source innovation*

Much of the allure of blockchain has been that anyone can participate in a public blockchain network. Vitalik Buterin, founder of Ethereum summarized this romance, *"I just love the idea that the thing (blockchains) can just run on a few thousand people's laptops, it doesn't require all of this billion dollars of capital, started up by people who are already here before and that would be impossible for any new group to match...if blockchains were only usable by the rich, the whole space would be much less interesting"* [CIGI, 2018a].

The notion that "anyone can participate" creates value by fostering a dynamic ecosystem. This in turns enables open source innovation when users are attracted to this platform (barriers to joining are low). A good idea can come from anywhere and the openness of a platform increases the likelihood of creating the killer blockchain app.

Matt Mullenweg, creator of WordPress, one of the most popular open source platforms for website publishing noted that an open and neutral platform results in the creation of unique and valuable services. For instance, *"WordPress has been translated and localized into many languages that there would be no commercial reasons to go into, including Klingon. When you are able to create a platform and a movement, not just a product, it doesn't just benefit one company, it benefits a whole ecosystem. For every dollar that Automattic (owns WordPress) makes, twenty dollars is made by the other companies in the WordPress ecosystem....it turns out, for the really successful (open) platforms, that ratio happens"* [CB Insights, 2017].

An open platform is likely to bring about differentiation of services and in doing so expand markets. Brynjolfsson *et al.* [2003] estimated that increased choice enabled by online platforms enhances consumer welfare by at least five times the welfare gain from more competitive prices. Open access can therefore, bring notable benefits. However, where blockchain differentiates from existing platforms such as WordPress is decentralization and disintermediation.

1.2.1.2 *Decentralized trust*

A key feature of blockchain technology is enabling decentralized or peer-to-peer exchanges. Decentralization eliminates intermediaries and alongside that, middlemen fees. For instance, money senders currently pay on average 8% for international money transfers [CB Insights, 2018a], while blockchain based alternatives can cut fees to 2% or less [Fintechnews Singapore, 2015]. Streamlining transactions by removing intermediaries also improves transaction speeds. Blockchain based alternatives for international money transfer for instance can cut transfer times to minutes rather than days.

Disintermediation also generates efficiency gains by bypassing central authorities who leverage market power to extract incumbency rents. On a blockchain network, coordination and verification of transactions rely on participation in the network rather than a central authority. The cost of coordination can be expected to reflect underlying costs more closely absent market power and associated monopoly mark-ups. Catalini and Gans [2017] refers to this as the 'cost of verification' and notes that the elimination of intermediaries by blockchain technology brings about the potential for *"costless verification"*.

Transparency and trust can enable consumption decisions based on new dimensions such as origin of production inputs; or in the case of music, how revenues are distributed to the artists versus others involved in the production. This widens choice and can bring about significant benefits associated with fulfilling long-tailed demand.

Providing information about the carbon footprint of a product/service is not exclusive to blockchain, the same can arguably be provided by a centralized platform. But centralized platforms act in their interests rather than interests of its users so the "truth" presented maybe only be partial. On a decentralized platform, the focus is on the users, hence services are likely to be developed in line with user preferences rather than commercial incentives of the platform. In effect, blockchain lowers privacy and censorship risk through disintermediation. The value of increased autonomy over privacy can be particularly pertinent where personal data protection legislation is cumbersome or has the unintended effect of increasing monopoly power [Schechner and Kostov, 2018].

1.2.1.3 *Tokenization*

Initial Coin Offerings ('ICOs') provide an alternative to traditional funding sources for blockchain startups. In 2017, blockchain startups have already raised far more funding via ICOs than traditional equity funding routes [CB Insights, 2018b]. Additionally, native tokens may serve to reward users of the platforms for contributing resources. This in turns creates the incentives for contributors (as opposed to 'investors' as projects may not constitute formal securities offerings) and users alike to grow the network, as an appreciation in token value would increase their payoff from the resources contributed or investment sunk. Therefore, token sales and token incentives help blockchain networks raise funds and scale quickly.

Tokenization can enable the creation of a digital twin to a physical asset. In turn, this could facilitate digital trade of this asset without the need for physical transfer of the asset. In addition, tokenization of physical assets allows for fractional investing that might be impractical in a non-blockchain world, either due to physical constraints (assets such as art would become worthless if broken down into pieces) or concerns over double spend in a mutable digital ledger. Fractional investing could create new markets not unlike the impact of online retail.

Trading a digital copy of a physical asset via blockchain would however require the digital copy to be inherently linked to its physical twin. This would require a unique physical property to be digitally recorded; or to link the blockchain and physical world by statute so that the blockchain ledger is legally valid. While there are some hurdles to overcome, tokenization has the potential to open access to funds, create new forms of commerce and serve new demand.

1.2.2 *The long road to digital champion*

There are blockchain alternatives to many existing digital services, including blogging and social networking (Steemit), ride sharing (LaZooz), search (BitClove) and storage (Filecoin). Yet for all its promise, blockchain alternatives have yet to make a dent on digital giants, this subsection explores why.

1.2.2.1 *Network effects*

Platform markets are characterized by network effects — the larger the platform, the more attractive it is to users. By a yardstick of scale, FAMGA is far ahead. For instance, Facebook has 2.1bn users. In comparison, the number of Bitcoin addresses with a positive balance is just under 22m (this overstates the Bitcoin user count as an individual might have multiple addresses but serves as a proxy) [Bitinfocharts, 2018]. Blockchain-based social media platform — Steemit's user count has been hovering around 60k in 2018 — a drop in the ocean.

A large part of the success of existing digital platforms has been the huge investment made in acquiring users, by offering free or discounted services. Khan [2017] notes that despite Amazon's success to date, it has rarely exited the red in the past twenty years a consequence of prioritizing growth over profits. Digital platform giants also invest heavily in retaining users, for instance, through investment to expand the scope of their platform and in loyalty programs — Amazon Prime being the prime example.

Blockchain startups do not have the deep pockets of these digital incumbents. To put into perspective, FAMGA have a combine market cap of just under US$4tn [Morningstar, 2018], in comparison the total market capitalization of all cryptocurrencies is just under US$440bn [Coinmarketcap, 2018]. It is almost silly to make such comparisons when the age of these firms would place them on different playing fields — you would not expect a startup have the same capitalization propensity as Amazon. Nonetheless, in the era of digital platform markets where scale, scope and investment are key determinants of a platform's success, digital incumbents are far ahead of their blockchain non-peers.

1.2.2.2 *Going mainstream*

Being far behind is one thing, catching up is another. Schumpeter destruction can happen rapidly in the world of digital platforms, or not at all if markets tip. Coyle [2018] notes that *"while longevity is not a definitive sign that disruptive challenge is impossible, it is suggestive"*. Bitcoin has had a run time of nearly a decade but has yet to become mainstream. While it may be that blockchain's decentralized architecture forces a longer road to maturity and being a general-purpose technology requires a longer diffusion period, there remains barriers to overcome to turn the 'if' question into a 'when' question.

Lack of regulatory clarity

One of the potential barriers is the lack of regulatory clarity over blockchains and cryptocurrencies in particular. Attempts in early 2018 to coordinate regulatory approaches at the G20 level have failed to reach consensus. Regulation, if any, has been quite ad hoc and regimes vary regionally as well as internationally.

Such a lack of consistency creates uncertainty and inhibits wider use of blockchain. For instance, even banks who use Ripple's blockchain technology for cross border payment settlement would not touch its native token XRP as *"there was no way they could use an instrument that regulators may never approve"* [Leising and Robinson, 2018]. Further, wide fluctuations in the value of cryptocurrencies prevents them from being a useful medium of exchange.

For blockchain to be pervasive, it must permeate the analogue world. There have been some movement on this front though developments remain experimental. Dubai has ambitious plans to secure all government documents on blockchain by 2020. Meridio has tokenized a three-story building in Brooklyn, enabling trade and investment of this property via blockchain. There is a project to put the genome code of the wildlife in the Amazonian rainforest on a blockchain and track use of this information to return value to the indigenous and traditional communities of the Amazon.

More generally, this will require tokenization of analogue assets to be supported by statute (discussed above), not unlike role of the United Nations Commission on International Trade Law's model laws that allowed electronic contracts to be legally binding. In addition, sensors and smart meters that digitalize new information and signals will widen the scope for blockchain applications. Here, regulation may be required to ensure economical access to this infrastructure.

Public trust and acceptance

Another potential reason for sluggish blockchain development is the paradoxical concept of decentralized trust. Centralized trust is easy to comprehend and accept because it has been the default. In markets where authorities do not command that sort of respect, decentralized trust may be attractive. Decentralized trust offered by blockchain is built on protocol designed incentives, implemented in code. That sets the bar for trust high as these protocols are not easily understood. As it is hard to trust something you do not understand, the core blockchain community has remained small.

This also means that non-code proficient users of blockchain (most of us) must delegate trust, via interpretation of code, to trusted parties or functions — for instance in the auditability of open source code or an establishment to provide oversight of the development of the code. This however represents a move back toward centralization and hangs a question mark over the value of decentralization.

It has not helped that cryptocurrencies have developed a reputation as medium for illegal activities. Bitcoin, the poster child for blockchain being the currency of choice for an underground drug bazaar (Silk Road) does not bode well for instilling trust. For all its promise of trust, blockchain's potential downfall is the lack of trust.

1.3 Regulation in a decentralized economy

Regulation can help address concerns associated with blockchain technology and foster development. As trust is increasingly delegated to protocols and code, there will be an increasing public safety dimension to the work of software engineers and developers carry out. Regulatory oversight to ensure that digital architectures and systems of tomorrow are developed with public safety in mind will help instill public trust in code.

The Centre for International Governance Innovation suggests some form of self-regulation via a Code of Ethics akin to that in the civil engineering profession [CIGI, 2018b].

Self-regulation would shift the burden of regulation to more parties rather than rely solely on the government, allowing regulation to be nimble and relevant. On the other hand, self-policing schemes tend to suffer from moral hazard issues and may lack effectiveness. It is important therefore, for market forces and societal norms to impose constraints on the conduct of firms.

The present concern over economic and political power amassed by digital giants provides an important lesson in ensuring competitiveness of markets. Competition policy and law therefore need to be alert to the potential competition issues in blockchain markets.

1.3.1 *What constitutes a monopoly?*

Conceptually, one would think that decentralization is the antithesis of monopolization, so what would a monopoly look like in a blockchain world?

In competition law, a dominant entity is defined to have monopoly power if it has the autonomy to act independently, without due regard to its rivals [ECJ, 1978]. Typically, this is reflected in the ability to raise prices and/or lower quality without significant harm to the profitability of the business.

In blockchain networks, there are a few dimensions that could allow an entity to act independently of other rivals. First relates to mining or voting power that determines who gets to write onto the ledger. An entity with majority of voting or mining power can influence which transactions get committed to the ledger first, which in turn enables some influence over the costs of committing transactions and by implication the cost of services provided on top of the blockchain. This impact may be particularly pertinent in blockchain systems with transaction fees only and no block reward.

Furthermore, miners or nodes collectively participate in maintaining a blockchain network and any rule or protocol changes can only be implemented if mining community adopts these changes ('runtime consensus'). Controlling a majority stake in mining and voting power therefore affords the ability to dictate the underlying architecture and functioning of a blockchain network.

In reality, public blockchain networks are less decentralized than we may think. The number of entities controlling more than 50% of the mining or voting power in some of the most popular public blockchain networks is between one to three [Palmer, 2018]. The controversial hard fork of the Ethereum blockchain following The DAO hack also underscores the possibility for an influential entity (in this case, the Ethereum Foundation led by Vitalik Buterin) to orchestrate the mining community toward accepting the hard fork proposal. However, as with the dangers of jumping to "big is bad" assertions in traditional competition assessments, market structures created by a concentration of mining/voting power should ultimately be judged on its effects on market harm.

Second, a concentration of tokens is held. For blockchains that run Proof of Stake consensus, a concentration of tokens can potentially be akin to a concentration of voting power and the above concerns would apply. Furthermore, as services provided on a blockchain are priced in the native token of the blockchain, a concentration of tokens held presents a strong influence over the value the services provided and the value of the whole network. This risk is evident from Ripple locking away 55% of its native token, XRP, in escrow to manage concerns associated with market flooding.

Third, the concentration of ability to implement code changes. In a world where code is law, controlling the code is akin to controlling the network. In addition to concentration of mining/voting power discussed above, there is the ability to write the code (coding resources), the gatekeeper power to implement code changes (for Bitcoin, the gatekeeper is Bitcoin Core for example) and achieving runtime consensus amongst blockchain constituencies who run nodes — exchanges, wallets and merchants. In the same way data is a key input to the digital centric business models of today, concentration of key resources enabling the creation of new applications and services on blockchain could afford an entity market power in a blockchain world.

Overall, blockchain markets may not be immune to monopolization. Quite the opposite, being characterized by network effects suggests markets will eventually rationalize toward oligopolistic or monopolistic structures. However, the indicators of market power may be different to traditional markets. Concentration of influence in the protocol layer is likely to be important because it dictates differentiation of services. For instance, the way a blockchain implements zero knowledge proof can have direct impact on privacy preserving features of applications built on it. This is unlike traditional digital platforms where majority of the value capture is in the application layer. For blockchain networks, it is likely to be in the protocol layer. Therefore, accumulating control over the protocol layer should be considered in addition to typical considerations when defining relevant markets and assessing market power.

1.3.2 *Applying competition law in a blockchain world*

1.3.2.1 *On whom and how would legislation apply*

One immediate concern about regulating blockchain networks is the practicality of regulating ownerless and stateless entities. Public blockchain networks such as Ethereum can exist as open source code owned by no one. The network is collectively maintained but no one actually owns this infrastructure. This could well extend to applications and agreements built on such blockchains. For instance, Decentralized Autonomous Organizations (commonly 'DAOs') are formed via a series of smart contracts on Ethereum. Such an "origination" is created and defined in code but has no formal identity and can be stateless. On whom and how would existing legislation apply to such stateless cooperatives?

Even where the legal liability of such ownerless architecture can be defined, the distributed nature of blockchain networks may still pose considerable practical challenges in the enforcement of competition law (and indeed other legislation) across jurisdictions. This calls for coordinated action by governments globally and for open dialogue to take place between the blockchain community and government to facilitate a meeting of minds. Early dialogue is also important for blockchain as it is protocol driven. Protocols are hard to amend once widely implemented. For instance, there may be a need to reconcile the right to be forgotten with the immutability of a blockchain where personal data is at stake.

1.3.2.2 *Complex competition dynamics*

In general, competition law focuses on ensuring consumer welfare by setting rules on what sellers can lawfully do in commerce. Blockchain is likely to increase the prevalence of peer-to-peer markets and give rise to the 'prosumer' (producer who is also the consumer). This may mean evaluating both demand and supply incentives of a single entity and reconciling the two based on the incentives at play.

This may be difficult to do given the complex competition dynamic at play. On one hand, actors have joint stakes in the network and are incentivized to work collectively toward maximizing the value of the network. This may mean weaker incentives to foreclose rivals as having more diverse participation increases network value (due to network effects). On the other hand, where resources are scarce and finite, incentives to maximize gains over rivals may be stronger, creating the urge to consolidate and monopolize. Therefore, it may be challenging to evaluate whether business conduct in a blockchain market is ultimately exclusionary.

Furthermore, there is the overlay of token signals and incentives to account for. There may be a need to consider token signals (in cryptocurrency) alongside or instead of traditional price signals (in fiat currency); and more generally the interaction of blockchain and non-blockchain market dynamics. This is difficult if the value of cryptocurrencies fluctuates widely and interactions with price signals are hard to predict. Changes to token incentives over time and potential incentive compatibility issues associated with Proof of Stake systems could add further complexities.

The circular market dynamic (market participants switching between consumer and producer roles) also makes it difficult to define relevant markets and assess market power. Although there has been considerable research on how to define relevant markets in two or multisided market [Evans and Schmalensee, 2012], [Filistrucchi *et al.*, 2013], participants on either side of a blockchain network may be dynamic rather than static, adding complexity.

Overall, this calls for new frameworks and tools capable of capturing dynamic incentives in circular market structures whilst accounting for token signals and the interplay with non-blockchain markets.

1.3.2.3 *Private blockchains and collusion*

A final area of concern relates to if and how private blockchain networks could facilitate collusive behavior amongst selected market participants. If it does facilitate collusion, the standard of proof to enforce against this may be high as competition law requires evidence of intent or of agreement to act in concert. Participating in a private blockchain and using a common set of protocols to provide services may not present such proof. A similar concern involving collusion via the use of algorithms is subjected to review in several jurisdictions and may yield relevant insights here. If the burden of proof to enforce against collusive behavior ex post is high, it may be necessary to impose certain principles ex ante to ensure that private blockchain protocols abide by competition law.

1.4 Conclusions

In search of the antidote to monopolization, it is worth bearing in mind that digital platforms such as Facebook and Google have brought about significant benefits to users. There are concerns over digital giants monopolizing markets and blockchain can offer a decentralized alternative but will only succeed if it brings greater value to users. Ultimately, systems of centralized and decentralized trust can and will co-exist. The key is to ensure markets remain competitive so the relative efficiencies from either system will benefit the wider economy.

Policy makers should be alert to how regulatory certainty can contribute to an enabling environment for blockchain development by ensuring that the delegation of trust to code is handled with due regard to public safety and for competitive markets to foster. Network effects create large platforms — both centralized (Facebook) and decentralized (Bitcoin) — which may not be identified as monopolies traditionally but may cause new forms of monopolistic harm (Facebook — loss of privacy). New definitions of monopolies for a digital network era is likely important given the significance of these large, transnational network projects. Competition policy should be alert to market power arising from concentration of influence over the protocol layer of blockchains. Further research on circular competition dynamics in peer-to-peer markets and the interaction of token signals with existing market dynamics would help futureproof competition policy.

References

Barrera, C. (2018). The Blockchain Effect: Network Effects without Market Power Costs, 29/3/2018. https://medium.com/mit-cryptoeconomics-lab/the-blockchain-effect-86bd01006ec2 (accessed 22/4/2018).

Bitinfocharts. (2018). https://bitinfocharts.com/top-100-richest-bitcoin-addresses.html (accessed 29/04/2018).

Brynjolfsson, E. Smith, M. D. and Hu, Y. (2003). Consumer Surplus in the Digital Economy: Estimating the Value of Increased Product Variety at Online Booksellers, *Management Science* Vol. 49, No. 11.

Brynjolfsson, E. Eggers, F. Gannamaneni, A. (2018). Using massive online choice experiments to measure changes in well-bring. Working Paper 24514. National Bureau of Economic Research.

Catalini, C. and Gans, J. (2017). Some Simple Economics of the Blockchain, 21/9/2017.

CB Insights. (2017). The future of publishing, interview with Matt Wullenweg, CB Insights Aha Conference 2017. https://www.youtube.com/watch?v=ClMeanZtISs (accessed 22/04/2018).

CB Insights. (2018a). How Blockchain Can Disrupt Banking, 8/2/2018.

CB Insights. (2018b). Blockchain Startups Absorbed 5X More Capital Via ICOs Than Equity Financings In 2017, 18/1/2018.

CIGI. (2018a). When new tech and dated policies collide, a conversation with Vitalik Buterin. https://www.youtube.com/watch?v=KlIFQ7GIdBA (accessed 22/4/2018).

CIGI. (2018b). Governance vacuums and how code becomes law. https://www.cigionline.org/multimedia/video-governance-vacuums-and-how-code-becoming-law (accessed 22/4/2018).

Cohen, P. Hahn, R. and Hall, J. Levitt, S. Metclfe, R. (2016). Using big data to estimate consumer surplus: The case of Uber.

Coinmarketcap. (2018). https://coinmarketcap.com/tokens/ (accessed 22/4/2018).

Coyle, D. (2018). Practical competition policy implications of digital platforms. Forthcoming, Antitrust Law Journal.

ECJ (1978). Judgment of the Court of 14 February 1978.United Brands v Commission of the European Communities — Chiquita Bananas. Case 27/76.

Evans, D. and Schmalensee, R. (2012). The antitrust analysis of multi-sided platform businesses, Coase-Sandor Institute for Law & Economics Working Paper, No. 623, 2012.

Facebook. (2018). Company Info. https://newsroom.fb.com/company-info/ (accessed 22/4/2018).

Farahoor, R. (2017). Silicon Valley has Too Much Power', *Financial Times*, 14/5/2017.

Filistrucchi, L. Gerardin, D. van Damme, E. and Affeldt, P. (2013), Market Definition in Two-Sided Markets: Theory and Practice, Dipartimento die Scienze Economiche, Universita degli Studi di Firenze, Working Paper, 05/2013.

Fintechnews Singapore. (2015). CoinPip: Bringing Bitcoin to Southeast Asia, 22/10/2015.

Gapper, J. (2017). Business is Becoming A Battle of the Giants', Financial Times, 6/12/2017.

Khan, L.M. (2017). Amazon's Antitrust Paradox. The Yale Law Journal, Vol 126, No 3, pp. 564-907, January 2017.

Leising, M and Robinson, E. (2018). Ripple Wants XRP to Be Bitcoin for Banks. If Only the Banks Wanted It. Bloomberg 25/1/2018.

McKinsey Global Institute. (2018). Solving the productivity puzzle: The role of demand and the promise of digitalization, February 2018.

Morningstar. (2018). Amazon.com Inc. http://www.morningstar.com/stocks/xnas/amzn/quote.html (accessed 22/4/2018).

Palmer, J. (2018). Are we decentralized yet. https://arewedecentralizedyet.com/ (accessed 22/4/2018).

Schechner, S. and Kostov, N. (2018). Google and Facebook likely to benefit from Europe's privacy crackdown, 23/4/ 2018, *Wall Street Journal*.

Shapiro, C. (2017). Antitrust in a Time of Populism. Forthcoming, *International Journal of Industrial Organization*, 24/10/2017.

Statscounter. (2018). Search engine market share worldwide. http://gs.statcounter.com/search-engine-market-share (accessed 22/04/2018).

Stiglitz, J. (2017). America Has a Monopoly Problem—and It's Huge. The Nation, 23/10/2017.

The Economist. (2016). The Superstar Company: A Giant problem, 17/9/2016.

Part 2

Blockchain Economic Open Network Innovation

Chapter 4

Financing Small & Medium Enterprises with Blockchain: An Exploratory Research of Stakeholders' Attitudes

Alex Kayal

Exact Business Software, the Netherlands

Jingwen Yao

Exact Business Software, the Netherlands

Judith Redi

Exact Business Software, the Netherlands

Erich C.G. Schnoeckel

3Thin.gs Blockchain Consultancy, the Netherlands

Abstract

Obtaining the necessary financing can be a challenging task for small and medium enterprises (SMEs). To obtain such financing, SMEs must go through a lengthy assessment procedure that is costly for them as well as for financiers. Experience shows issues of trust, administrative costs, repetition, and data sensitivity may be at the root of these costs. With the emergence of blockchain technology, an opportunity arises whereby a shared ledger could alleviate these issues and support the financing procedure. In this paper, we conduct an exploratory research into the appetite of the stakeholders involved in two traditional financing procedures, namely invoice factoring and inventory finance, for adopting the blockchain technology in their part(s) of the procedure, as well as the envisioned changes to their respective careers. The results show the potential of blockchain in the financing procedure, and highlight the areas where it would have the highest impact.

1.1 Introduction

The recent blockchain revolution has been taking the world of fintech by a storm. The success of bitcoin, followed by the rise of a newer generation of decentralized protocols (e.g. Ethereum[a]) along with smart contracts, has given an opportunity for many banking, accounting, and auditing institutions to consider experimenting with the trustless realm. In this paper, we envision how Blockchain could disrupt yet another traditional way of doing business: that of credit financing for Small and Medium Enterprises (SMEs).

Keeping a projected positive cash flow is one the most challenging issues for SMEs. Having access to credit at the right moment, in the right quantity and against affordable conditions allows SMEs to pay suppliers and employees on time, as well as develop plans to grow the company by accepting new orders or investing in new equipment and marketing campaigns.

Unfortunately, late payments of clients or money tied up in inventory and unfinished projects often negatively influences cash flow. This involves billions of Euros worldwide: in the Netherlands alone it is over 1 billion per year that restrains an SME from growing [1]. In fact, a Dutch SME has (on average) a cash flow need per year that is 3.7 times of what can be covered by their existing credit facilities. Usually the involved amounts add up to no more than €20.000 at a time [1].

---

[a] https://www.ethereum.org/.

To receive extra credit from their banks, SMEs are asked to prove the healthiness of their business via an assessment that generates a credit rating. Credit rating agencies and banks compute this rating based on models that ingest past information, such as past (quarterly) audit reports, outstanding invoices, current obligations, deposited annual statements, questionnaires sent to the suppliers and clients of the SME, amongst others. This information is stored in separate, centralized databases, which makes the exchange of it quite difficult. Discrepancies, mistakes or changes that are identified by the SME are very unlikely to change their creditworthiness or reputations, possibly leading to the refusal of financing when instead a healthy situation is at hand [2, 3]. In addition, credit rating is an expensive process, both in terms of time and money, that quite often costs much more than SMEs can afford [2, 3].

Alternatives to banks, crowd funders, factoring companies, and new Internet-based lenders require less documents or securities to provide loans — though they may charge significantly higher fees for their services[b]. The majority of SMEs can therefore afford neither of these two choices; eventually either resorting to the use of their own private funds or family resources (if available) or simply going bankrupt.

Blockchain technology can be a powerful tool to tackle the financing problems of SMEs. By implementing a shared ledger where all transactions and invoices of the SMEs are logged and stored, timely and accurate estimates of the finances, assets and paying behavior of an SME's debtors can be obtained, based on the most recent, immutable data. Indicators of financial virtuosity of SMEs can be maintained and provided to credit lenders, with the guarantee that these indicators are derived from untampered, timely data and hence represent an accurate picture of their creditworthiness. In addition, the shared ledger, so transparently logging all activities of many SMEs, may potentially stimulate virtuous behavior (e.g. timely payment) of SMEs, through peer pressure.

Disruptive technologies such as blockchain, however, often encounter a bumpy road toward adoption — literature shows that people tend to resist the acceptance of new technologies [5]. Since to the best of our

---

[b] According to our customers, including participants in this study, fees can amount to double digit percentages for this type of funding.

knowledge, little or no research is conducted on whether (and how) the different parties involved in financing processes (accountants, SMEs, banks, auditors, etc.) may be willing to adopt such technology, we were set out to conduct an exploratory research to (1) discover the possible potential (and obstacles) for blockchain in the financing process, (2) assess the appetite of the various stakeholders in this process for adopting a technology of the such, and (3) validate many assumptions made regarding decentralization in financing at this point in time.

In the following sections, we first provide more detail on how blockchain may disrupt credit financing, in the specific cases of invoice and inventory financing (Section 1.2). We then present our research methodology in Section 1.3 and the outcomes of the research in Section 1.4. We finally provide our conclusions and outlook in Section 1.5.

1.2 Use cases

1.2.1 *Invoice financing (or factoring)*

The name Invoice Financing comes from this process's focus on lending money based on emitted invoices. It is traditionally served by *factoring companies*, who are willing to lend on higher risk profiles than banks are, for commensurately higher commissions and fees. Specifically, Factoring companies are willing to pay (a large percentage of) an invoice's value in advance to SMEs, to then retain a (conspicuous) fee when the SME's debtor pays off the invoice within or after payment terms. This is advantageous for SMEs because it allows them access to much-needed cash well before the invoice's payment deadline. On the other hand, in order to obtain this service from factoring companies, the SME needs to demonstrate the solidity of its financial profile as well as the trustworthiness of its debtors. Accountants usually take a leading role in this demonstration process nowadays, assisting SMEs to gain more trust from factoring companies.

We propose that augmenting the invoice factoring process with blockchain may facilitate this process—the new workflow would proceed as follows: whenever an SME sends an invoice to a client through a regular process (e.g. digital in XML or UBL format plus PDF), the invoice will be stored in an accounting software package (the supplier's administration) and the hash (i.e. a digital signature) of the invoice and a pointer to that document will be stored in a blockchain. A copy of the invoice will also be stored in a separate trusted data storage. At this point, the invoice will have an open status, a timestamp of the moment of sending, and a link to the stored hash (and/or invoice) in the Blockchain (additional the added storage).

The receiving SME (the client) will receive the invoice in the traditional way or through its preferred channel. The technology will allow to verify the sender first, checking for e.g. ghost senders. The invoice will then be accepted, booked and scheduled for payment; otherwise, in presence of errors or defections from what was agreed, there will be a possibility of rejection. In both cases, similar to what happens when sending, all status changes will be reflected in stored hashes and new pointers on a blockchain.

Once the invoice is accepted and paid, the cycle will be closed, and every action involved in the process will result in a hash and pointer stored on a blockchain. Based on this information, it will be possible to create indicators describing the behavior of the involved SME in terms of (1) the quality of the invoices sent, reflecting the extent to which the sending SME respected agreements with customers and (2) the payment behavior of the SME debtors in relation to the agreed terms (including timeliness indicators).

These indicators reflect how the SME has acted in the past, and how it may act in the future under similar circumstances-- thereby constituting proxy indicators for financial health and trustworthiness, being grounded in timely and untampered data.

1.2.2 *Inventory finance*

A more complex mean of financing for SMEs is Inventory Finance. Similar to invoice factoring, inventory finance is also a short-term loan, where the SME's inventory serves as collateral in the case that this loan could not be repaid. Compared to Invoice factoring, the approval of inventory financing loans is a much more complex-- the physical flow of goods and its whereabouts and ownership at any given moment during it production (and consumption) life cycle adds further complexity to the process. And though the invoice remains the main source of information, quality audits, (Internet-of-things based) location information, bills of lading, and additional data are also relevant to the process, in order to keep track of location (e.g. different warehouses) and (projected) value of these goods at all time.

This type of information exists in a variety of systems that need to be connected in a consistent way. In this case, trust between different parties becomes a crucial factor in the validation process, as almost all information will needs to be verified multiple times by a number of stakeholders. Specifically, the parties involved in a typical inventory finance processes are:

(1) Small and medium enterprises (SMEs), the business entities that apply for financing.
(2) Accountants, the assistants and advisors of SMEs.
(3) Logistic services providers (LSPs) that provide services such as warehousing, transportation, financing advice, etc.
(4) Auditors, who provide quality audit reports on physical goods.
(5) Financial services providers (FSPs), e.g. banks or smaller loan-providing platforms, who receive financing applications and may offer the SMEs financing based on these applications.

With such complexity, blockchain may be leveraged to simplify the tracking of all the operations performed by the different stakeholders in the process. In line with what is described in the scope of the blockchain-based invoice factoring concept, every status change in the life cycle of the process from ordering to delivery could be registered on a blockchain. The assumption here is that by storing immutable digital signatures of this process, trust between the stakeholders will gradually increase, leading to a better flowing procedure with potentially better financing conditions. A simplified lifecycle of the inventory financing process can be described as follows:

(1) The SME, potentially with the assistance of the LSP, prepares a financing application based on their inventory.
(2) The SME will have their goods transported to the LSP's warehouse.
(3) The LSP reviews and submits the application to the FSP.

(4) An auditing team visits and audits the inventory at the LSP's warehouse, on behalf of the FSP.
(5) The auditing team submits its report to the FSP.
(6) The FSP validates the data in the audit report, possibly involving the LSP in the process.
(7) The FSP provides the SME with a financing package including terms and condition that correspond to the inventory and the audit report.

The above process is depicted in Figure 1.

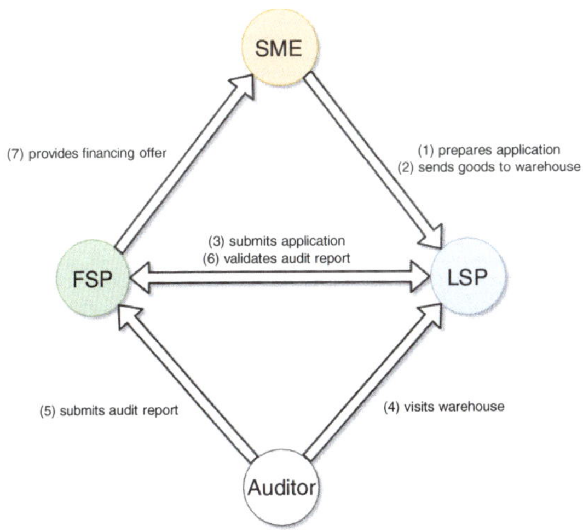

Figure 1. The (simplified) steps of the inventory financing process.

1.3 Research objectives and methodology

We have up to this point, and based on business experience, made the assumption that financing (whether based on invoices or inventory) is a long, complex, and costly procedure with a sizable amount of overhead and unnecessarily repeated work. We also assumed that one factor leading to this complication is the lack of trust amongst the participating parties– small businesses, accountants, financiers, logistic services providers (LSPs), and auditors on either side tend to repeat the work of others in order to protect their own interests.

In this section we detail the methodology we followed to investigate the openness of the different parties involved in invoice and inventory financing to the adoption of blockchain technologies, and the circumstances under which this adoption may take place.

1.3.1 *Assumptions*

Below are the key assumptions we made until this point, which the research intends to investigate. They were formulated based on the knowledge of our internal experts.

- Financiers usually take high risks when approving a loan to an SME.
- Loan conditions are unfavorable mainly due to the high risks they take and the time it costs.
- Financiers would like to acquire more customers to finance in general.
- Financiers would like to provide better loan conditions if the risks are reduced.
- Verifying invoices takes the most effort of financiers due to trust factors.
- Financiers have trust in blockchain based solutions.
- SMEs are comfortable with compromising some of their privacy in return for more favorable loan conditions.
- SMEs incur plenty of costs due to numerous administrative tasks.
- SMEs would stop manipulating relevant financial records in return for more favorable loan conditions.
- Accountants will embrace the automation of processes and gradually transition into advisory roles.

The assumptions above summarize the main requirements and challenges for the stakeholders involved in the financing process, that blockchain technology can help either support or alleviate.

1.3.2 *Research method*

The methodology we adopted for our research is loosely based on Co-Constructing Stories (CCS) [6], a semi-structured, participatory-design based qualitative research methodology that allows for a formative evaluation of technologies that are yet to be implemented. A session of CCS is composed of two phases: sensitization and elaboration. In the sensitization phase, interviewees are invited to share their current experiences regarding a certain event, habit, or process (in this case, financing). In the elaboration phase, an additional element (in this case, blockchain) is introduced, and the interviewees are then asked to construct the same story they discussed in the sensitization phase while trying to encompass the newly added element. The exact protocol used in the seven interviews is described in the following section.

We have interviewed seven different stakeholders in the processes of invoice factoring and inventory finance: (1) an accountant with a traditional accounting background, (2) an accountant with experience advising small and medium enterprises (SMEs) prepare for (and obtain) financing, (3) a manager of an auditing team in a commercial financing institution, (4) head of strategy at a major local bank, (5) managing director of an LSP, (6) co-founder of a loan facilitating platform, and (7) an SME with an experience of applying for inventory finance. In the remainder of this paper, we are going to refer to the SME as Business (B), to the head of strategy at a bank, the loan facilitator as Financiers (F); to the director of the Logistic service provider as (L), to the accountants as (A) and to the manager of the auditing team as Auditor (D). Before the interviews, we had no prior knowledge on the interviewees' experience with blockchain.

1.3.3 *Research protocol*

Interviews lasted between 30 and 60 minutes and followed a semi-structured approach. An interview consisted of two distinct parts: (1) a request to describe the financing process as it has been experienced by respective interviewee from that interviewee's point of view, and (2) a discussion on how the interviewee expected the process would change given the introduction of a blockchain solution (explained when required). The interviews were audio-recorded (with the consent of the interviewees) and later transcribed. The final transcriptions included over 100 pages of text, produced from almost 300 minutes of audio. The interviews started with an introductory session, during which the researchers and the research theme were introduced, and so was the goal of the project (albeit without explicitly mentioning blockchain to avoid bias); a consent form was also signed and the audio recording started.

Thereafter, the sensitization phase took place. This addressed the previous experiences of the interviewee, and lasted between 10 and 20 minutes. Specifically, the participant was asked:

"Could you walk us through the average financing (e.g. inventory finance or invoice factoring) procedure?"

We aimed at having the answer of the participant cover as much as possible of the assumptions listed above. The following questions were asked, depending on the background of the participant (B, F, L, D or A), in the case where the validation (or invalidation) of some of our assumptions was not touched upon:

- How was the experience in general? (B, F, L, D)
- What is your usual role during an invoice factoring (or auditing) process? (A, L, D)
- What are your main struggles when doing invoice factoring? (B)
- What are your main concerns when you do invoice factoring? (F)
- Which documents are required for this process (aside from invoices)? (B, F, L, A, D)
- Where in the procedure (or pertaining to which documentation) does trust pose an obstacle? (B, F, L, A, D)
- Do you think trust is often an issue when approving a loan? (A)
- Normally how long does it take to approve a loan based on this process (also solely on your part), and why? (B, F, L, A, D)
- Are you (or your institution) doing anything already to improve this situation? Are you satisfied with the current procedure? Either way, why? (B, F, L, D)
- Do you think it is necessary to improve the current situation? Where and why? (F, L, A, D)
- Is it in your interest to finance more SMEs and/or provide more favorable loan conditions? (F)

At this point, participants were led through the Elaboration phase (envisioned future experience, 10-20 mins). First, they were provided with a short explanation on the immutability of records and how they are stored, without explicitly using the word blockchain. Then, they were directly addressed:

"If you could use this system to solve a problem from question 1, how do you imagine the situation would be? Can you walk us through this new story?"

Again, a number of questions were defined that had to be addressed by the different interviewees:

- What do you need in order to trust such a system (on a functional level)? (B, F, L, D)
- Do you think some SMEs/Wholesalers will see this solution as a threat to their way of doing business? And why? (B, A, D)
- Is it enough to confirm the authenticity of invoices that way? Do we need to ensure the authenticity of any other transactions? (F, L, D)
- How do you believe such a solution would affect your profession? Why? (B, F, L, A, D)

A Wrap-up session, lasting about 5 minutes, concluded the interview. At this point, participants were explicitly asked about their familiarity with blockchain, their opinion about it and their potential trust in it. They were then debriefed and thanked for their participation.

1.3.4 *Data analysis*

A common method to analyze qualitative data is grounded theory [4]. Grounded theory aims to build concepts, themes, and relational models out of collected data, from the ground up. It usually follows four intertwined phases: (1) open coding, where quotes and paragraphs are coded (i.e. tagged) with specific concepts, (2) axial coding, where groups of concepts are put together as themes or concepts, (3) selective coding, where relevant codes, themes and concepts are selected and further refined, and (4) theory building, where analysts aim to build a hypothesis on the basis of the data and themes/concepts generated in the earlier steps. For this analysis we have used Atlas.ti[c], a qualitative data analysis software that facilitates the aforementioned procedure.

1.4 Findings

The outcome of the analysis was a conceptual model that links together three main themes involved in the financing process to the blockchain. These themes are:

(1) Risks: certain constructs that are responsible for the lack of favorable financing conditions by financiers, that may be alleviated by the blockchain.
(2) Process: steps and actions taken that make up the financing procedure, that may be replicated on the blockchain.
(3) History: SME financial and other data that may be verified through the blockchain.

Figure 2 shows the composition of these themes and how they are conceptually linked to the blockchain. This section will further detail our findings with respect to each theme. In addition, we also provide insights on how the different stakeholders believe that the introduction of blockchain may impact their profession.

[c] http://www.atlas.ti/.

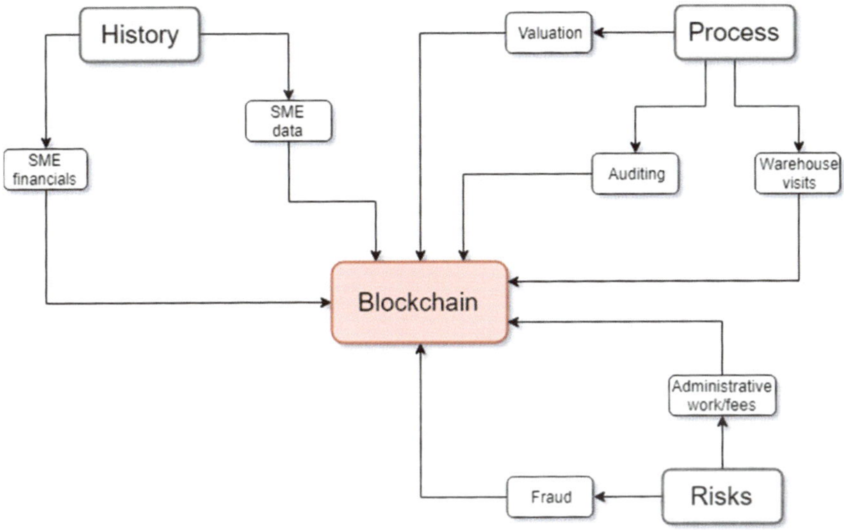

Figure 2. Thematic outcome of the research. The map outlines how Risks, History and Process could benefit from blockchain-based solutions.

1.4.1 *Risks (that blockchain-based finance can potentially overcome)*

1.4.1.1 *Fraud*

According to the head of an auditing team at a commercial financing institute, fraud always exists as a possibility whether you're dealing with invoice or inventory financing.

The risk of fraud is affected by 3 factors:

(1) The smaller the business entity, the higher the risk.
(2) The less history exists between the business entity and the financier, the higher the risk.
(3) Financing a foreign business carries a higher risk than a local one.

In other words, a financier would like to know how and when they will retrieve their investment in the case of bankruptcy. Other interviewees, including a financier and a director of a logistic services provider (LSP) director fully agree with these points.

1.4.1.2 *Administrative costs*

According to a traditional accountant, the 5% financier fee for an invoice is too high — too high for "doing nothing", that is. For inventory finance, the fees are usually much higher, ranging between 20% and sometimes up to 85%, as reported by the SME.

These high fees are primarily there to cover the risk of fraud, though they also cover the costs of the repetitive administrative work done on the part of the financier. "It's a long, complicated process", says the head of an auditing team. It takes roughly 20 days for invoice factoring, and for inventory finance it could take much more. The LSP's director asserts that "the banks will repeat all the work we do", and that they will reach to as much as possible of their clients' financial data before they make a decision.

1.4.2 *Process*

1.4.2.1 *Valuation is key*

The head of the auditing team conservatively shared the outline of a 9-step process that takes place every time an inventory financing application is received. As mentioned in the previous sections, the process could take numerous weeks, and it involves checks on the inventory's ownership, location, quality, and valuation. Due to the sensitivity of the process, we could not get a more detailed explanation — though we do understand that ownership, location, and quality audits happen less frequently (e.g. yearly) than valuation audits, which may be needed very often in the case of goods with fluctuating prices — and there is where most of the risk associated with the process lies. The head of strategy at a major local bank confirmed this as well. The head of the auditing team mentioned that for some types of inventory (e.g. metals) the value is easy to obtain through regulated stock markets, while for others, valuation takes on a much more complicated pattern (seasonal, etc.), and much more research is required. In any case, every inventory is investigated as a separate case, and a large part of the investigation involves offline processes. According to the head of the auditing team, LSPs possess accurate valuation data and models, due to the nature of their business — and interestingly enough, the manager of the LSP we interviewed suggests that LSPs do not mind sharing that data with financiers if that would benefit their clients (i.e. the SMEs), and possibly minimize the duplication of this work performed by the financiers.

On a related note, and according to the financier, human contact with the client will always be necessary, and that cannot be digitized.

1.4.2.2 *The inventory finance process may be very enduring for SMEs*

One of our interviewees was an SME with one experience in inventory-based finance. The process, in their experience, lasted somewhere between 2 to 3 months, partly because they have been in business for years and the financiers wanted to examine their complete financial history. Additionally, our interviewee mentioned that though the application was successful, the financiers required them to even reshuffle their company's structure. Moreover, and even though the head of the auditing team mentioned that there is sometimes room for negotiation, the SME members that we interviewed believed that the financiers possess almost all the power in shaping the final offer. The co-founder of the loan facilitator platform mentioned that sometimes, SMEs hire advisors to prepare such an application, pay the advisors some €4000 on average, yet sometimes end up having their application rejected. The SME also mentioned that, despite having successfully completed a financing application, the financier will go through the process all over again in case of a new application.

1.4.2.3 *Invoice finance may be easier for blockchain*

The head of the auditing team, an accountant who advises SMEs on financing, the head of strategy at a major local bank, as well as a loan facilitator all agree that financing based on invoices (i.e. cashflow) is a much simpler process than financing inventory. According to the head of the auditing team, the process of financing invoices will be easier to replicate on the blockchain as the financiers will only need to investigate the client's debtors, whose reputation can gradually be established on the blockchain. The process of inventory finance involves processes that are more difficult to replicate on the blockchain.

1.4.3 *History*

1.4.3.1 *Full financial overview*

The SME mentioned that during the process, the financiers wanted a complete overview of their finances — not only their inventory. According to them, the inventory itself, if not a majority of their assets, matters quite little: in the case of an emergency sale, the bank does not expect to get more than 10-15% of its actual value, and therefore provides an offer of such terms.

Moreover, according to the head of the auditing team, though a business entity's financial history sheds a great light on their financial health, it cannot fully predict future risk.

1.4.3.2 *Data privacy is key*

During the discussion with the SME, we've reached the point where we could evaluate a critical assumption that we've previously made. Since SMEs usually share most (if not all) of their financial data with their accountants, we've asked the SME we interviewed on whether they would be willing to share more data with more stakeholders in the inventory financing process (e.g. auditors, financiers, logistic service providers, ...) in case that would help them obtain better financing conditions. The answer was an undoubting "no": the SME wanted their data shared on a strictly need-to-know basis, regardless of whether it will lead to better financing conditions. The reason for that comes from the sensitivity of their data — were it to fall into the hands of their competitors, the risk of damage to their business would far exceed any potential improvement in financing conditions. They said they are also sure that most businesses would answer this question in exactly the same way.

1.4.4 *How do stakeholders view the effect of blockchain-based financing on their profession?*

1.4.4.1 *Financiers*

The head of strategy at a major local bank believes that a change in the way banking works will be quite slow. Banks are unlikely to be the first risk-takers and will only adopt blockchain-based solutions once others have accepted it. In other words, he believes adopting an SME financing solution will come from other types of financiers and trickle its way up the value chain. The head of an auditing team at a financing institution echoed that statement, mentioning that he is confident his team would adopt such a technology, but only when their institution starts financing SMEs.

1.4.4.2 *Accountants*

We interviewed two accountants. One is more of a traditional accountant and the other an advisor for SMEs. When discussing the potential influence of blockchain on their professions, both did not seem to think that blockchain is there to "replace" their profession — which, as one of them suggests, will still be relevant because they offer various services to their clients, not only bookkeeping. Both accountants were among the most enthusiastic to adopt a technology as such when it would exist, mentioning that it will make their job easier as well, as a part of an overall "digitalization" trend that is much needed in accountancy as many still rely heavily on paper work even in this day.

1.4.4.3 *SMEs*

Since SMEs would be the least of the stakeholders to interact with the blockchain, and since we've already covered the privacy aspect, we preferred to get the perspective of the loan facilitating platform founder on how SMEs may be affected with blockchain. He believes that enhancing trust and transparency with blockchain to improve financing conditions would "level the playing field". In other words, smaller and larger businesses will have more of an equal chance to obtain financing.

Moreover, and despite the privacy concerns highlighted in our previous post, he believes that the more transparent businesses will obtain better conditions — those who are not willing to be transparent may have something to hide. And in his view, blockchain will negatively affect these businesses, maybe rightfully so.

1.5 Discussion and conclusions

Based on the outcomes of the research, we clearly see the benefit of Blockchain in supporting inventory and invoice financing.

By providing a trustworthy and detailed history of all of the SME transactions, blockchain would allow financiers to accurately evaluate the risk of fraud. In addition, this detailed and trustworthy history would allow minimizing double checks and repeated work from the different stakeholders, possibly minimizing administrative costs (and fees as a consequence).

Though our analysis highlighted that invoice-based financing is more accessible than inventory finance at the time being, and thus readier to adopt blockchain, it also pointed out that there is much more room for improvement in the more complicated inventory finance process, and specifically the room for blockchain to improve the processes of valuation and data validation. Tracking the status of an SME's goods in a blockchain would certainly lower the costs of research, administrative costs, and the overall time spent on each inventory valuation case. This will gradually lead to improvements on the already poor financing conditions that SMEs receive, because of these impediments.

On the more sensitive issue of financial data privacy, our findings confirm the need for zero-knowledge proofs [7], and that what is stored on a blockchain accessible to multiple stakeholders should be limited to digital signatures (e.g. hashes) of financial data, instead of the data itself.

Finally, analysis showed that the blockchain may potentially "level the playing field" in the financing game for SMEs, transition the traditional book-keeping role of accountants into more of an advisory one, while financial institutions are likely to be the last of the stakeholders to adopt this disruptive technology.

In conclusion, we believe that the outcome of this exploratory should encourage the majority of stakeholders involved in the financing procedure to implements proofs-of-concept to gain a first-hand experience into the possible benefits and obstacles that will arise as the blockchain technology becomes more mature. A development of this sort would allow for a forthcoming, summative evaluation in the form of a quantitative user study.

References

1. Interim Justitia (2017). "The 2017 European Payment Report", released may 2017.
2. Beck and A. Demirgüç-Kunt (2006). Small and medium-size enterprises: Access to finance as a growth constraint. Journal of Banking & Finance, 30(11):2931–2943.
3. R. Canales and R. Nanda (2012). A darker side to decentralized banks: Market power and credit rationing in SME lending. Journal of Financial Economics, 105(2): 353–366.
4. Strauss, A. and Corbin, J. (1998). Basics of Qualitative Research: Techniques and Procedures for developing Grounded Theory. Sage Publications Inc.
5. Venkatesh, V., Morris, M. G., Davis, G. B., and Davis, F. D. (2003). User acceptance of information technology: Toward a unified view.
6. Ozcelik Buskermolen, D. and Terken, J. (2012). Co-constructing stories: a participatory design technique to elicit in-depth user feedback and suggestions about design concepts. In Proceedings of the 12th Participatory Design Conference: Exploratory Papers, Work-shop Descriptions, Industry Cases - Volume 2, PDC '12, pp. 33–36, New York, NY, USA. ACM.
7. A. Kosba, A. Miller, E. Shi, Z. Wen and C. Papamanthou (2016). "Hawk: The Blockchain Model of Cryptography and Privacy-Preserving Smart Contracts," 2016 IEEE Symposium on Security and Privacy (SP), San Jose, CA, pp. 839–858.

Chapter 5

Blockchains for Accelerating Open Innovation Systems for Sustainability Transitions

Rumy Narayan

Doctoral Researcher, School of Management, University of Vaasa, Finland

Annika Tidström

Professor, School of Management, University of Vaasa, Finland

Abstract

Challenges related to climate change, inequality, environmental degradation, and resource scarcity threaten our ability to sustain ourselves while ensuring an equal and prosperous future. The inherent complexity and interconnectedness of these challenges demand a rethinking of our traditional approach toward organizing our production and consumption systems. Transitions toward sustainability require systemic changes, implying a wide network of actors coordinating for new forms of organizing. This chapter proposes that blockchains could offer opportunities for such organizing by leveraging the various combinations of skills, capabilities, and knowledge across open innovation networks to facilitate transitions. The characteristics of open innovation networks and their significance to blockchains are discussed, and their relevance in sustainability transitions. Democratizing access to knowledge and coding trust and consensus through smart contracts make new and innovative economic spaces and opportunities possible. Firms may have to rethink traditional modes of organizing to seize the multiple opportunities that blockchain-enabled open innovation systems present.

1.1 Introduction

Blockchain technologies offer opportunities to reinvent various categories of monetary markets, financial services, payments, and economics in addition to a highly effective model for organizing activities that could enable possibilities for reconfiguration across industries, including most areas of human activity [Swan, 2015]. Such possibilities could potentially help facilitate transitions to sustainability, for instance, through new forms of peer-production and decentralized infrastructures supporting applications such as shared economies, finance, cloud databases, and mesh networks.

Based on existing research, this chapter explores how blockchains could enable networks for open innovation. We focus on the characteristics of these open innovation networks and their contribution to sustainability transitions. By developing an understanding of the key characteristics and their relatedness to the ideas driving blockchains, this chapter addresses the relevance of such characteristics in open innovation processes guiding sustainability transitions. It proposes that blockchain technologies could play an important role in harnessing open innovation markets by radically reorganizing our production and consumption systems through decentralization; and thus enable transitions toward sustainable systems.

Sustainability transitions gain importance as societies globally face significant long-term challenges related to climate change, population, resource scarcity, food security and pollution. In addition, deepening inequality and slowing economic growth have further exposed the need for a reconsideration of the traditional models of production and consumption toward more sustainable ones. [Blok *et al.*, 2015]. However, there are strong path-dependencies and lock-ins within the current system that resist change [Markard *et al.*, 2012; Ahman and Nilsson, 2008; Unruh, 2000].

Established technologies are socialized through user behavior, practices and lifestyles, aided by complimentary technologies that maintain the business models, value chains, organizational and institutional structures and regulations [Rip and Kemp, 1998]. The transition to electric vehicles where the internal combustion engine is giving way to battery technologies is not limited to the energy source but includes the sociotechnical system that supports them. The established alliances within current sociotechnical systems lean toward incremental rather than radical changes thus limiting capabilities for addressing sustainability challenges [Markard *et al.*, 2012; Frantzeskaki and Loorbach, 2010; Dosi, 1982]. This has highlighted the need for ways and means of promoting and governing a fundamental transformation of sociotechnical systems toward sustainable modes of production and consumption.

An emerging body of literature on transitions to sustainable sociotechnical systems is contributing toward understanding the complex and multi-dimensional shifts that are necessary for societies and economies to adapt to sustainable models of production and consumption, encompassing areas like energy, transport, housing, and food [Coenen *et al.*, 2012].

This transition process is defined by innovations that are systemic and are characterized by shifts toward sociotechnical configurations involving new technologies along with corresponding changes in markets, user practices, policy and cultural discourses, and governing institutions [Markard *et al.*, 2012; Geels and Schot, 2010; Geels *et al.*, 2008].

In the context of firms, this translates into navigating beyond product and process innovations toward a more systemic level of innovation that include products, services, and technologies along with new business and organizational models [Xavier *et al.*, 2017; Adams *et al.*, 2016; Montalvo, 2014; Boons *et al.*, 2013], involving a wider stakeholder engagement. It is increasingly evident that such radical transitions requiring systems level innovations involving a diverse set of actors demand enabling tools for effective and efficient coordination.

There is now a growing consensus that the ideas, policies, and narratives that have traditionally defined and governed firm competitiveness are changing and this changing landscape calls for collaborative innovation systems, as the issues are complex and interrelated [Loorbach and Wijsman, 2013]. Sustainability transitions therefore imply systemic changes requiring open innovation systems comprised of diverse actors such as businesses, research organizations, universities and governments.

Innovation is a multi-dimensional process characterized by changes in product, production process, markets, supplies/inputs, and organization [Schumpeter, 1934]. Innovation in the context of transition to sustainability needs to extend beyond economic potential to include societal changes that result from such innovation activities and the consequences for environmental and social sustainability, thus broadening both the problem framing as well as the analytical perspectives [Jacobsson and Bergek, 2011; Smith *et al.*, 2010]. In drawing attention to the co-evolution of technology along with social networks and institutions, the innovation systems literature conceptualizes innovation as a process driven by multiple actors [Geels, 2010]. Innovation conceptualized in this form, from the perspective of the firm, corresponds to the idea of open innovation.

It is important to note that in practice, openness is implicit in innovation processes, however, innovation literature makes a distinction between open and closed innovation [Huizingh, 2011]. Chesbrough [2003] used the term 'open innovation' as an umbrella construct that connected and integrated a range of activities, and in doing so enabled scholars and practitioners to visualize the design of innovation strategies in an increasingly networked and interconnected world [Huizingh, 2011].

Studies on open innovation offer deep insights into how firms negotiate environmental uncertainty and the complexities of innovation and knowledge recombination, and diffusion through increased organizational permeability initiated by interactions with a wide range of actors [Felin and Zenger, 2014]. This notion of innovation that encompasses diverse sets of actors has resulted in a range of alternatives ranging from contests and tournaments, to alliances and joint ventures, and corporate venture capital, licensing, open source platforms, and even participation in various development communities [Felin and Zenger, 2014]. Increase in such external linkages demonstrates improved innovation outcomes and better financial performance [Leiponen and Helfat, 2010; Love *et al.*, 2014]. Additionally, firms that repurpose their focus toward mitigating negative social and environmental impacts by moving beyond just optimizing individual performances could fundamentally restructure existing systems and encourage a rethink within wider networks [Loorbach and Wijsman, 2013].

Described as a 'new paradigm for organizing activity with less friction and more efficiency', blockchains offer global scope and scale for disintermediated transactions and automated resource allocation of physical as well as human assets [Swan, 2015]. We propose that firms that reorient themselves toward sustainable transition markets stand to gain by taking advantage of opportunities and blockchain technologies offer such firms the ability to do so. Blockchain technologies may offer alternate ways of 'spontaneous' organizing along with the governance properties of commons [Allen and Potts, 2016a,b; Davidson *et al.*, 2016] in open innovation processes directed toward solving issues related to sustainability.

More importantly, by enabling secure, end-to-end, and computationally validated transfer of value (this can be money, assets, or contractual agreements), it creates a new form of 'algorithmic trust' [Swan, and De Filippi, 2017], thus offering new opportunities for open innovation collaborative platforms aimed at resolving sustainability related challenges.

1.2 Open Innovation Networks for Sustainability

Transitions toward sustainable production and consumption systems require involvement of a variety of disciplines and approaches [Grin *et al.*, 2010; Reid *et al.*, 2010] including new business models and advanced management approaches incorporating new ways of determining business performance and success [Loorbach and Wijsman, 2013]. This means making intentional changes to the underlying philosophy and values that drive the current system; and to imagine this possibility while operating within the constraints of the incumbent system can be a daunting task [Kemp *et al.*, 1998; Geels, 2002; Garud and Gehman, 2012; Adams *et al.*, 2016; Bollier, 2016].

However, open innovation arenas could enable such transition processes. Technology and innovation management studies present why open innovation systems may explain how firms leverage their capabilities and appropriate value more effectively, [Gassmann *et al.*, 2010]. Some firms have internalized the idea that the value of business models that incorporate and encourage a continuous interaction of ideas within wider networks is far greater than those that do not [Chesbrough, 2003; Chesbrough and Appleyard, 2007; Gassmann *et al.*, 2010]. Chesbrough [2003] described this shift from a predominantly closed system to an open one as a 'paradigm shift' (in the sense of Kuhn, 1962). Industrial marketing literature has identified the various actors in such innovation processes; comprised of firms, research organizations, universities and governments, it offers insights into how these complex innovation networks should be managed [Rampersad *et al.*, 2010]. The dynamics of such innovation processes, that include not only market introduction and social embedding, but also the extent to which existing technological capabilities and market linkages need to be changed, have been discussed as well [Abernathy and Clark, 1985; Deuten *et al.*, 1997; Van de Ven *et al.*, 1999; Rip and Schot, 2002; Rip, 2012].

There have been efforts [Moore *et al.*, 2014; Seyfang and Haxeltine, 2012] to provide an understanding of innovation processes for sustainability by reflecting on the normative orientations of such processes along with social and political aspects of knowledge production and technology development. This has contributed to innovation studies by connecting innovation theory with science and technology studies (STS); resulting in the examination of interactions within socio-technical transitions [Smith *et al.*, 2010].

Successful open-innovation efforts require a shared initiative, a pool of incentivized individuals and the organization of individual efforts. Blockchains, by allowing untrusted networks of participants to agree on shared states for decentralized and transactional data securely without any central control or supervisor [Tasca and Tessone, 2017] facilitates new modes of transactions. It offers a layer of societal mobilization by making activities for open innovation possible through software protocols and provides an opportunity to understand its role in the socio-technical transition process toward sustainability.

1.3 Blockchain Technologies

The potential of blockchain technologies for initiating practices that go beyond payment reconciliation systems toward a value-creating paradigm implying societal benefits has been discussed widely [Böhme *et al.*, 2015; Swan, 2015; Davidson *et al.*, 2016; Walport, 2016; Kewell *et al.*, 2017]. Blockchain technologies hold the promise of managing the contracts and records that define our economic, political, and social systems, through digitally engineered trust. Blockchains are open and distributed ledgers capable of recording transactions between two parties in a verifiable and permanent manner [Swan, 2015; Iansiti and Lakhani, 2017].

The potential of the blockchain can be gauged by its ability to embed contracts in digital codes that are stored in transparent and shared databases, protected from deletion, tampering, and revision. This would enable the identification, validation, storage, and sharing of all agreements, processes, tasks, and payments, thus making intermediary roles played by brokers, lawyers, and bankers, redundant.

Smart contracts on the blockchain are both defined as well as executed by the code automatically, making them autonomous, self-sufficient and decentralized [Swan, 2015]. Autonomy means that upon initiation of the contract, the initiating agent can cease any engagement with the contract, self-sufficiency offers such contracts to raise funds and allocate resources for specific activities, and decentralization means they are not dependent on any single centralized entity but distributed and self-executed across network nodes [Swan, 2015; Beck *et al.*, 2016, 2017].

The true potential of the blockchain can be realized when individuals, organizations, machines, and algorithms begin freely interacting and transacting with one another with very little friction [Iansiti and Lakhani, 2017]. This is already evident from the financial industry's willingness to leverage blockchains for cost reductions and increased efficiencies in several business processes involving networks of global transactions in goods, services, and legal contracts. Blockchains enable real-time settlements, which reduce operational costs, its immutability reduces the risk of fraud and the use of smart contracts eliminates operational errors [Tasca and Tessone, 2017].

This could have deeper implications for the structure and operation of society as current established power relationships and hierarchies could easily lose their effectiveness [Swan, 2015]. Blockchain-led innovations will have transformational effects on our social, economic, and political systems and in doing so, they could potentially create new foundational infrastructures for these systems [Swan, 2015; Iansiti and Lakhani, 2017].

Firms, within this context, could cease to be stable entities and morph into dynamic networks that will coalesce into temporary enterprises by pooling knowledge residing in millions of nodes to complete tasks and projects, or to solve problems, with limited or no centralized control. The protocols will enable cooperation, and along with smart contracts, make new economic spaces possible.

1.4 Blockchain Powered Open Innovation Platforms for Sustainability Transitions

The call for a redesign of our economic institutions within which human activities are conducted, with the right incentives for creating societal and environmental resilience, is a long standing one [Arrow *et al.*, 1995]. Blockchains present the potential for developing the tools for creating such incentives at multiple levels through smart contracts, decentralization, and consensus [Swan, 2015].

The boundary spanning and dynamic nature of blockchains resonates with the core characteristics of open innovation. The idea of open innovation is synonymous with rapid technological change, where the challenge is to create openness to possibilities and options, and success depends on the re-combinations of these options and contribution from diverse actors [Chesbrough, 2003; Chesbrough and Appleyard, 2007]. Within this frame of reference, open innovation networks geared toward sustainability transitions would necessitate an extension of technological capabilities and market linkages that result in ecological, economic and social values in addition to economic value. This implies reframing innovation for addressing wider challenges linked to sustainable and inclusive growth that spans beyond the boundaries of the firm.

An open innovation model incorporating economic, social and environmental aspects while engaging with diverse actors would have a distributive characteristic. The interconnectedness of the challenge amplifies the importance of all entities on the platform, thus eliminating any hierarchy in the interactions.

Firms in transition could use blockchain powered open innovation platforms for testing new ideas and models for sustainability. Such platforms would create opportunities for enacting complex interactions allowing technology to shape the development process and vice versa. This could enable problem solving not through adaption but through mobilizing collective intelligence and resources for radical new solutions, which is the core purpose of open innovation, the potential of which has remained under exploited so far [Gassmann *et al.*, 2010].

Take the example of the open innovation platforms evolving around Circular Economy (CE), a framework that presents the potential for businesses to conceptualize economic activity along with environmental and social wellbeing in a sustainable manner [Geissdoerfer *et al.*, 2017]. As a global partner of the Ellen Macarthur Foundation[i], a CE platform, Nike initially developed a sustainable material index in a bid to understand and manage the impact of its material consumption. Subsequently, it offered this information as a freely downloadable application, as users (designers and producers) increase their consumption of sustainable materials, the actual impact will be greater, and in addition, as more actors make the transition, the cost of these materials will fall, creating an important incentive for making the transition.

Now imagine this playing out on a blockchain and the range of product ideas and business models increase exponentially. The sustainable material index could be like an InterPlanetary File System (*IPFS is a global and always accessible filesystem that can be drawn upon for resolving any issues related to the Internet*) for anyone wanting to work with sustainable materials. Through smart contracts, Nike could license its proprietary technology or even offer consulting services for business processes and strategies. This could create an avenue for revenue generation that it can leverage to justify cutting back on selling more

---

[i] https://www.ellenmacarthurfoundation.org/about.

products and contributing more effectively to a larger sustainability goal, that of bringing down the level of consumption in our societies. Nike, in this context, morphs into a key knowledge provider in the network, from a mere product company. Opendesk[ii] is another example of an online market place that hosts independent furniture designs while connecting customers to local makers, as an alternative to mass manufacturing and shipping; it claims to build a distributed and ethical supply chain through a global maker network.

Such models are possible for sustainable food, energy, mobility, and other consumer products leveraging the enormous volumes of data generated every day. This data includes historical records, messages, videos, GPS signals, and transactions, in addition to health records, land registry, education and employment. Organizations draw insights from the collection and analysis of data to optimize decision-making, personalize services and predict future trends. Ecco[iii], the Danish shoe brand is collecting data from customers in stores to explore the possibility for delivering affordable handmade bespoke shoes, for example. Further, advances in artificial intelligence (AI) is making it easier to draw relevance from disparate data sources and blockchains are becoming increasingly effective in addressing concerns related to privacy [Zyskind *et al.*, 2015].

Being tamperproof and transparent generates trust and open up opportunities for collaborations, and decentralization of governance make blockchains effective in storing, protecting, and sharing data effectively. The ability to decentralize governance means that open innovation networks can emerge to solve issues at the micro levels while drawing resources from other parts of the network at very low costs.

As a new and evolving technology, blockchain itself is an interesting case study providing insights into the governance of innovation commons. Discovering complementary uses of new technologies reduces transaction costs and while the immediate gains from new technologies or ideas might

---

[ii] https://www.opendesk.cc.

[iii]https://www.economist.com/science-and-technology/2018/05/22/shoemakers-bring-bespoke-footwear-to-the-high-street?cid1=cust/ddnew/email/n/n/20180522n/owned/n/n/ddnew/n/n/n/nap/Daily_Dispatch/email&etear=dailydispatch&utm_source=newsletter&utm_medium=email&utm_campaign=Daily_Dispatch&utm_term=20180522.

not be visible, innovation commons hold the promise of reaping the economic benefits of the continuous information exchange and coordination. [Allen, 2017]. Therefore, blockchain is a natural ally and could be a powerful driver for open innovation platforms for sustainability transitions.

1.5 Conclusion

Blockchain technologies facilitate a new paradigm by creating decentralized currencies, smart contracts or self-executing digital contracts, and creation of intelligent assets, while enabling participatory and decentralized governance systems [Wright and De Filippi, 2015]. Blockchains have the potential for revolutionizing how we think about innovation and enable the deployment of open innovation platforms for transitions toward sustainability.

Such innovation platforms could also, influence the governance norms of the blockchain. Lessing [1999] identifies law, social norms, markets, and architecture (for example, code) as the elements that influence behavior and norms, and calls for a larger ecosystem approach for influencing individuals, and open innovation platforms for sustainability transitions could provide such an ecosystem. Open innovation platforms could help understand and shape the blockchain governance structures and the blockchain in turn could enable these platforms to flourish.

To manage complex transition processes, we need to rethink firms as dynamic networks with various combinations of skills and knowledge capabilities. Open innovation platforms could help pool the abundance of skills, knowledge, and capabilities for powerful problem solving capacity. Open innovation networks offer creative solutions as such platforms would attract diverse groups of problem solvers and diverse groups have been known to outperform groups of high-ability problem solvers [Hong and Page, 2004]. Blockchains can provide the right tools for capturing the full potential of such open innovation platforms, but it also has the potential for affecting a far more radical change in the very way we think about our economic systems.

In playing the role of a coordination mechanism, blockchain brings down all costs and barriers related to intermediations, and in doing that, it puts an end to scarcity as the driving logic of our economic system and replaces it with abundance [Swan, 2017]. Open innovation networks facilitate the process of bringing together valuable assets and knowledge that organizations can use and learn from and blockchain helps create a financial model for doing this. As digital, decentralized, and distributed ledgers, blockchains have the ability to store data structured by rules and validated through consensus. Through this, blockchains derive the ability to confirm identities, status, and authority thus mapping the economic and social interactions that underpin our societal networks. Opportunities emerge within these interactions and financial models could surface from unlimited combination of such opportunities.

Blockchains also guides us in conceptualizing change as a process of becoming as it shifts the focus from entities toward connections and relationships, resulting in radical changes in our traditional belief systems. The network of connections increases possibilities for creating value far more than what strategic moves alone might have provided. In the process of becoming, entities are able to explore multiple possibilities through the network of connections and leverage the same connections for making those possibilities work. There is a continuous process of pursuing possibilities and maintaining a certain level of stability as the possibilities are acted on.

Firms are commonly understood, in organizational theory, as entities that are continuously adapting to the changing environment; this perspective restricts possibilities that are activated when change is associated with becoming. The idea of becoming indicates that entities are in a state of continuous change by responding to connections with new ideas and other entities. [Nayak and Chia, 2011].

Sustainability is incredibly hard to define but such abstraction need not be problematic. Firms as part of open innovation networks powered by blockchains could continuously experiment with ideas and models for capturing opportunities in transitions to sustainability through introduction, testing and diffusion of new products, services and processes. Operationalizing these processes on blockchains through smart contracts will bring down transaction costs [Davidson *et al.*, 2018].

An open innovation process like this would also distribute the responsibilities and benefits associated with the product or service across the value chain and this in turn will create incentives for all stakeholders to be involved in the process. The Internet democratized information but the ability of blockchains to record events, verify facts, and enforce norms helps in organizing this information for value creation at each of these levels. Decentralized governance makes this effective.

Decentralized governance is still evolving and needs reframing to include not just the rules that govern blockchains-based networks and applications but also the rules that govern the infrastructure that these networks and applications depend on. There is an endeavor to induce mechanisms for self-governance, along with bottom-up and multi-stakeholder governance and as this discussion develops and matures, it will provide valuable insights for governance of open innovation networks for sustainability transition governance on blockchains.

What is being proposed here will have deep implications how we conceptualize firms and this thought echoes often within the emerging scholarship on blockchains [see Davidson *et al*., 2018; Swan, 2017; Swan and De Filippi, 2017]. It is increasingly evident that value resides at the nodes where information is understood, processed, validated, and exchanged. We conclude that blockchains could provide the dynamic organizational capability vital for organizations intent on capturing these values, through open innovation networks for addressing the complex and interrelated societal challenges to sustainability. To do this effectively, organizations will need to decentralize themselves while collaborating and sharing far beyond their traditional comfort zones.

References

Adams, R., Jeanrenaud, S., Bessant, J., Denyer, D., and Overy, P. (2016). Sustainability-oriented innovation: a systematic review. International Journal of Management Reviews, 18(2), 180-205.

Åhman, M., and Nilsson, L. J. (2008). Path dependency and the future of advanced vehicles and biofuels. Utilities Policy, 16(2), 80-89.

Allen, D. (2017). Blockchain Innovation Commons. Papers.ssrn.com. Retrieved 18 January 2018, from https://papers.ssrn.com/sol3/papers.cfm?abstract_id=2919170.

Allen, D., and Potts, J. (2016a). How innovation commons contribute to discovering and developing new technologies. International Journal of the Commons, 10(2).

Allen, D., and Potts, J. (2016b). The origin of the entrepreneur and the role of the innovation commons. Paper presented to 86th Annual Meeting of the Southern Economic Association Conference, Washington, D.C., 19-21, November 2016.

Arrow, K., Bolin, B., Costanza, R., Dasgupta, P., Folke, C., Holling, C.S., Jansson, B.O., Levin, S., Mäler, K.G., Perrings, C., and Pimentel, D. (1995). Economic growth, carrying capacity, and the environment. Ecological Economics, 15(2), 91-95.

Beck, R., and Müller-Bloch, C. (2017). Blockchain as radical innovation: a framework for engaging with distributed ledgers. In: Proceedings of the 50th Hawaii international conference on system sciences, Waikoloa Village.

Beck, R., Czepluch, J. S., Lollike, N., and Malone, S. (2016). Blockchain — the gateway to trust-free cryptographic transactions. In: Proceedings of the 24th European Conference on Information Systems, Istanbul.

Blok, V., Long, T. B., Gaziulusoy, A. I., Ciliz, N., Lozano, R., Huisingh, D., Csutora, M., and Boks, C. (2015). From best practices to bridges for a more sustainable future: advances and challenges in the transition to global sustainable production and consumption: Introduction to the ERSCP stream of the Special volume. Journal of Cleaner Production, 108, 19-30.

Böhme, R., Christin, N., Edelman, B., and Moore, T. (2015). Bitcoin: Economics, technology, and governance. Journal of Economic Perspectives, 29(2), 213-238.

Bollier, D. (2016). Commoning as a transformative social paradigm. The Next System Project.

Boons, F., Montalvo, C., Quist, J., and Wagner, M. (2013). Sustainable innovation, business models and economic performance: an overview. Journal of Cleaner Production, 45, 1-8.

Chesbrough, H. (2003). Open Innovation: The New Imperative for Creating and Profiting from Technology. Harvard Business Press.

Chesbrough, H. W., and Appleyard, M. M. (2007). Open innovation and strategy. California Management Review, 50(1), 57-76.

Coenen, L., Benneworth, P., and Truffer, B. (2012). Toward a spatial perspective on sustainability transitions. Research policy, 41(6), 968-979.

Davidson, S., De Filippi, P., and Potts, J. (2018). Blockchains and the economic institutions of capitalism. Journal of Institutional Economics, 1-20.

Davidson, S., De Filippi, P., and Potts, J. (2016). Disrupting governance: The new institutional economics of distributed ledger technology.

Dosi, G. (1982). Technological paradigms and technological trajectories: a suggested interpretation of the determinants and directions of technical change. Research Policy, 11(3), 147-162.

Felin, T., and Zenger, T. R. (2014). Closed or open innovation? Problem solving and the governance choice. Research Policy, 43(5), 914-925.

Frantzeskaki, N., and Loorbach, D. (2010). Towards governing infrasystem transitions: reinforcing lock-in or facilitating change? Technological Forecasting and Social Change, 77(8), 1292-1301.

Jasper Deuten, J., Rip, A., and Jelsma, J. (1997). Societal embedding and product creation management. Technology Analysis and Strategic Management, 9(2), 131-148.

Garud, R., and Gehman, J. (2012). Metatheoretical perspectives on sustainability journeys: Evolutionary, relational and durational. Research Policy, 41(6), 980-995.

Gassmann, O., Enkel, E., and Chesbrough, H. (2010). The future of open innovation. R&D Management, 40(3), 213-221.

Geels, F. W. (2010). Ontologies, socio-technical transitions (to sustainability), and the multi-level perspective. Research Policy, 39(4), 495-510.

Geels, F.W., and Schot, J., (2010). Part 1: The dynamics of sociotechnical transitions: a sociotechnical perspective., In: Grin, J., Rotmans, J., and Schot, J. (Eds.). Transitions to Sustainable Development: New Directions in the Study of Long Term Transformative Change. Routledge: London, pp. 11-104.

Geels, F. W., Hekkert, M. P., and Jacobsson, S. (2008). The micro-dynamics of sustainable innovation journeys. Technology Analysis and Strategic Management, 20(5), 521.

Geels, F. W. (2002). Technological transitions as evolutionary reconfiguration processes: a multi-level perspective and a case-study. Research Policy, 31(8-9), 1257-1274.

Geissdoerfer, M., Savaget, P., Bocken, N. M., and Hultink, E. J. (2017). The Circular Economy–A new sustainability paradigm? Journal of Cleaner Production, 143, 757-768.

Grin, J., Rotmans, J., and Schot, J. (2010). Transitions to sustainable development: new directions in the study of long-term transformative change. Routledge.

Hong, L., and Page, S. E. (2004). Groups of diverse problem solvers can outperform groups of high-ability problem solvers. Proceedings of the National Academy of Sciences of the United States of America, 101(46), 16385-16389.

Huizingh, E. K. (2011). Open innovation: State of the art and future perspectives. Technovation, 31(1), 2-9.

Iansiti, M., and Lakhani, K. R. (2017). The truth about blockchain. Harvard Business Review, 95(1), 118-127.

Jacobsson, S., and Bergek, A. (2011). Innovation system analyses and sustainability transitions: Contributions and suggestions for research. Environmental Innovation and Societal Transitions, 1(1), 41-57.

Kewell, B., Adams, R., and Parry, G. (2017). Blockchain for good? Strategic Change, 26(5), 429-437.

Kuhn, T. S. (1962). The structure of scientific revolutions. Chicago: University of Chicago Press.

Lessig, L. (1999). Code and Other Laws of Cyberspace. New York: Basic Books.

Loorbach, D., and Wijsman, K. (2013). Business transition management: exploring a new role for business in sustainability transitions. Journal of Cleaner Production, 45, 20-28.

Love, J. H., Roper, S., and Vahter, P. (2014). Learning from openness: The dynamics of breadth in external innovation linkages. Strategic Management Journal, 35(11), 1703-1716.

Markard, J., Raven, R., and Truffer, B. (2012). Sustainability transitions: An emerging field of research and its prospects. Research Policy, 41(6), 955-967.

Montalvo, C. (2014). Global innovation and production networks: new rationales and policy challenges. Can policy follow the dynamics of global innovation platforms? 125.

Moore, M.L., Tjornbo, O., Enfors, E., Knapp, C., Hodbod, J., Baggio, J., Norström, A., Olsson, P. and Biggs, D. (2014). Studying the complexity of change: toward an analytical framework for understanding deliberate social-ecological transformations. Ecology and Society, 19(4).

Nayak, A., and Chia, R. (2011). Thinking becoming and emergence: process philosophy and organization studies. In Philosophy and organization theory (pp. 281-309). Emerald Group Publishing Limited.

Rampersad, G., Quester, P., and Troshani, I. (2010). Managing innovation networks: Exploratory evidence from ICT, biotechnology and nanotechnology networks. Industrial Marketing Management, 39(5), 793-805.

Reid, W. V., Chen, D., Goldfarb, L., Hackmann, H., Lee, Y. T., Mokhele, K., Ostrom, E., Raivio, K., Rockström, J., Schellnhuber, H.J., and Whyte, A. (2010). Earth system science for global sustainability: grand challenges. Science, 330(6006), 916-917.

Rip, A. (2012). The context of innovation journeys. Creativity and Innovation Management, 21(2), 158-170.

Rip, A., & Kemp, R. (1998). Technological change. Human choice and climate change, 2, 327-399.

Rip, A., and Schot, J. W. (2002). Identifying loci for influencing the dynamics of technological development. Shaping technology, guiding policy: Concepts, spaces and tools, 155-172.

Seyfang, G., and Haxeltine, A. (2012). Growing grassroots innovations: exploring the role of community-based initiatives in governing sustainable energy transitions. Environment and Planning C: Government and Policy, 30, 381-400.

Schumpeter, J.A., 1934 (2008), The Theory of Economic Development: An Inquiry into Profits, Capital, Credit, Interest and the Business Cycle, translated from the German by Redvers Opie, New Brunswick (U.S.A) and London (U.K.): Transaction Publishers.

Smith, A., Voß, J. P., and Grin, J. (2010). Innovation studies and sustainability transitions: The allure of the multi-level perspective and its challenges. Research Policy, 39(4), 435-448.

Swan, M. (2017). Is technological unemployment real? An assessment and a plea for abundance economics. In Surviving the Machine Age (pp. 19-33). Palgrave Macmillan, Cham.

Swan, M. (2015). Blockchain: Blueprint for a new economy. O'Reilly Media, Inc.

Swan, M., and De Filippi, P. (2017). Toward a Philosophy of Blockchain.

Tasca, P., and Tessone, C. J. (2017). Taxonomy of Blockchain Technologies. Principles of Identification and Classification.

Unruh, G. C. (2000). Understanding carbon lock-in. Energy policy, 28(12), 817-830.

Van de Ven, A. H., Polley, D. E., Garud, R., and Venkataraman, S. (1999). The innovation journey. Oxford University Press, New York.

Walport, M. (2016). Distributed Ledger Technology: Beyond Blockchain. UK Government Office for Science (p. 19). Tech. Rep.

Wright A., and DeFilippi P. (2015) Decentralized blockchain technology and the rise of lex cryptographia. Unpublished manuscript, Yeshiva University and Université Paris II. Retrieved 20 January 2018, from https://papers.ssrn.com/sol3/papers.cfm?abstract_id=2580664.

Xavier, A. F., Naveiro, R. M., Aoussat, A., and Reyes, T. (2017). Systematic literature review of eco-innovation models: Opportunities and recommendations for future research. Journal of Cleaner Production, 149, 1278-1302.

Zyskind, G., & Nathan, O. (2015, May). Decentralizing privacy: Using blockchain to protect personal data. In Security and Privacy Workshops (SPW), 2015, IEEE (pp. 180-184). IEEE.

Part 3

Social Science and Behavioral Economics

Chapter 6

Blockchain and the Future of Work: A Self-Determination Theory Approach

Horst Treiblmaier

Head of the Department of International Management

MODUL University Vienna, Austria

horst.treiblmaier@modul.ac.at

Uwe J. Umlauff

Chairman of the Executive Board at the City of Blockchain, Vienna, Austria;

Director of Steinbeis Transfer Institute Innovation & Business Creation, Munich, Germany

u.j.umlauff@steinbeis-sti.de

Abstract

Similar to the Internet several decades ago, Blockchain technology is expected to become a highly disruptive technology that will presumably impact society and economy alike. In this paper we present various scenarios as to how Blockchain might affect the future of work. We build on Self-Determination Theory, which takes into account different types of human needs and motivations, as a theoretical framework. We conducted 24 qualitative interviews with Blockchain experts and created three different scenarios that outline potential future developments. The experts' opinions range from predicting no significant impact of Blockchain on the work environment toward substantial changes that can have both beneficial and adverse consequences for the work force. In this chapter we detail the three scenarios and further illustrate Blockchain's potential implications for basic human needs in the context of the future of work.

1.1 Introduction

Blockchain technology has been given many labels. While some authors call it a "blueprint for a new economy" [Swan, 2015] or even a "revolution" [Tapscott and Tapscott, 2016], others simply refer to it as a "hype" [Kaminska, 2017]. Dedicated supporters are praising it as a panacea for many societal, economic and organizational ailments [Tapscott and Tapscott, 2016] while skeptics claim that it merely constitutes a highly overrated buzzword [Roubini, 2018]. Thorough academic research is therefore needed to critically and objectively assess the potential of Blockchain against the backdrop of contradictory opinions and to evaluate the extent to which Blockchain can meet the high expectations of many technology enthusiasts.

Outside of computer science and cryptography communities, the vast majority of the existing literature has been published in outlets targeting practitioners and mainly focuses on technological issues or on economic implications of Blockchain [Narayanan *et al.*, 2016; Swan, 2015]. As yet, few academic authors have scrutinized its potential implications for organizational processes with a specific focus on human resources and the future of work in general. Given the huge importance of the working world for economic and societal stability [Junankar, 2011] as well as personal well-being [Linn *et al.*, 1985], the question arises as to how Blockchain might quantitatively and qualitatively impact the way in which we will spend our professional lives and earn money in the future.

The transformation of the working world started long ago with the development of primitive stone tools for facilitating certain tasks. The oldest stone tools known to be used by predecessors of the genus homo were found at a site in Kenya and date back 3.3 million years [Harmand, 2015]. Since that time, humans have continually developed tools and machinery and streamlined processes in order to make their work more efficient and thus to increase productivity. Starting in the 18th century, the industrial revolution had significant repercussions not only for economic growth, but also led to major transformations of work processes, living conditions and work ethics [Sterns, 2013]. Productivity enhancements over the centuries led the proportion of people working in industry to increase steadily as farming became less labor-intensive. As industrial machinery became increasingly sophisticated, the service sector started to absorb much of the labor force, and this represents the current state in most industrialized countries [CIA, 2018]. The present situation has been shaped by the digital revolution, which started with centralized mainframe technology in the 1970s[a], was followed by the unexpected success of personal computing, and eventually led to technologies such as distributed client server systems, the Internet, mobile computing, cloud computing and ubiquitous computing. One of the most recent technological advancements is Blockchain, a distributed ledger technology (DLT)[b] that

---

[a] It should be noted, however, that the foundation for this development was laid many centuries ago. Already in the 17th century Wilhelm Schickard, Blaise Pascal and Gottfried Leibniz had built sophisticated calculating machines. During the heyday of the industrial revolution, Charles Babbage and Ada Lovelace worked on the analytical engine, the first mechanical general-purpose computer.

[b] It is beyond the scope of this paper to detail different types of Blockchain and DLT as well as their technical subtleties. Rather, it is the basic properties which most types of

possesses several key characteristics such as decentralization, immutability of the data, transparency, and fault tolerance that bear significant potential for novel applications such as the digital transfer of value [Narayanan *et al.*, 2016].

In this chapter we investigate if and how the specific characteristics of Blockchain and its potential future applications may impact the future of work. Qualitative data was gathered from interviews with Blockchain experts. In the following sections we will briefly introduce Self-Determination Theory, which constitutes our theoretical framework, followed by a short discussion of our methodological approach, the discussion of our findings and several implications for future research.

1.2 Work and Self-Determination Theory

Although it is largely undisputed that work constitutes an important part of human life, the nature of jobs and their respective perceptions vary widely, with some individuals pursuing rewarding, interesting and valued activities and others performing underpaid and frustrating tasks [Ryan *et al.*, 2010]. In order to be a satisfying part of one's life, work must contribute to the fulfillment of human needs, which are frequently depicted in a hierarchical pyramid founded on the most basic of needs, physiological requirements and safety, before progressing to the higher-level needs of belonging, esteem, and self-actualization [Maslow, 1943]. It has been argued that the very nature of human work can potentially fulfill all of these needs by providing a living, guaranteeing job security, allowing for good work relations, prestige, status and, finally, providing opportunities for achievement and advancement [Thomson, 2016]. All too often, however, this is not the case and work turns out to be a non-fulfilling experience which may even cause physiological and psychological

---

Blockchain or DLTs share that are of interest for this research. In the remainder of this paper we therefore use only the term Blockchain, but acknowledge that similar effects can be caused by other types of DLTs.

suffering [Steinmetz and Schmidt, 2010]. Explanatory models are therefore needed that go beyond the mere depiction of need hierarchies and show how specific work characteristics have the potential to affect the underlying motivational antecedents for better or for worse.

Previous research has shown that Self-Determination Theory (SDT) provides a useful and comprehensive framework to elucidate the link between motivation, well-being, and work performance [Ryan and Deci, 2000]. Figure 1 depicts the three major antecedents, which, taken together, form the basic psychological needs: need for autonomy (i.e., feeling in control of one's behavior and goals), need for competence (i.e., deeming oneself effective in interacting with the environment), and the need for relatedness (i.e., experiencing interaction and connection to other people). In turn they impact an individual's motivational continuum that stretches from amotivation (i.e., complete lack of motivation) to intrinsic motivation that is completely triggered by inner motives. In between lie different stages of extrinsic motivation that are strongly driven by external rewards: external regulation refers to contingencies external to a person (e.g., only working when the boss is watching); introjected regulation has been internalized, but has not been accepted as one's own (e.g., working because it makes me a worthy person); identified regulation refers to behavior which is fully congruent with individual goals and identities; and, finally, in a state of integrated regulation the behavior becomes an integral part of one's personality [Gagne and Deci, 2005]. Similarly, the level of autonomy can be depicted as a continuum with low levels corresponding to a higher degree of externally triggered extrinsic motivation. Deci *et al.* [2017] evaluated the current application of SDT in the assessment of work organizations and conclude that SDT has been successful in explaining organizational performance and employees' wellbeing.

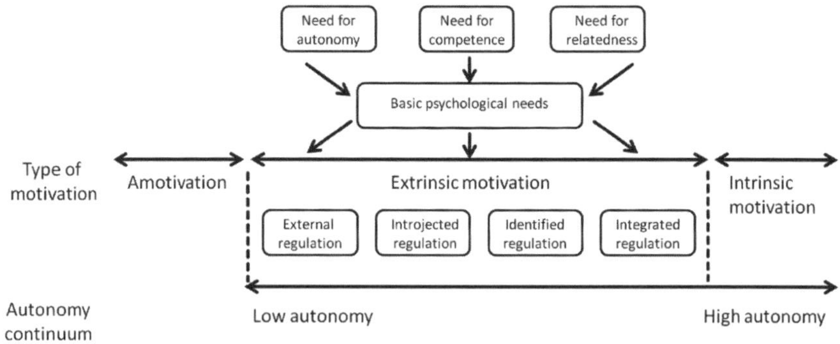

Figure 1. Self-determination continuum (based on Ryan and Deci [2000, 2007]).

It is the very nature of Blockchain which yields the potential to fundamentally alter the conditions of many jobs through the characteristics of traceability, accountability, transparency, control, and immutability. Based on SDT, in the following sections we focus on the positive and negative implications of Blockchain for the quantity and quality of work and on human needs for autonomy, competence and relatedness.

1.3 Method

Between January and February 2018 we conducted 24 qualitative interviews with Blockchain experts via telephone. The interviews each lasted between 12 and 23 minutes. All interviews were recorded, transcribed and analyzed following the standards of qualitative content analysis and grounded theory [Glaser and Strauss, 1967; Hsieh and Shannon, 2005]. The experts were selected from the member directory of a large Blockchain interest group in Austria and included representatives of organizations from various industries (e.g., finance, energy, transportation), interest groups, consulting agencies, governmental institutions and educational institutions. All of the experts had previous experience with Blockchain technology such as the implementation and evaluation of use cases, industry consulting projects, or the mining of cryptocurrencies. We used a rough interview guide and asked the experts to briefly outline their expectations as to how Blockchain might impact the future of work. All questions were open-ended and we frequently used follow-up questions to eliminate uncertainties. The interview transcripts were analyzed using inductive content analysis, which included open coding, the creation of categories and abstraction. Axial coding was used to make connections between categories and subcategories. Finally the emerging concepts and categories (i.e., groups of concepts) related to organizational work contexts were grouped into themes, some of which included an assumed causality [Martin and Turner, 1986].

1.4 Results

In the following sections the main themes that emerged from the interviews are discussed sequentially. Initially, we report the experts' expectations pertaining to the further development of Blockchain in general and its anticipated positive and negative consequences. Next, we present three different scenarios for the overall labor market and, finally, a thorough investigation of proposed changes pertaining to the exogenous constructs in SDT.

1.4.1 *Positive and negative effects of Blockchain*

The development of the core concepts underlying Blockchain started decades ago, but only attracted attention in specialized computer science and cryptography communities [Narayanan and Clark, 2017]. In 2008, Satoshi Nakamoto, a pseudonym representing an as yet unidentified person or group of persons, published a seminal paper in which various existing technical components were combined in an ingenious manner resulting in the cryptocurrency Bitcoin [Nakamoto, 2008]. The first Bitcoin client was released in January 2009 without a significant impact on industry or society. It was not until the massive price increase of Bitcoin several years later that the general public started to take notice of the underlying technology, Blockchain, and its wide-ranging potential applications. In their "Hype Cycle for Emerging Technologies 2017", Gartner [2017] positioned Blockchain in the category labeled as "Peak of Inflated Expectations", which indicates an intensive public discussion and many conflicting opinions regarding the subject. Similarly, our respondents exhibited a broad range of differing opinions, ranging from seeing Blockchain as being "*overrated*" to "*offering a huge number of untapped possibilities*". One expert summarized the current discussion by stating that *"some people might say it is great while others consider it to be awful"*. Additionally, the respondent added: *"However, Blockchain is only a technology, which by itself is neither good nor bad. It is completely up to us how we deploy it*".

Figure 2 shows the three main categories that emerged from the interviews, which are clustered into positive and negative outcomes respectively. The categories show the impact of the Blockchain on industry as well as on individuals' work and private lives. In short, Blockchain technology can be seen as a double-edged sword demonstrating a huge potential to positively impact economies and society alike. However, hidden dangers may be lurking in potential applications that might lead to severe negative consequences. As far as industry in concerned, Blockchain is seen as a potential innovation driver that could impact organizational processes in various ways and lead to higher productivity: for example, by reducing transaction costs. Furthermore, various use cases were mentioned in which the transfer of money and increased transparency of transactions lead to beneficial outcomes for organizations. Then again, numerous ambiguities exist pertaining to the legal situation and doubts about the applicability of Blockchain technology for many alternative use cases. Furthermore, the restructuring of business processes may lead to so-called self-cannibalization, destroying, for example, existing distribution channels and business relationships. Jumping on the "Blockchain bandwagon" might also lead to substantial losses pertaining to time and money invested in dubious projects with futile outcomes.

As far as the "human factor" is concerned, the experts expect Blockchain to lead to increased efficiency and a reduction in the use of labor for routine activities which can be accomplished by automating processes or sharing common access to immutable data. The use of objective performance records may result in the development of new rewards systems, which, in turn, could lead to increased motivation. Furthermore, certain Blockchain applications bear the potential to increase employee participation by allowing, for example, for shared database

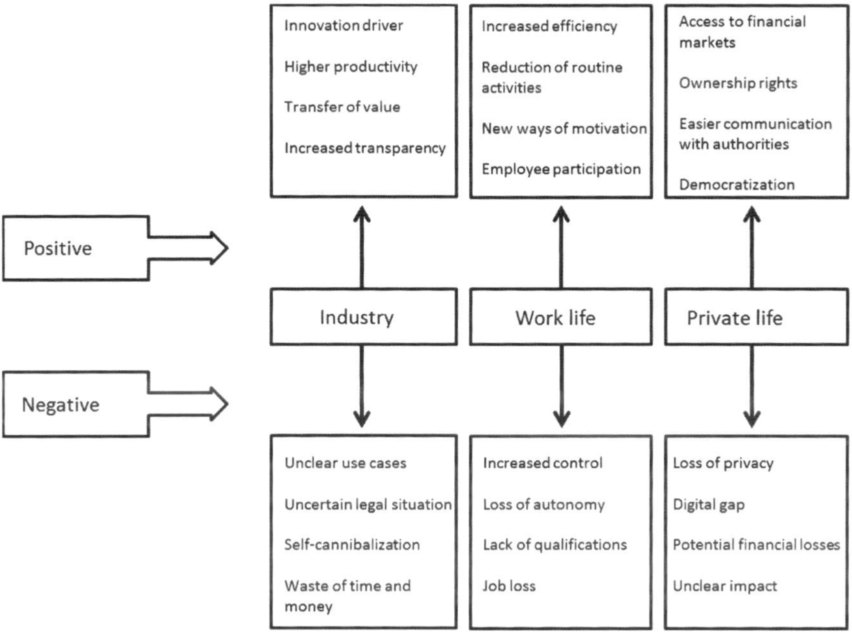

Figure 2. General effects of blockchain.

access. However, the experts also warn against increased control, which may arise due to the permanent and immutable storage of data. As a consequence, workers' autonomy may be restricted with single job tasks being exactly prescribed, measured and evaluated. Existing qualifications and skills may lose value, which ultimately might even lead to job losses.

The experts also mentioned several potential positive implications of Blockchain for individuals' private lives. These include easy access to financial markets, as has happened during the recent rise of ICOs (Initial Coin Offerings), and the guarantee of ownership rights. In the public sector, communication with authorities may be easier and more traceable. Taken together, these effects could potentially give more power to the people and foster a process of increased democratization. However, negative side effects may also appear, including a general loss of privacy due to greater data transparency and facilitated data access, and the widening of the "digital divide" caused by lack of technological skills in some parts of the population. Potential financial losses may occur on investments made in the wake of enthusiastic media coverage of Blockchain-based technologies. As the long-term consequences of Blockchain are unclear, this creates uncertainty on the side of private consumers. In the following sections, the impact of Blockchain on working lives is investigated in more detail.

1.4.2 *Quantitative and qualitative changes of the working world*

Ever since the advent of stone tools for facilitating work, humans have simultaneously worked on reducing and improving work processes. The success of these long-lasting efforts is reflected in the shift of the labor force from manual labor, first in agriculture and later in manufacturing, toward the service industry. However, all these efforts have also led to the somewhat paradoxical situation that humans are constantly trying to reduce the actual amount of physical and mental work they need to accomplish, while at the same time acknowledging that work constitutes an essential part of their well-being and self-actualization [Spreitzer *et al.*, 2005]. Consequently, high unemployment rates are viewed with aversion by politicians, among others, due to their effects on humans on a societal and individual level alike. The question arises as to whether Blockchain technology has the potential to directly affect the quantity (i.e., the sum total of all tasks to be completed by humans, as reflected by the size of workforce needed) and quality (i.e., cognitive challenges involved in completing specific tasks) of work. Based on our classification and the categories that were developed from the expert interviews, three different scenarios emerged (see Figure 3). In our framework we differentiate between total demand for work in three manifestations (i.e., decrease, stable, increase) and two qualitatively different types of work, namely routine work and skilled labor, with the latter including challenging problem-solving tasks which demand specialized knowledge.

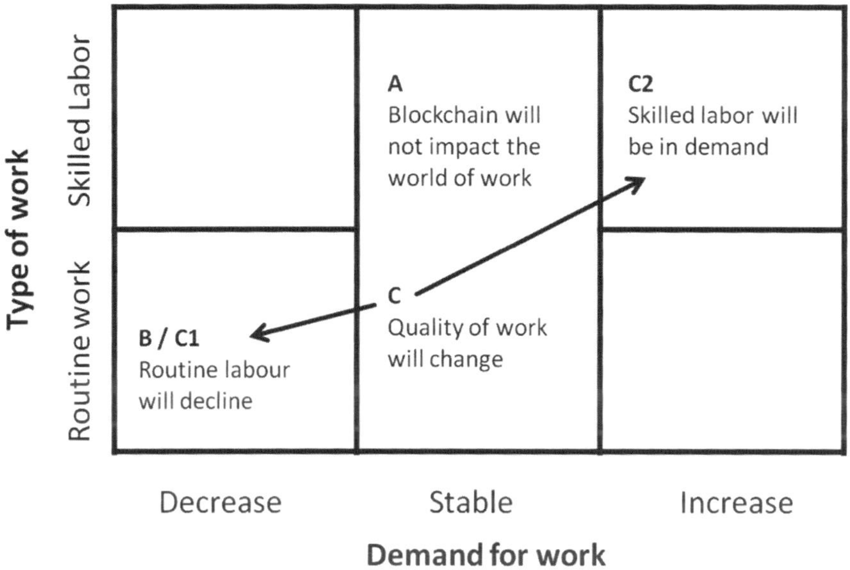

Figure 3. Blockchain and the working world.

- Scenario A: Blockchain will not impact the world of work

Several experts expressed the opinion that Blockchain will not lead to any important changes in the overall quantitative and qualitative composition of the work force. Exemplary statements included "*Similar to what has happened with the introduction of other technologies before, Blockchain will not result in a reduction in employment*", "*Blockchain will impact society in general, but I do not see any specific implications for the work force*", and "*I do not see how Blockchain will affect the work in a major way*". Others mentioned that Blockchain is only part of a general digitalization trend and does not have any specific effects: "*Blockchain is just part of the digitalization process we are facing right now. It is an evolution, not a revolution*".

- Scenario B: Routine labor will decline

A minority of experts expect Blockchain to result in a general decline in the quantity of work: in other words, to a reduction in employment that is not offset by the creation of new jobs. This is attributed to specific qualities of Blockchain that allow for more efficient processes to replace existing tasks. All of the experts in this category agreed that routine work that does not demand specific skills will be most affected: "*Many back-office activities will be substituted by Blockchain*". One respondent highlighted the importance of individuals' willingness to change: "*Some people should be afraid of losing their jobs if they are not willing to conform*". Finally, several experts indicated that changing transaction costs might lead to structural organizational changes in several industries: "*Banks and notaries will still exist in the future, but they will have to focus on their core competencies*".

- Scenario C: The quality of work will change

The third scenario is composed of two opposing effects which neutralize each other when it comes to the overall magnitude of the required workforce. It was this development that was deemed most likely by the vast majority of experts. They predict that a decline in routine labor (C1), which corresponds to scenario B, will be offset by a simultaneous increase in demand for highly qualified labor (C2), which in most cases includes computer specialists but might also offer new opportunities for legal or financial experts: "*Smart contracts, for example, need to be designed. This is not less work, but simply different activities*". One respondent called it a "*zero sum game*". The general sentiment was that "*the overall requirements for employees will definitely increase, but I do not believe that we will lose jobs in the long run*" or "*some jobs will definitely become redundant, but we need regulation [...] and new jobs will be created in this area*". There was some level of agreement about the future role of human workers: "*Humans will be needed for the complicated tasks, everything that a machine cannot decide*". Several experts pointed out that the existing shortage of highly skilled workers will become more pronounced: "*There will be a shortage in several areas. We especially need people with interesting CVs. For example, IT specialists that engage in cryptography or programmers that understand legal issues*". It was also highlighted that the proportion of female specialists needs to be increased: "*It is a fact that we do not have enough women in the field*". Historical reflection enabled some experts to provide an optimistic outlook: "*In the long run, technological progress has always created more and better jobs than were lost in the first place*".

1.4.3 *Self-Determination Theory: Blockchain and psychological needs*

As already outlined in previous sections, Blockchain development is seen as an ongoing process which simultaneously entails advantages and disadvantages: "*the danger is there, but I also expect a lot of innovation. Some people feared the steam engine, electrification, computers and DNA analysis. It is a process we simply cannot stop*". Substantial changes in the qualitative nature of work are also expected: "*the way we work will be significantly altered. Blockchain will change all kinds of organizational processes, data exchange, traceability, communication, settlements*". This might even lead to fears and social tensions: "*Blockchain will lead to an extreme change for humans and we should be careful about it. We need to remember that the industrial revolution gave birth to the luddites*". SDT can help to investigate whether the anticipated qualitative changes in the nature of work have the potential to impact individuals' motivation and their perception of autonomy in the workplace. As shown in Fig. 1, autonomy, competence and relatedness constitute three basic antecedents for human motivation and their consequent social development and well-being [Ryan and Deci, 2000]. Figure 4 shows potential positive and negatives effects of Blockchain on the respective antecedents.

Given the current shortage of Blockchain-related skills, an expert predicted that personal autonomy in the workplace will increase, since "*the number of highly skilled jobs will grow, and these typically provide greater autonomy and flexibility for employees*". Furthermore, "*they will be able to oversee business transactions in their entirety*" since "*Blockchain makes transactions immutable and transparent. Everyone gets the same view*" and "*they will be in control of complete transactions*". Similarly, another respondent commented that "*employees will be empowered. They will be responsible for more complex tasks*". However, it is also possible that Blockchain impacts autonomy in a negative way by making certain tasks superfluous: "*certain activities will not be needed anymore. This can affect especially middle management since decision processes can be outsourced to algorithms*". Similarly, it is feared that "*algorithms will be in control*" and that "*it will be machines who measure human performance. They will finally decide who is doing a good job*". This might potentially intensify perceived stress: "*employees will be under increased pressure. They would not be able to act independently anymore*".

Blockchain is also expected to impact competences in both positive and negative ways. It might demand an increase in job skills ("*for example, smart contracts have to be designed. This is a challenging task*"), which suggest careful consideration of education choices: "*for the millennial generation this poses a great opportunity, if they are smart enough to choose the right type of education. You simply need to give them the right perspectives*". Greater flexibility and an increased locus of control (i.e., the extent to which people believe that they control the outcome of events in their lives) will be caused by "*jobs that are simply more demanding*". It is further expected that employees take on more personal responsibility. Finally, Blockchain will also allow for a fair evaluation of individual performance: "*now it is possible to track performance of individual employees. This will allow for a fair measurement of an employee's performance*". Negative impacts on competence might stem from an increase in the fragmentation of labor ("*Tasks can be split into sub-tasks that can be more easily controlled*") and by replacing humans with machines: "*Smart contracts are really good for standardized products. They can be copied and shared and others can also use them. We will need less lawyers*". One expert even mentioned that they found that artificial intelligence produced a superior result: "*We once used AI for smart contracts. After a while we figured out that the algorithm produced a solution that was superior to those of our lawyers*". However, one respondent highlighted the danger of over-reliance on certifications based on "objective" measurement: "*In some cases, certifications might not be enough. You need some common-sense, and this is not reflected on paper. Your CV might look better on paper than your qualifications are in reality*". This goes hand in hand with the problem of measuring social skills: "*We only talk about technical certifications. Social skills belong exclusively to humans and a computer will never be able to assess whether you are a team player*".

Finally, Blockchain is expected to influence the way in which people interact. Positive effects are expected from joint problem solving: "*Employees share the same view of business transactions. This makes communication easier*". As a side-effect of immutable and shared data, the experts anticipated that the level of trust inside and between organizations will increase: "*Trust in business partners will be increased. There will be less haggling and fewer complaints*", and "*Processes inside the company will become more transparent, which will foster trust and communication*". In case individual performance can be tracked objectively this will lead to impartial assessments: "*Work performance can be recorded permanently. This improves the fairness of evaluations and subsequently also corporate culture*". However, Blockchain might also exert a negative impact on relatedness, for example by reducing the need for direct human interaction ("*in case contracts will be executed automatically, communication between employees will suffer*"), which might also affect relations between superiors and subordinates: "*Supervision might be taken over by machines. This makes relations inhuman*". Eventually this might result in a situation where personal relations become superfluous: "*in an increasingly automated world the importance and the value of personal relations decreases*". Finally, a respondent raised concerns about the potential of Blockchain to exert control, which might even lead to a general paranoia: "*I do not want to live in a surveillance state, so we have to be careful about how we deploy Blockchain*".

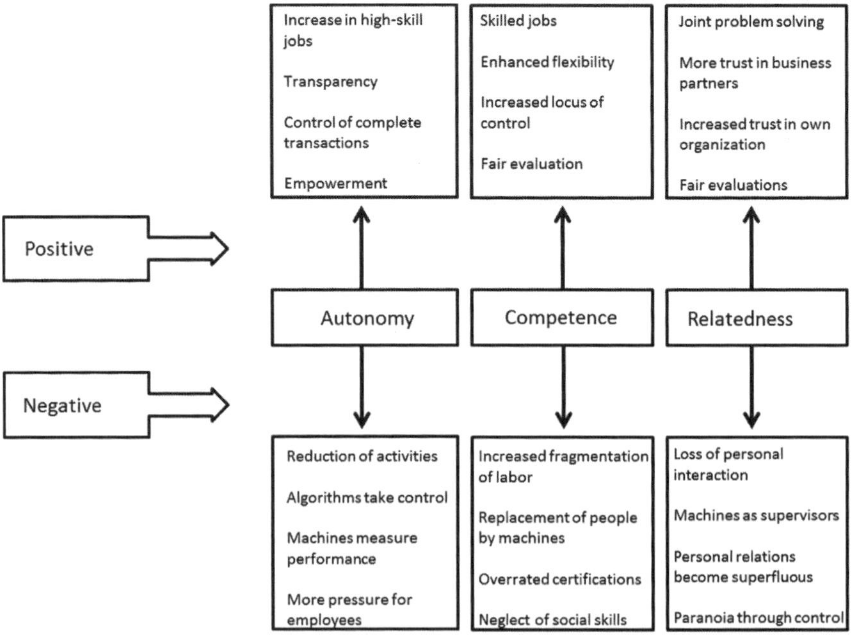

Figure 4. Blockchain and human psychological needs.

As we have shown in the previous sections, the potential positive and negative effects of Blockchain on the basic psychological needs of autonomy, competence and relatedness are manifold. This does not mean that all of these effects are inevitable consequences, or that they will all manifest with the same force. The huge array of potential implications just highlights the importance of current Blockchain-related developments for working lives of the future. As was outlined in the description of SDT, perceived fulfillment of individual needs impacts the level of motivation as well as the perception of personal autonomy. In turn, these factors influence work performance and personal well-being. Blockchain thus has the potential to decrease the level of extrinsic motivation toward a state of introjected regulation or even external regulation, which eventually might result in a motivation. Conversely, there exists a vast potential for job enrichment which might lead to states of identified and integrated regulation and, ultimately, intrinsic motivation. This in turn impacts the regulatory processes needed to control, supervise and reward employees.

1.5 Conclusion and Implications

Recently Blockchain has gained a lot of attention in scholarly and practitioner literature. The general impact of the technology on society and economy is expected to be huge. Naturally, this also includes the working world, the importance of which has already been acknowledged by the industry [PwC, 2017]. To date, however, rigorous and theory-based academic research in this field is missing. In this paper we therefore lay the foundation for further studies by presenting the results from 24 qualitative interviews that were analyzed following the principles of qualitative research. SDT was used as a guiding framework and helped us to position our findings within the scope of a well-established theory. Our results show that Blockchain has the potential to heavily influence the working world for better or for worse by impacting the exogenous variables of SDT. In light of the anticipated effects we suggest that future academic research closely investigates the nature and strength of Blockchain-related implications. We have further shown that SDT provides an ideal starting point for doing this by offering a tested theoretical framework and well-established measurement instruments. Additionally, action research might help to design and implement systems that not only boost organizational performance, but simultaneously take into account the needs and desires of the work force. Such an approach would bridge the gap between academia and industry, which is looking for solutions to practical problems. Employers, for example, could use our framework to carefully assess the potential implications of Blockchain. In a broader sense this could also inform policy makers who are responsible for legal matters that affect the design of the working world. It is the responsibility of academic research to guide the industry on how different Blockchain implementations might impact employees' quality of life as well as organizational performance, and how an appropriate organizational design can help to improve the quality of working life. The findings of this study present the first step toward establishing a solid theoretical foundation for future academic research investigating the implications of Blockchain on the working world. Future studies can build on our framework and develop it further by integrating it into a broader theoretical framework or refining the three scenarios we presented.

References

CIA (2018). The World Factbook, https://www.cia.gov/library/publications/the-world-factbook/fields/2012.html, accessed January 10, 2018.

Deci, E. L., Olafsen, A. H. and Ryan, R. (2017). Self-Determination Theory in work organizations: The state of a science, Annual Review of Organizational Psychology and Organizational Behavior, 4(1), pp. 19-43.

Gagne, M. and Deci, E. (2005). Self-determination theory and work motivation, Journal of Organizational Behavior, 26(4), pp. 331-362.

Gartner (2017). Top trends in the Gartner Hype Cycle for emerging technologies, www.gartner.com, accessed February 9, 2018.

Glaser, B. and Strauss, A. L. (1967). *The Discovery of Grounded Theory: Strategies for Qualitative Research.* Aldine Publishing Company, Chicago.

Harmand, S. *et al.* (2015). 3.3-million-year-old stone tools from Lomekwi 3, West Turkana, Kenya. Nature, 521(7552), pp. 310-315.

Hsieh, H.-F. and Shannon, S. E. (2005). Three approaches to qualitative content analysis, Qualitative Health Research, 15(9), pp. 1277-1288.

Kaminska, I. (2017). Growing scepticism challenges the blockchain hype, *Financial Times*, https://www.ft.com/content/b5b1a5f2-5030-11e7-bfb8-997009366969, accessed February 17, 2018.

Linn. M. W., Sandifer, R. and Stein, S. (1985). Effects of unemployment on mental and physical health, American Journal of Public Health, 75(5), pp. 502-506.

Junankar, P. N. (2011). The global economic crisis: Long-term unemployment in the OECD, Institute for the study of labor, IZA, Discussion paper no. 6057.

Martin, P. Y. and Turner, B. A. (1986). Grounded theory and organizational research, Journal of Applied Behavioural Science, 22(2), pp. 141-157.

Maslow, A. H. (1943). A theory of human motivation, Psychological Review, 50(4), pp. 370-396.

Nakamoto, S. (2008). Bitcoin: A peer-to-peer electronic cash system, https://bitcoin.org/en/bitcoin-paper, accessed August 12, 2017.

Narayanan, A. and Clark, J. (2017). Bitcoin's academic pedigree: The concept of cryptocurrencies is built from forgotten ideas in research literature, ACM Queue, 15(4), pp. 1-30.

Narayanan, A., Bonneau, J., Felten, E., Miller, A., and Goldfeder, S. (2016). *Bitcoin and Cryptocurrency Technologies: A Comprehensive Introduction.* Princeton University Press: Princeton, USA.

PwC (2017). How will blockchain technology impact HR and the world of work?, pwc, report, https://www.pwc.co.uk/issues/futuretax/how-blockchain-can-impact-hr-and-the-world-of-work.html?lipi=urn%3Ali%3Apage%3Ad_flagship3_pulse_read%3BDgmOD4mxRbmImEvX4l0CwA%3D%3D, accessed January 10, 2018.

Roubini, N. (2018). Blockchain's broken promises. www.brettonwoods.org/sites/default/files/publications/Blockchain%E2%80%99s%20Broken%20Promises%20by%20Nouriel%20Roubini%20-%20Project%20Syndicate.pdf, accessed February 17, 2018.

Ryan, R. M., and Deci, E. L. (2000). Self-Determination theory and the facilitation of intrinsic motivation, social development, and well-being, American Psychologist, 55(1), pp. 68-78.

Ryan, R. M., and Deci, E. L. (2007). Active human nature: Self-determination theory and the promotion and maintenance of sport, exercise, and health. In M. S. Hagger and N. L. D. Chatzisarantis (Eds.), Intrinsic motivation and self-determination in exercise and sport, Human Kinetics: Champaign, IL, pp. 1-19.

Ryan R. M., Bernstein J. H. and Brown K. W. (2010). Weekends, work, and well-being: psychological need satisfactions and day of the week effects on mood, vitality, and physical symptoms, Journal of Social and Clinical Psychology, 29(1), pp. 95–122.

Spreitzer, G., Sutcliffe, K., Dutton, J., Sonenshein, S., and Grant, A. M. (2005). A socially embedded model of thriving at work, Organization Science, 16(5), pp. 537-549.

Steinmetz, H. and Schmidt, P. (2010). Subjective health and its relationship with working time variables and job stressors: Sequence or general factor model? Work & Stress, 24 (2), pp. 159-178.

Sterns, P. N. (2013). *The Industrial Revolution in World History.* Westview Press: Boulder Colorado, USA.

Swan, M. (2015). *Blockchain: Blueprint for a New Economy.* O'Reilly Media: Sebastopol, CA, USA.

Tapscott, D., and Tapscott, A. (2016). *Blockchain Revolution: How the Technology Behind Bitcoin is Changing Money, Business, and the World.* Penguin: New York.

Thomson, I. (2016). Putting workplace theories into practice, https://blog.sodexoengage.com/applying-maslows-hierarchy-of-needs-theory-to-hr-responsibilities, accessed January 10, 2018.

Chapter 7

How Value is Created in Tokenized Assets

John Hargrave

Bitcoin Market Journal

Navroop Sahdev

UCL Centre for Blockchain Technologies, United Kingdom

Olga Feldmeier

Ludwig-Maximilians-Universität München, Germany

Abstract

A tidal wave of change is coming to the world of Economic Science. Digital tokens — including bitcoin, altcoins, and cryptocurrencies — will require a fundamental rethinking of valuation, in the same way that the introduction of the stock market required a new understanding of value. As of this writing, the total value of all tokens stands at $500 billion. How do investors place value on computer code, with no central bank or physical asset to support it? Drawing from the literature on behavioral economics and cognitive psychology, we provide a clear understanding of how investors are valuing these new digital assets, making this the first study of applied behavioral economics on token valuation. Using a new instrument called the **Framework for Token Confidence,** we show how value can be created out of "thin air," and how tokens — indeed, our entire economic system — operate as something like a "vote of confidence."

1.1 Introduction

In May 2010, an early bitcoin developer named Laszlo Hanyecz made the first public purchase using bitcoin.[1] He sent 10,000 bitcoin to another digital currency enthusiast, who placed an order for two pizzas to be delivered to Hanyecz's home. At the time, those bitcoin were worth about $40; today they would be worth $100 million.

The most common interpretation of this story is that Hanyecz overpaid for the pizzas. We suggest another view, which is that Hanyecz created enormous value by *building confidence* in the new technology. In fact, this purchase could be remembered as the historical equivalent of Alexander Graham Bell's first words spoken into the telephone: "Mr. Watson, come here — I want to see you." By making a real-world purchase using bitcoin, Hanyecz showed that bitcoin could have real-world monetary value. He gave confidence to the nascent developer community that bitcoin could be used as a new kind of digital currency.

That confidence was contagious. It has not only propelled bitcoin to a 2,500,000% increase since that historic purchase,[2] it has also created an entirely new digital asset class of "tokenized assets," currently valued at $500 billion. In that sense, the pizzas were a deal.

How do investors value these digital assets? In most cases, they are not backed by assets, revenues, or guarantees. To dismiss the entire asset class as speculative, as some economists have done, is shortsighted. Why are some tokenized assets worth $10,000, and others worth practically nothing? By observing hundreds of new token launches, and measuring the success rate of each, what can we learn about investor behavior? Using this knowledge, can we predict which tokens are likely to increase in value? Can we identify the next bitcoin?

In this paper, we answer these questions using the well-understood concept of *investor confidence*. We lay out a new theoretical framework for how investors mentally value tokenized assets, when there are no "hard numbers" to evaluate. Finally, we introduce an analytical tool for token valuation, for the benefit of both token creators and investors: the Framework for Token Confidence.

1.2 Explaining tokenized assets

In 1997, the rock musician David Bowie introduced a novel investment vehicle called the "Bowie Bond." The brainchild of investment banker David Pullman,[3] the Bowie Bond offered an interest rate of 7.9% with an average life of ten years (a ten-year Treasury note returned only 6.3%). The bond was backed by the expected revenues on David Bowie's back catalog of 25 albums, which could be reasonably expected to hold their earning potential over time.

Investors could be confident in the bonds, since they were given an investor-grade rating by Moody's,[4] and ultimately purchased by Prudential Insurance Company of America for $55 million.[5] Bowie used the proceeds to buy back some of his master recordings, while still retaining ownership over his catalog. Rather than selling the rights to his music, in other words, Bowie used the bonds to buy them back.

The Bowie Bond is instructive, as it proved early on that even an intangible asset like digital music could be securitized. If digital music, then why not digital computer code? This is precisely what has happened with the new class of digital assets — including bitcoin and so-called "altcoins" like Ethereum, Ripple, and countless others — that we refer to as **tokens**. Like a traditional security, a token can be understood as a fractional share of value in an underlying asset or enterprise. We propose the following taxonomy:

- **Currency tokens** like bitcoin can be used to buy and sell real-world goods;
- **Platform tokens** like Ethereum can be used as "payment" to run transactions on a blockchain platform;

- **Asset-backed tokens** are tied to an underlying physical asset like real estate, fine art, or collectibles.

Today, blockchain technology is the "fuel" that allows users to store and transfer ownership of these tokens, since blockchain offers features like decentralized ownership and control, novel consensus mechanisms, immutability of data, trustless protocols and new governance models.[6] While there are a wide range of use cases, *all tokens represent decentralized ownership of some underlying value*. Indeed, it is likely that we are entering a new "tokenized economy," where investors will be able to buy fractional ownership of any asset of value, from sports teams to cities and governments, with each transaction recorded on blockchain technology.

Given this transformative trend, it is imperative to understand how investors value tokenized assets. In the case of the Bowie Bond, it was backed by the expected future earnings from the artist's music. How do investors value tokens, which are not backed by companies or expected future revenues? Where does the value come from?

1.3 Tokenized assets: From concrete to abstract

To answer these questions, we will first consider digital tokens backed by **assets of known value**, then **assets of uncertain value**, then **new tokenized assets**. We propose this taxonomy in order to move us from the concrete to the abstract, to better illustrate the mental shortcuts that investors use to place a monetary value on tokens.

1.3.1 *Tokens backed by assets of known value*

Consider a token that represents some underlying physical asset where the approximate price is known (e.g., gold, real estate, fine art, etc.). Like the Bowie Bond, these tokens are backed by a real asset or predictable revenue stream. As blockchain technology improves, it is likely that we will see a tremendous increase in the number of tokenized "real" assets. For example:

- **Real estate:** Investors in Mumbai will be able to own a piece of real estate in Manhattan, which will appreciate in line with the New York real estate market;
- **Collectibles:** Art lovers will be able to own a token backed by a Van Gogh painting, which will hold its value as long as Van Gogh's work remains popular;
- **Firms:** Venture capital firms will issue their own tokens, which will appreciate in value as investors develop more confidence in the firm's portfolio companies.

In each case, the token represents a fractional ownership of the underlying asset's value, but *not the asset itself*. (The very definition of a token is "a thing serving as a visible or tangible *representation* of a fact.")[7] In this sense, tokens are unlike securities, which represent true ownership. With tokens, it is more accurate to say they represent a share of *perceived value*.

When the U.S. dollar was still on the gold standard, it was backed by physical gold. When the U.S. went off the gold standard, it was backed by a *social contract*: because it was widely agreed that the dollar has value, it has value.

The same social contract holds with tokens: as long as enough investors agree they have value, they have value. As more investors enter the market, or as investors grow more confident in the future value of tokens, they rise in value. When investors lose confidence, they fall.

Imagine a future in which the works of David Bowie are backed by the "Bowie token." The estate of David Bowie would then do everything possible to increase investor confidence in David Bowie's back catalog: licensing it for popular films, holding Bowie-themed music festivals, and so forth. In this way, they would be creating value for investors, and for themselves.

Thus, the value of a token backed by an asset of known value can be simply calculated as:

$$\frac{\text{Asset value}}{\text{Tokens outstanding}}$$

1.3.2 *Tokens backed by assets of unknown value*

With most altcoins, however, there is no "real-world peg" to the underlying asset. Yet the social contract determines that it does have value: billions of altcoins are bought and sold on digital exchanges every day. From where does this value arise?

One way of approaching this problem is through **network effects**. Metcalfe's Law states that the value of a network increases in proportion to the number of users in the network. For n users in a network, the value to each user is proportional to the number of total users:[8]

$$n \text{ x } (n-1) = n^2 - n$$

Let us imagine a simple blockchain platform that is backed by a pool of 100 tokens. If each token has a value of $1 for every user on the network, then 10 users create a total value of $100, or $1 per token. Metcalfe's Law suggests that for every 10x increase, the network increases 100x: as the network grows from 10 to 100 users, for instance, the total value of the network grows from $100 to about $10,000. However, *the number of tokens remains fixed*, so the token value increases from $1 to $100.

Indeed, this is precisely what we find when analyzing the growth in blockchain wallets vis-à-vis the total market capitalization of all blockchain assets:

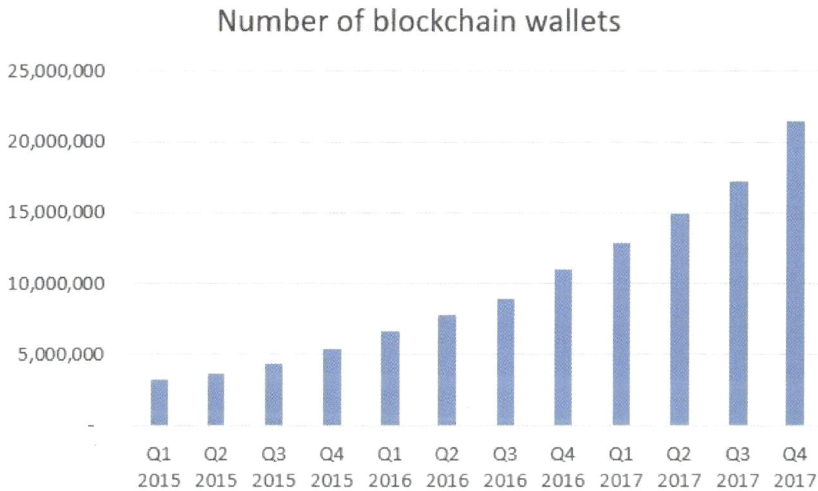

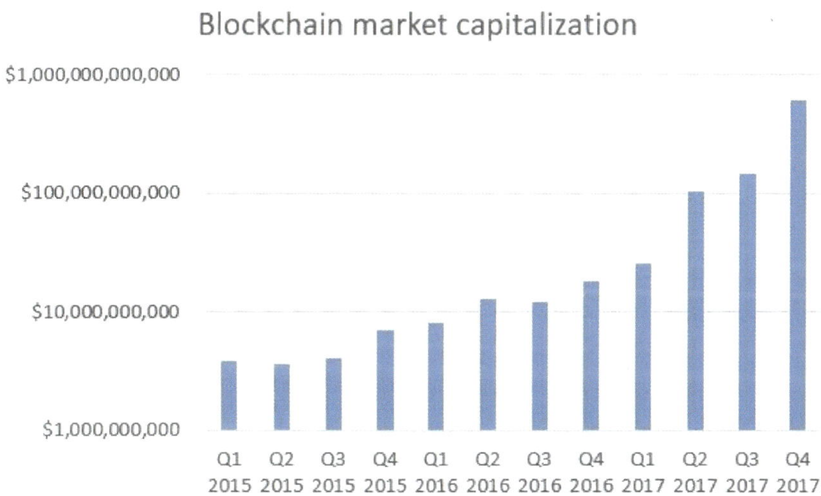

Sources: Statista,[9] *CoinMarketCap*[10]

This finding is significant, as it shows that Metcalfe's law applies to the value of digital tokens, but with a twist: since the number of tokens remains constant, the tokens see a disproportionate rise in value. This makes tokens unlike fiat currency: more people using dollars does not increase the monetary value of the dollar. Thus, the tokens that are likely to increase in value are the tokens with a large and established user base that is likely to grow in the future.

It should be remembered that distributed ledgers are powered by a decentralized nexus of computers that lend computing power to the network by solving complex mathematical problems, commonly known as "hashing." For so-called "Proof of Work" blockchains like bitcoin, the total computing power, or "hash power," is another way of measuring the value of the total network. Since hashing involves the real cost of electricity, it can be used as another measure of the total "value" of the network, as per Metcalfe's Law.

1.3.3 *New tokenized assets*

Where a new token is being created, without an underlying asset and without a network of users (e.g., through an Initial Coin Offering, or token sale), investors calculate prices subjectively, using whatever reference points they can.

To investigate how investors make these decisions, we held working sessions with approximately 250 token investors over a period of several months. We created a series of "blockchain investor meetups" in Boston and Cambridge, Massachusetts; for each meeting, we chose several highly-rated Initial Coin Offerings to analyze and discuss as a group.[11] We asked participants to review the white paper for each ICO in advance, which laid out the business plan and technical specifics behind the project. We then facilitated the discussion around each ICO, observing the decision-making process of the investors. Finally, we asked participants to vote on whether they would personally invest in the ICO.

We found that investors looked for a variety of factors, including:

- **Team**: Does the founding team have a demonstrated track record of success?
- **Idea**: Does the token solve a real-world problem in some believable way?

- **Market**: Is the market strong and growing, or a shrinking niche?
- **User adoption**: How will they get both buyers and sellers to actually use the token?
- **Buzz**: What are other investors saying about the token? Is there a good deal of favorable PR?

We identified two types of ICO investors: those who planned to buy and hold for the long term, and those who planned to buy and sell as quickly as possible (hopefully at a profit). The slang term for long-term investing was "hodl,"[12] where short-term investing was often called "pump and dump." Where the former were interested in strong ideas led by strong teams, the latter were more interested in the "hype cycle," hoping that a first-day trading spike would allow them to exit profitably.

Building on the Timmons Model of Entrepreneurship,[13] we created a rigorous method of evaluating ICO investment opportunities, identifying those that are most likely to lead to long-term user adoption, and thus enjoy the network effects of valuation outlined above. This model, the Framework for Token Confidence, is explained below. To understand its foundation, let's first look into the investor's mind: given future uncertainty and the lack of past performance as an anchor, what builds investor confidence in the first place?

1.4 Building investor confidence in tokens

Confidence is an essential ingredient in any financial transaction. The buyer and seller must have confidence in each other; they must have confidence in the market in which they participate; and the market must have confidence in the institutions that govern it. A number of indices have been created to measure investor confidence, including the Yale Investor Confidence Index,[14] the ZEW Investor Confidence Index,[15] and the State Street Confidence Index.[16]

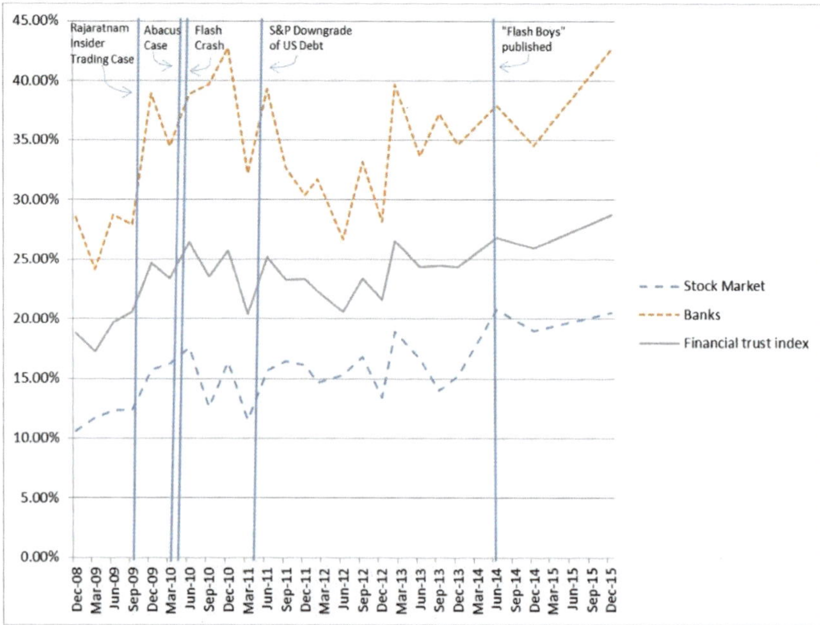

Investor Confidence Indices

Source: U.S. Securities and Exchange Commission Division of Economic and Risk Analysis[17]

The figure above shows that market movements are highly correlated with investor confidence, as measured by the Investor Trust Index.[18] We also accept this as a common-sense fact: the Fed chooses its words carefully to keep "market sentiment" high; the financial press talks about market downturns as "rattling" or "spooking" investors. These are all measures of confidence.

If confidence and market growth are correlated, how can the creators of new blockchain tokens create confidence, *before* the token has been assigned a value on public exchanges? Recent findings in behavioral economics, particularly the foundational work of Daniel Kahneman and Amos Tversky,[19] provide some tantalizing clues into the minds of investors, and how savvy blockchain startups can focus their efforts to build investor confidence.

Familiarity: We trust what we know. This is the principle behind advertising, religious upbringing, and political dynasties. As Larry Jacoby demonstrated in his paper *Becoming Famous Overnight*,[20] we are likely to view a new piece of information more favorably if we are already familiar with it. Expose test subjects to random names, and they are more likely to "remember" the names positively later on, even if they cannot remember *how* they remember. Tokens that are able to build wide awareness are more likely to build confidence, and thus more value.

In our analysis of over 750 Initial Coin Offerings,[21] we found that sometimes founders were able to drive awareness through a larger advertising budget or better public relations, but often it was due to "grassroots" efforts — for example, building a strong development community, or leveraging existing networks of blockchain enthusiasts. The lesson is not that a larger marketing budget is necessary, but that token creators should focus on *building a strong network of users*.

The Halo Effect: We tend to assume that good-looking people are more intelligent.[22] This is known as the "halo effect," where one easily-recalled attribute is conflated with another attribute which is more difficult to discern.[23] When investors view a company or a brand in a positive light, that tends to "rub off" on their view of the leadership team.

When deciding whether to participate in a new token offering, investors tend to attribute the "halo effect" to a founding team that comes from well-regarded companies or academic institutions. For example, the Dragonchain blockchain technology was originally developed by a team while working at Disney; when Dragonchain launched its $13.7 million ICO, Disney became part of the media story, even though Disney had no formal affiliation with the token.[24]

To measure confidence in a new token, investors look for other symbols of confidence. When the token is connected with well-known technology brands (Uber, Google, Facebook), financial brands (Visa, PayPal, Apple Pay) or educational brands (Harvard Business School, Stanford, MIT), these are good signals that the halo effect is at work.

Intuition: The American economist Herbert Simon studied how humans make decisions, and his ideas were profoundly shaped by his pioneering work in the field of artificial intelligence. One of the topics that fascinated him was intuition: was it a distinctly human trait, or could machines also be taught intuition? He came to believe that intuition is nothing more than subconscious pattern recognition:[25] we've "seen this movie before." In other words, there is nothing magical or mystical about intuition: it is based on familiarity, which is why experts often "know" without "knowing how they know" (as popularized in Malcolm Gladwell's bestseller *Blink*).[26]

When intuition is put head-to-head with simple algorithms, however, the algorithms win. Daniel Kahneman devotes a whole chapter to "Intuitions vs. Formulas" in his landmark book *Thinking, Fast and Slow.* His conclusion, after reviewing dozens of academic studies measuring "expert predictions" vs. "simple formulas": the formulas are more likely to predict winning outcomes.[27]

The reason that intuition is unreliable when evaluating token offerings is that they are simply too new: no one has the requisite "10,000 hours"[28] of experience in reviewing them to make intuitive judgments. Kahneman's work shows that investors would be better off making a simple formula of five to six different heuristics to evaluate an Initial Coin Offering. It is this framework that we offer below.

1.5 The Framework for Token Confidence

Babson College professor Jeffrey Timmons developed the Timmons Model of Entrepreneurship in order to assess the attractiveness of entrepreneurial ideas. It can be used by entrepreneurs seeking to develop a new product, as well as investors looking to evaluate an entrepreneur's idea. By rigorously asking the same questions across several different categories, the angel investor or entrepreneur can have an "apples to apples" comparison of different business ideas.

We have built upon the Timmons Model to make it more relevant to token offerings. For each question in the list, assign a value from 1 (lower potential) to 5 (higher potential). The score for each question is averaged at the end of each section, and the score for each section is averaged at the end (Table 1).

Table 1. Framework for token confidence.

	Higher potential (5)	**Lower potential (1)**	**Value**
Market			
Problem that it solves *Is there a clear problem solved by this token?*	Identified	Unfocused	
Customers *Can you clearly identify who will use this token (job title, demographics, etc.)?*	Reachable and receptive	Unreachable or unlikely to adopt	
Value created *If a user adopts this token, how much value will be added to his/her business or lifestyle?*	High and identified	None	
Market structure *What is the composition of the market this token will serve?*	Emerging or fragmented	Concentrated or mature	
Market size *Is the potential market too small, too large, or just right?*	$100 million+	<$10 million	
Regulatory risks *How likely are further regulations on this market, and tokens in general?*	Low	High or highly regulated	
AVERAGE MARKET SCORE *Average the six scores above*			
Competitive Advantage			
Technology/blockchain platform *Is the token built on a well-known standard blockchain, or it built from scratch?*	Existing blockchain	New blockchain	
Lead time advantage *Does the team have a head start on companies working on a similar idea?*	Strong	None	

(Continued)

Table 1. (*Continued*)

Contacts and networks *What is the team's ability to access key players in this market?*	Well-developed	Limited	
AVERAGE COMPETITIVE ADVANTAGE SCORE *Average the three scores above*			
Management Team			
Entrepreneurial team *Does the team have a demonstrated track record of success?*	All-star "supergroup"	Weak team or solopreneur	
Industry/technical experience *Does the team have "10,000 hours" of experience in this industry?*	Super track record	Newbies	
Integrity *Does the team demonstrate scrupulous honesty, and complete transparency?*	Highest standards	Questionable	
AVERAGE MANGEMENT SCORE *Average the three scores above*			
Token Mechanics			
Token required *Does the problem truly require a problem, or is it a "bolt-on blockchain"?*	Impossible without	Token unnecessary	
Value added *Does the token add a new type of value, or is it "another one of those"?*	Highly differentiated	Copycat token	
Decentralized *Is it truly decentralized (like a mesh network), or is it run by the company (like a cell tower)?*	Users do the work	Company does the work	

(*Continued*)

Table 1. (*Continued*)

Token supply *Is there a known quantity of tokens, or can more be issued in the future, diluting the value?*	Fixed, predictable	Uncertain, inflatable	
Public exchange *On which digital exchanges will the token be listed?*	Known, reputable	Unknown or disreputable	
MVP *Is there an existing product, or a Minimum Viable Product?*	Functioning product	White paper only	
AVERAGE TOKEN SCORE *Average the six scores above*			
User Adoption			
Technical difficulty *Will a non-technical person be able to understand this idea?*	Non-technical	Highly technical	
Halo Effect *Is the token strongly associated with well-regarded brands or institutions?*	Strong halo effect	Weak or no halo	
Buzz *Are people talking about it? Or is there silence?*	High social buzz	Low social buzz	
AVERAGE INVESTOR FRIENDLINESS SCORE *Average the three scores above*			
Overall Score *Average the five section values above*			

In practice, an overall score of around 3 is common, as most tokens (by definition) are average. A token with a score approaching 2 shows low investor confidence and should probably be avoided, while a score of around 4 indicates high investor confidence and is worth a closer look. As with any investment, this is not meant to be the end of the process, but a strong beginning.

For investors, the Framework for Token Confidence should be viewed as a tool for filtering out less attractive opportunities. For tokens that score highly, the investor will want to interview the founding team, seek out users of the token, and do a deeper competitive analysis.

For entrepreneurs or founding teams, the Framework for Token Confidence can be used as a tool for strengthening the idea. Better still, a knowledgeable third party is best positioned to fill out the Framework for Token Confidence most objectively, as founders are likely to score themselves more optimistically than an unbiased outside source. This is due to information asymmetries that exist between token creators and token investors, as well as the cognitive bias where "we can be blind to the obvious but also blind to our blindness."[29]

1.6 Conclusions

A tidal wave of change is coming to our economic system, in the form of blockchain technology. New asset classes — cryptocurrencies, altcoins, and tokens — are growing rapidly, and investors are looking for frameworks to value these new "tokens."

The key contribution of this paper is to provide an "industry standard" for token valuation. Our **Framework for Token Confidence** can be used as an "investor scorecard" to rate new tokens, much as the Morningstar Rating™ is used to rate mutual funds — indeed, we expect that companies will begin using our framework to develop high-value research on new token offerings.

Our work builds on well-developed literature in behavioral economics and entrepreneurship studies, illustrating how investors think about new token investments, and how to correct for the mental biases that investors may bring to the table. Hence, the study is simultaneously a first for the academic community, as well as investors and companies. The next step of the study is to test the framework in the real world by augmenting it with actual data on the performance of tokens over time.

Tokens that are backed by a "real" asset (real estate, royalty streams, or precious metals) are fairly straightforward to value. The value of tokens not backed by a real asset — e.g., an altcoin like Ethereum or

Ripple — can be estimated by looking at the total number of network users or total hash power (not to be confused with total tokens), in accordance with Metcalfe's Law. New token offerings — popularly known as Initial Coin Offerings — can be valued using the proposed Framework for Token Confidence, as these are likely to be valued more highly if they first build *investor confidence.*

Confidence is a critical ingredient for the successful functioning of our economic system. If enough people believe that something is valuable, it is — until they stop believing it. This is why we create elaborate structures around our largest societal institutions: the songs and stories of religion, the pomp and circumstance of politics, the rituals and rules of Wall Street. It is why bankers wear lapel pins with their bank logo, and why doctors wear white coats. These structures create confidence in these institutions, which gives them their legitimacy.

Aspiring entrepreneurs who wish to launch a new token, then, would be wise to build investor confidence through (a) attracting a strong network of users, (b) associating the token with well-known companies, and (c) building familiarity with the token among investors in the blockchain space. This is sometimes called "building a brand," but an enduring global institution goes far beyond a brand. What is the brand of America? Islam? The military? These institutions are complex, with a "mental architecture" that stretches back centuries, each generation adding its own layer of interpretation.

To build long-term value in a token, then, it is necessary to build long-term confidence through institutional structures. Just as a religion has stories, scriptures, and songs, tokens that seek to build long-term value will incorporate origin stories, taglines, and advertising jingles. They will enlist the help of "elders," in the form of well-regarded advisory teams, and they will constantly convey their values in speech, habits, and dress. As an example, the founders of the Ripple token regularly appear at blockchain conferences wearing a lapel pin with the Ripple logo, in the manner of politicians.

Building investor confidence takes time. Investing in believable projects also takes time. Using the Framework for Token Confidence, both token creators and token investors can focus on building long-term value for the blockchain economy, and for the world.

References

1. Bitcoin Wiki (retrieved February 24, 2018). Laszlo Hanyecz. https://en.bitcoin.it/wiki/Laszlo_Hanyecz.
2. CoinMarketCap (retrieved February 24, 2018). Cryptocurrency market capitalizations. https://coinmarketcap.com/currencies/bitcoin/historical-data/.
3. Knight Ridder/Tribune Business News (2008). Investment Banker Hopes to Issue More Rock 'n' Roll Bonds. https://www.highbeam.com/doc/1G1-53133655.html.
4. Boulden, J. (2016). David Bowie made financial history with music bond, *CNN Money*. http://money.cnn.com/2016/01/11/media/bowie-bonds-royalties/index.html.
5. Christman, Ed. (2007). The whole story behind David Bowie's $55 million Wall Street trailblaze. *Billboard Magazine*. https://www.billboard.com/articles/business/6843009/david-bowies-bowie-bonds-55-million-wall-street-prudential.
6. Sahdev, N. (2017). Navroop Sahdev, Governance structures on blockchain technology.
7. Oxford Living Dictionary (retrieved February 24, 2018). Token. https://en.oxforddictionaries.com/definition/token.
8. Shapiro, C. and Hal R. V. (1999). *Information Rules: A Strategic Guide to the Network Economy*. Harvard Business Press.
9. Statista (retrieved February 24, 2018). Number of blockchain wallet users worldwide. https://www.statista.com/statistics/647374/worldwide-blockchain-wallet-users/.
10. CoinMarketCap (retrieved February 24, 2018). Cryptocurrency market capitalizations. https://coinmarketcap.com/charts/.
11. ICOs were first rated using our Framework for Token Confidence.
12. Bitcoin Market Journal (retrieved February 24, 2018). What does hodl mean? https://www.bitcoinmarketjournal.com/what-does-hodl-mean/.
13. Timmons, J. and Stephen S. (2009). *New Venture Creation: Entrepreneurship for the 21st Century*. McGraw-Hill Higher Education.
14. Yale Investor Confidence Index (retrieved February 25, 2018). Yale School of Management. https://som.yale.edu/faculty-research/our-centers-initiatives/international-center-finance/data/stock-market-confidence-japan.
15. ZEW Indicator of Economic Sentiment (retrieved February 25, 2018). Zentrum für Europäische Wirtschaftsforschung. http://www.zew.de/en/publikationen/zew-gutachten-und-forschungsberichte/forschungsberichte/konjunktur/zew-finanzmarkt report/.
16. State Street Investor Confidence Index (retrieved February 25, 2018). http://www.statestreet.com/ideas/investor-confidence-index.html.
17. Ko, Jeremy (2017). Economics note: investor confidence. Securities and Exchange Commission. https://www.sec.gov/files/investor_confidence_noteOct2017.pdf.
18. Financial Trust Index. Chicago Booth/Kellogg School. http://financialtrustindex.org/.
19. Kahneman, D. (2011). *Thinking, Fast and Slow*. Farrar, Straus and Giroux (USA).

20. Jacoby, L. *et al.* (1989). Becoming famous overnight. *Journal of Personality and Social Psychology*, 56, pp. 326-328.
21. Bitcoin Market Journal (retrieved February 24, 2018). Completed ICOs. https://www.bitcoinmarketjournal.com/completed-coin-offerings/.
22. Kanazawa, S. (2009). Beautiful people are more intelligent. *Psychology Today.* https://www.psychologytoday.com/blog/the-scientific-fundamentalist/200903/beautiful-people-are-more-intelligent-i.
23. Rosenzweig, P. (2007). *The Halo Effect.* (Free Press, USA).
24. Dale, B. (2017). Blockchain startup with Disney roots completes $13.7 million ICO. Coindesk. https://www.coindesk.com/dragonchain-ico-13-7-million-disney-roots/.
25. Frantz, R. (2003). Herbert Simon: Artificial intelligence as a framework for understanding intuition. *Journal of Economic Psychology*, 24, pp. 265-277.
26. Gladwell, M. (2005). *Blink: The Power of Thinking Without Thinking.* Back Bay Books (USA).
27. Kahneman, *Op. cit*. pp. 222-233.
28. Gladwell, M. (2008). *Outliers: The Story of Success.* Little, Brown and Company, pp. 39-42.
29. Kahneman, *Op. cit*. p. 247.

Part 4

Financial Theory and Complexity Science

Chapter 8

Consensus Algorithms: A Matter of Complexity?

Renato P. dos Santos

Associate Professor and Blockchain Researcher

The Lutheran University of Brazil, Brazil

renatopsantos@ulbra.edu.br

Abstract

This chapter discusses whether PoW, PoS, and hybrid consensus-based blockchains could be considered complex systems and, if so, whether chaotic ones. A positive response would raise concerns about their likelihood of entering a chaotic regime, with catastrophic consequences for financial systems as a potential result. This study was accomplished with the help of Information Theory of Complex Systems, in general, and Crutchfield's Statistical Complexity measure, in particular. Contrasting to PoW consensus algorithms that were shown to be highly non-complex, the PoS consensus methods studied show an outstandingly higher measure of complexity, what is undesirable for what should be a simple computational system. This chapter is a work-in-progress and undoubtedly prone to incorrectness as consensus algorithms continue to evolve. As a final thought, however, considering that the presence of capital gains-seekers in cryptocurrency markets may introduce non-linearity and, consequently, cause the emergence of chaotic regimes, one may wonder whether the recent surge of blockchain technology-based start-ups and use-based trading volume, even discounting all the scam ICO cases, could help to reduce non-linearity and prevent chaos.

1.1 Introduction

1.1.1. *Consensus algorithms*

Consensus algorithms are the essential operating feature of distributed ledgers. In computer science, consensus algorithms are protocols used to achieve agreement on a single data value or state among distributed processes or systems. In distributed ledgers, similarly, consensus algorithms are the process of the distributed peer-to-peer nodes in the network coming to agreement upon updates states of the ledger per executed transactions. Consensus algorithms are mechanistic and automated. As such, they provide the *trustless* software mechanism for the automatic execution of blockchain transactions between parties that do not need to know or trust each other.

While the concept of decentralized digital currency has been around for decades (see, e.g. Wei Dai's b-money, 1998[a]), Satoshi Nakamoto's consensus algorithm [2008], known as “proof of work” (PoW), was a breakthrough because it simultaneously provided:

1. A simple and moderately effective consensus algorithm for collective agreement on a set of updates to the state of the Bitcoin ledger.
2. A mechanism that allowed free entry into the consensus process while preventing Sybil attacks[b] [Buterin, 2014].

---

[a] http://www.weidai.com/bmoney.txt.

[b] In a Sybil attack, the attacker attempts to take control of a network by filling it with clients that they control through forged identities. The name comes after a case study of a woman diagnosed with dissociative identity disorder.

1.1.2. *Problem context: Systemic risk*

Systemic risk (the risk of large-scale failure in financial systems) is a problem in global financial markets that is challenging to classify, measure, and predict. It is unclear whether markets are more or less risky since the 2008 financial crisis and as a result of flash crashes (rapid price declines due to programmatic trading). The impact of blockchain technology implementations on financial market risk is also unknown. A general problem is a lack of methods for assessing financial risk in global markets. A specific problem is the need for assessment tools to evaluate the financial market risk of distributed ledger consensus algorithms. Economics and financial markets are a domain of complexity [Kirman, 2010], and therefore complexity methods are methodologically appropriate for their study. The novel contribution of this chapter is a demonstration case that applies mathematical complexity methods to the study of economics, in particular, to distributed ledger consensus algorithms.

1.1.3. *Complexity*

Before proceeding with our analysis, it must be understood that some authors merely assume that the whole blockchain code possesses a high degree of complexity; they apparently confuse the high complication (of the code) with an eventual complexity of the resulting blockchain and Bitcoin ecosystem. To obscure things further, there is no concise definition of a complex system, which has been associated with properties such as non-linearity, chaotic behavior, and emergent order, as well as oft identified with complicated or random (stochastic) systems. Besides, the term "complexity" has been so much used by so many authors, both scientific and non-scientific, that the word has, unfortunately, almost lost its meaning [Feldman and Crutchfield, 1998].

Complex systems are often quite loosely defined as those constituted by many different components in strong interaction and showing some self-organisation and emergent structured collective behavior. One should then notice that this pseudo-definition finds an echo in the characterisation of the blockchain as the result of "the asynchronous interaction of a resilient network of thousands of uncomplicated, independent nodes, all following straightforward, algorithmic rules to accomplish a myriad of financial processes" [Antonopoulos, 2014, p. 177].

Consequently, blockchain seems to worth an analysis through the lenses of Information Theory of Complex Systems to clarify this issue.

1.1.4. *Volatility*

Another observation that should be made is on attempts of understanding chaotic regimes in terms of high volatile ones. Volatility is habitually defined as a statistical measure of dispersion around the average of any random variable such as market parameters [Belev and Todorov, 2015], assuming that price follows a Gaussian random walk or a similar distribution and that some regression toward the mean always happens. Majdandzic *et al.* [2013] studied real-world dynamical networks and observed that, in their model, nodes always display a recovery process after events such as the 6 May 2010 "flash crash" of the US stock markets, irrespective of the failure of the nodes being due to internal or external causes. Mt. Gox, the DAO, and hacking scandals in general, might be seen as unpredictable but post-facto explainable, massively impactful, high-volatility events, usually called "black swans" [Taleb, 2007].

It should be noticed, however, that Mandelbrot has already shown that financial markets are characterised by "wild randomness," in which the price changes do not follow a Gaussian distribution, but rather Lévy stable distributions having infinite variance [Mandelbrot, 1963]. Therefore, a small shift in structural parameters of some markets may suffice to generate chaotic time paths of volatility, in which prices become highly unpredictable, which can be related back, e.g. to the 1987 stock market crash [Shaffer, 1991]. Vuorenmaa and Wang [2004] modeled that same 2010 flash crash as a "hot-potato effect," derived from a fast feedback loop system collectively created by a network of high-frequency automatic traders and triggered by a massive, possibly unintentional, institutional sell. Considering that we now live in a multi-species [Swan, 2015] trading world in which at least half of market volumes come from algorithmic trading programs, the presence of chaos in those networks may lead to catastrophic market crashes without such a desirable recovery process. In other words, ordinary volatility is expected and even desirable to some degree as it provides profitable opportunities; chaotic regimes are a menace to any market.

In Econophysics research, chaos theory has been applied to monetary, power, labor, international exchange rate, crude oil, gold, electricity, stock exchange, equity, currency, commodity, and sovereign markets[c]. As an example, Tsionas and Michaelides [2017] studied the stock markets from USA, UK, Switzerland, Netherlands, Germany, and France, from 2003 to 2014, and identified chaos both before and after the 2008 financial crisis. Closer to this work, a recent study of Lahmiri and Bekiros [2018] focused on investigating the presence of chaos, randomness, and multi-scale temporal correlation structure in prices and returns data from the Bitcoin market using the largest Lyapunov exponent, Shannon entropy, and the multi-fractal detrended fluctuation analysis, respectively.

Siddiqi [2014] studied the presence of chaos in the Bitcoin market, as characterized not only by positive feedback mechanisms, in the sense that the greater the number of users that accepts it as a currency the stronger is the incentive for outsiders to join in, but also by negative feedback ones, as the sole objective of capital gain seekers is to realize capital gains before the bubble bursts. Siddiqi's result [2014] is that the price dynamics are modeled by

$$C_t = aC_{t-1}(1 - b/a\, C_{t-1}) + aqC_{t-2}$$

where C_t is the total number of capital gain seekers at any time t and a, b, and q, are constants of proportionality, which is a delay logistic model equivalent to the Hénon map[d]. Consequently, in Siddiqi's modeling, depending on the values of those constants, the Bitcoin market might enter a chaotic regime in which the number of participants in the market

---

[c] See, e.g. [Lahmiri & Bekiros, 2018], for references.

[d] See [Skiadas & Skiadas, 2008, p. 91] for details of the associated chaotic attractor.

oscillates dramatically, as their expectations become irrational and unpredictable.

In this work, instead of focusing on market returns, we will study the presence of complexity on the underlying blockchain structures themselvcs.

1.2 Information Theory of Complex Systems

Due to the difficulties mentioned above in defining complexity in a consistent form, the systems' complexity is analyzed here, as in the previous paper [dos Santos, 2017], using the Crutchfield's Statistical measure of complexity [Feldman and Crutchfield, 1998]. This choice is justified as Ladyman *et al.* [2013] showed that it was the measure of complexity available in the scientific literature that best captures the qualitative notion of the complexity of systems.

1.2.1 *Measures of complexity*

According to Shannon's significant contribution to the modern theory of communication [Shannon, 1948], the amount of information I_k a process encodes in some event k can be calculated (in bit units) as the negative base-2 logarithm of its probability p_k

$$I_k = -\ln_2 p_k$$

Furthermore, Shannon also showed that the averaged uncertainty over the set of possible events k, the source entropy rate,

$$-\sum_k p_k \ln_2 p_k$$

is a fundamental property that determines how compressible the outcomes of an information source are.

Nevertheless, Shannon's entropy can only express the notions of randomness, order, or complexity of a complete set of objects under some distribution rather than of a single object. Combining notions of computability and statistics, Solomonoff, Kolmogorov, and Chaitin formulated independently in the mid-sixties what became known as the *Kolmogorov–Chaitin complexity* [Kolmogorov, 1959] or *algorithmic complexity*. In terms of Universal Turing Machines, for an object, such as a binary string of text, its algorithmic complexity equates the length of the shortest computer program (in a predetermined programming language) that produces that object as output.

Unfortunately, however, Kolmogorov–Chaitin complexity requires the exact replication of the target string and, therefore, is being dominated by its eventual randomness. In other words, it is not a measure of structure but rather a measure of its randomness [Crutchfield, 2012]. To account for that, the usual solution is to discount for randomness by again describing the complexity in ensembles of behaviors [Crutchfield, 2012]. Besides, Chaitin [1969] demonstrated that, for most objects, it is not possible to compute even a lower bound for its Kolmogorov complexity let alone its exact value. In other words, as it happens with many other complexity measures, Kolmogorov complexity is not computable.

1.2.2 *Crutchfield's statistical complexity*

Crutchfield's alternative approach to complexity stems from Computational Mechanics, an extension of Statistical Mechanics that describes not only a system's statistical properties but also how it stores and processes information — how it computes [Crutchfield, 2012]. This approach consists then of encoding the structures of the discrete process under study in reconstructed computational models, referred to as *ϵ-machines*, Turing Machines that can guess, in Crutchfield' words [Crutchfield, 1994]. All one must do is to uncover the system's initial physical configuration, the computation whose performing corresponds to the temporal sequence of changes in the system's internal state, and the state to which the system relaxes [Crutchfield, 1994]. Once the reconstruction is complete, one can discuss the structure of the original process from the statistical complexity of the corresponding ϵ-machine, which measures the structure of the minimal ϵ-machine [Crutchfield, 1994].

Three optimality theorems ensure that the ϵ-machine representation of a process captures all the process's properties, including its randomness and organization from the available, indirect measurements that some instrument provides [Crutchfield, 2012]. These measurements may be arranged in histories from which predictions about everything that is predictable about the system can be defined. Two histories are said to be equivalent if they lead to the same prediction and, from them, classes σ of equivalent histories may be then constructed. These equivalence classes σ are called the "causal states" of the process, as they themselves retain all the relevant information for predicting the future of the system [Crutchfield, 2012].

Given this framework, the statistical complexity C_μ can be calculated as

$$C_\mu = -\sum_{\sigma \in S} P(\sigma) log_2 P(\sigma)$$

where S is the set of all the causal states and $P(\sigma)$ is the probability distribution over them [Crutchfield, 2012].

For a system with only two (complementary) causal states σ_1 and σ_2, Figure 1 shows how the Crutchfield's Statistical Complexity measure C_μ varies as a function of the ratio between their probabilities $P(\sigma_1)$ and $P(\sigma_2) = 1 - P(\sigma_1)$.

The maximum value of this complexity measure occurs when both causal states have the same probability, and the measure is minimal when

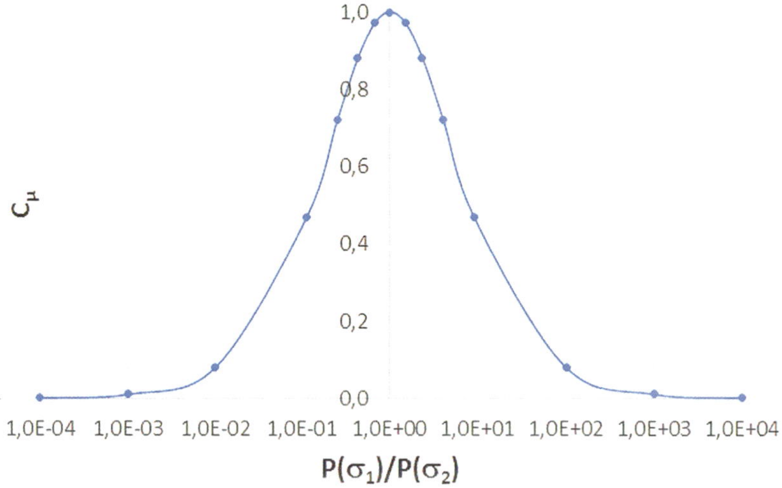

Figure 1. Crutchfield's Statistical Complexity measure C_μ as a function of the ratio between the probability $P(\sigma_1)$ of some causal state σ_1 and of its complementary state σ_2, $P(\sigma_2) = 1 - P(\sigma_1)$.

one causal state is much less probable than the other, a conclusion that can be generalized for systems with more than two causal states. Nevertheless, this dependence on causal states should not be confused with one on traditional system states, e.g. of the fair-coin flip. Rather this system is unpredictable: all different histories of measurements are equivalent in their inability to predict this system's future behavior. There is only one class σ of equivalent histories, whose probability is consequently $P(\sigma) = 1$, and its statistical complexity, from the formula above, is $C_\mu = 0$.

1.3 Analysis

In this section, we will proceed to calculate the Statistical Complexity of the stream of blocks provided by a few different consensus protocols to infer whether the resulting blockchains can be considered complex systems.

1.3.1 *PoW complexities*

To proceed with our analysis, it is worth quoting Charles Moore, author of the original "Block Chain Ledger" and "Inter Ledger Protocol" patent [AU2000030225, 2005], that the Bitcoin blockchain "is a sequential time machine." "Within Bitcoin, the difficulty in finding a conforming hash acts as a clock. A universal clock, if you will, because there is only one such clock in the universe. It does not matter that this clock is imprecise. What matters is that the this is the same clock for everyone and that the state of the chain can be tied unambiguously to the ticks of this clock" [Moore, personal communication, May 23, 2018].

Moore's understanding supports our previous paper's [dos Santos, 2017] assumption, following Crutchfield and Young [1989], that the Bitcoin blockchain can be reconstructed (modeled) as a *semi-infinite-string-production ϵ-machine* (Figure 2), one block per tick.

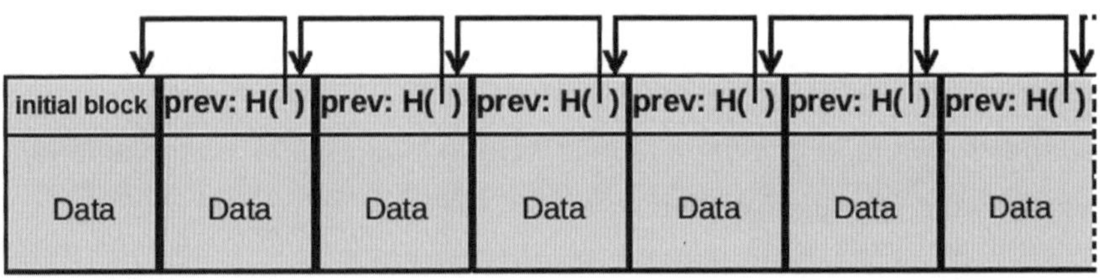

Figure 2. Bitcoin blockchain as seen as a semi-infinite-string-production ϵ-machine.

This machine oscillates about every 10 minutes between two states (Figure 3), like a clock's tick and tock:

1. σ_m (mining state): A new block was just incorporated into the blockchain, and the machine starts mining a new block that includes most of the pending transactions collected from around the world into the *transaction pool*. Hashes are generated and tested against the network's *difficulty target*.

2. σ_b (broadcasting state): A nonce that results in a hash smaller than the target is found, the validated block is broadcast to the P2P network for inclusion into the blockchain.

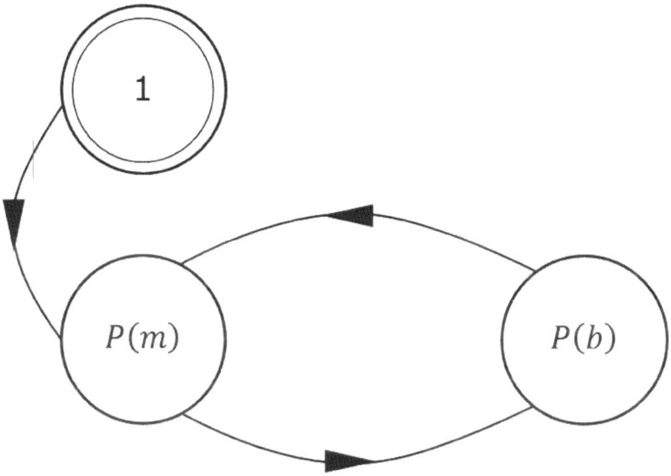

Figure 3. Bitcoin blockchain as seen as a semi-infinite-string-production ϵ-machine. After the start-state corresponding to the generation of the origin block, indicated by the inscribed circle, it oscillates between the two states σ_m and σ_b.

To calculate the Crutchfield's Statistical Complexity measure of Bitcoin's blockchain, consider that new blocks are created about every 10 minutes [Antonopoulos, 2014, p. 2], or 600 seconds, and that, for a network production rate value of 27.8 exa (10^{18}) hashes per second, it takes on average $(2.78 \times 10^{19}) \times 600 \cong 1.66 \times 10^{22}$ hashes to find one that is lower than the target. Therefore, the probability of the broadcasting state is

$$P(\sigma_b) = 1/(1.66 \times 10^{22}) \cong 6.0 \times 10^{-23},$$

the probability of the complementary mining state σ_m is

$$P(\sigma_m) = 1 - P(\sigma_b) \cong 1 - 6.0 \times 10^{-23}$$

and the statistical complexity C_μ, with only these two causal states $S = \{\sigma_m, \sigma_b\}$, results[e]

$$C_\mu = -[P(\sigma_m)log_2P(\sigma_m) + P(\sigma_b)log_2P(\sigma_b)]$$

$$C_\mu = -\big[(1 - 6.0 \times 10^{-23})\log_2(1 - 6.0 \times 10^{-23}) + (6.0 \times 10^{-23})\log_2(6.0 \times 10^{-23})\big]$$

$$C_\mu \cong 4.51 \times 10^{-21}$$[f].

Now, applying this procedure to a few PoW cryptocurrencies, using their respective network production rate values on May 12, 2018, we obtain the results shown in Table 1.

Table 1. Crutchfield's Statistical Complexity measure C_μ calculated for a few PoW cryptocurrencies.

Currency	Bitcoin	Ether	Bit. Cash	BTC Gold	Litecoin	Dash	Monero	Eth. Classic
Block time†	10 min	0.25 min	10 min	10 min	2.5 min	2.5 min	2 min	0.25 min
Hashrate (hash/s)†	2.78×10^{19}	$2.77\times10^{+14}$	$4.62\times10^{+18}$	$3.50\times10^{+07}$	$2.98\times10^{+14}$	$1.80\times10^{+15}$	$4.32\times10^{+08}$	$7.70\times10^{+12}$
C_μ	4.51×10^{-21}	1.28×10^{-14}	2.62×10^{-20}	1.70×10^{-09}	1.27×10^{-15}	2.19×10^{-16}	7.15×10^{-10}	4.17×10^{-13}
Currency	Zcash	Vertcoin	Dogecoin	Feathercoin	BlackCoin	Namecoin	Auroracoin	
Block time†	2.5 min	2.5 min	1 min	1 min	1 min	10 min	1 min	
Hashrate (hash/s)†	$4.23\times10^{+08}$	$1.02\times10^{+12}$	$2.21\times10^{+14}$	$5.45\times10^{+09}$	$9.61\times10^{+13}$	$2.20\times10^{+19}$	$1.37\times10^{+15}$	
C_μ	5.88×10^{-10}	3.18×10^{-13}	4.14×10^{-15}	1.21×10^{-10}	9.33×10^{-15}	5.68×10^{-21}	7.00×10^{-16}	

† Obtained on May 12, 2018, from https://bitinfocharts.com.

[e] Due to $P(\sigma_b)$ being much smaller than 1, we used Padé Approximation $\log_e(1-x) \cong -x\,(6-x)/(6-4x)$ to increase the precision of calculation of the $(1-P(\sigma_b))\log_2(1-P(\sigma_b))$ term.

[f] The complexity measure of Bitcoin's blockchain was previously estimated (dos Santos, 2017), for the then current network production rate of 4.27 exahashes per second, as approximately $C_\mu \cong 1.56 \times 10^{-20}$, a higher but still extremely low value.

These extremely low statistical complexity C_μ results (see Figure 1) lead us to the conclusion that PoW-based blockchains, in general, can hardly be considered complex. What confirms and extends to all these cryptocurrencies is the statement about Bitcoin from Charles Moore: "Block Chain Ledgers are very simple, they are just ledgers with a hash chain applied to them. [...] I build these things and I can only build simple systems. Complex ones will always fail and cannot be secured. [*sic*]" [Moore, personal communication, April 20, 2017]. The functioning of these blockchains may indeed be regarded as algorithmically complicated, but not complex.

1.3.2 *PoS complexities*

PoW was undoubtedly crucial to give birth to Nakamoto's breakthrough. However, its computing power-intensive nature implies that PoW cryptocurrencies are dependent on energy consumption, as is demonstrated in practice. That introduces significant costs in the operation of those networks that are compensated via a combination of inflation and transaction fees. As the mint rate slows in the Bitcoin network, reducing the block reward that the successful miner takes, it is putting pressure on raising transaction fees to sustain a preferred level of security, as predicted by King and Nadal [2012].

Due to the likely increasing energy consumption of the PoW algorithm, and consequent pressure on rising transaction fees, there has been a burst of popularity in favor of the cryptocurrencies that use the alternative algorithm known as "Proof-of-Stake" (PoS) for choosing the block creators. In the PoS protocol structure, the forger of the next block is chosen in a deterministic, pseudo-random way, and the chance of being selected depends on its wealth (the stake). PoS calculates the weight of a node according to its currency holdings and not its computational resources [Buterin, 2014]. That is why, in PoS cryptocurrencies, the blocks are usually said to be forged (in the blacksmith sense of this word) or minted [Popov, 2016].

For example, the Nxt[g] consensus algorithm chooses the account to generate the next block according to the number of coins it has. The wealthier the account is, the higher the chance that it will be selected to generate the next block and receive the corresponding transaction fees. Habitually, one assumes that this probability should be precisely proportional to the account's balance, although this is not entirely accurate for Nxt [Popov, 2016].

In Nxt, to obtain the right to forge (generate) a block, each active Nxt account "competes" by waiting for a new round, with each passing second that no block is generated, until its particular *target* value surpasses its own random 'hit' value. This is calculated by applying a SHA256 hashing function to its account public key and the generating signature of the current block. The bigger the account stake is, the higher and faster-growing will be its target, making it easier to surpass its hit [Nxt community, 2016; Nxt Wiki contributors, 2017]. In other words, in Nxt, the "chance" of an account to forge a block hinges only on its current 'stake' (which is a property of each account), the time passed since the last block was forged (which is shared by all forging accounts) and the base target value (which is also shared by all accounts). The process is smoothed such that the generation block time between blocks is ensured to be of 60 seconds in average [Nxt community, 2016].

Instead of a global target against which nodes keep generating their hashes until the target is hit, in Nxt, the individual hits are calculated beforehand, and new, increased target values are generated each second until one that satisfies the $hit < target$ condition is found [Andruiman, 2014].

Consequently, PoS-based blockchains can also be modeled as semi-infinite-string-production machines that oscillate between two states about every minute:

1. σ_t (targeting state): A new block was just incorporated into the blockchain. Each active forging account k generates its own random hit value H_k and starts generating new, increasing

[g] http://nxtplatform.org/.

individual target value T_k each second that no block is generated, until some of them surpass their own hit values.

2. σ_b (broadcasting state): One or more accounts hit their own target and win the right to forge candidate blocks. Each one of them bundles up to 255 unconfirmed transactions into a new block along with all its required parameters and broadcasts it to the network as a candidate for the blockchain.

Consequently, we apply the same procedure above to Nxt to evaluate its statistical complexity C_μ. In Nxt, a block is forged about every 60 seconds and new targets are generated each second. It takes on average 60 targets to find one that is bigger than its own hit. Therefore, the probability of the broadcasting state (σ_b) is

$$P(\sigma_b) = 1/60 \cong 1.67 \times 10^{-2},$$

the probability of the complementary targeting state (σ_t) is

$$P(\sigma_t) = 1 - P(\sigma_b),$$

and the statistical complexity C_μ, with only these two causal states $S = \{\sigma_t, \sigma_b\}$, results[h]

$$C_\mu = -[P(\sigma_t) log_2 P(\sigma_t) + P(\sigma_b) log_2 P(\sigma_b)]$$

$$C_\mu = -[(1 - 1.67 \times 10^{-2})\log_2(1 - 1.67 \times 10^{-2}) + (1.67 \times 10^{-2})\log_2(1.67 \times 10^{-2})]$$

$$C_\mu \cong 0.122,$$

a value of Crutchfield's Statistical Complexity measure that is 10 to 20 orders of magnitude bigger than those of Table 1. Consequently, serious

---

[h] Due to $P(\sigma_b)$ being much smaller than 1, we used Padé Approximation $\log_e(1 - x) \cong -x\,(6 - x)/(6 - 4x)$ to increase the precision of calculation of the $(1 - P(\sigma_b))\log_2(1 - P(\sigma_b))$ term.

concerns are raised about the possibility of Nxt entering a chaotic regime at any time without notice.

Differently from above Siddiqi's modeling [2014] of the presence of chaos in a cryptocurrency market, however, the emergence of a chaotic regime in a blockchain itself could mean disruption of the network communication, due extreme flutuaction of the number of connected nodes, bursts of excessive number of transactions in the pool, high number of rejected blocks and/or unconfirmed transactions, all of which could be exploited by a 51% attacker.

The PoS protocol has since been improved and implemented in many conceptually different versions and blockchain projects. Notable examples include "Proof of Stake Version 2" by Pavel Vasin (2014) and "Proof of Stake Version 3" (PoS 3, or SPoS) by Patrick Dai *et al.* (2017), implemented in Qtum[i], as well as lesser-known projects.

In Qtum[j], as the blocks are forged about every 2 minutes (120 s), and new targets are generated every 16 seconds, it takes on average $120/16 =$ 7.5 targets to find one that is bigger than its own hit, and the probability of the broadcasting state (σ_b) is

$$P(\sigma_b) = 1/7.5 \cong 0.133,$$

and the statistical complexity C_μ, with only these two causal states $S = \{\sigma_t, \sigma_b\}$, results

$$C_\mu = -[(1 - 0.133)\log_2(1 - 0.133) + (0.133)\log_2(0.133)]$$

$$C_\mu \cong 0.566,$$

Table 2 exhibits these results for NxT and Qtum (PoS)

[i] http://qtum.org.

[j] http://qtum.org.

Table 2. Crutchfield's Statistical Complexity measure $\boldsymbol{C_\mu}$ calculated for Nxt and Qtum (PoS) cryptocurrencies.

Currency	NXT	Qtum
Block time‡	60 s	2 min
Hashrate (hash/s) ‡	1.0	0.0625
C_μ	0.122	0.556

‡ Obtained from their respective whitepapers.

1.3.3 *Other PoS protocols*

There are also other PoS protocols with conceptually different implementations. For example, the probability of being selected may also depend on the time the coins stay in the account without being spent or transferred (the so-called *coin age*) [Popov, 2016]. Coin age can be defined merely as currency amount times holding period [King and Nadal, 2012].

The concept of coin age was known to Nakamoto at least as early as 2010 and used in Bitcoin to help prioritise transactions, but it did not play much of a critical role in Bitcoin's present security model. Scott Nadal and Sunny King independently rediscovered the concepts of PoS and coin age in October 2011, whereby realizing that PoS could indeed replace most PoW's functions with a careful redesign of Bitcoin's minting and security model [King and Nadal, 2012].

Another PoS variation is Proof of Stake Velocity (PoSV), implemented in Reddcoin[k], which intends "to encourage both ownership (Stake) and activity (Velocity), which directly correspond to the two main functions of Reddcoin as a real currency: a store of value and a medium of exchange" [Ren, 2014]. The anonymity of wallet addresses, however, implies the inability to obtain an accurate measure of the velocity since it is impossible to know which coins were spend on goods or merely transferred back to their owner. Reddcoin takes Velocity into account by changing the form of the coin-ageing function from a linear to an

[k] http://reddcoin.com/.

exponential decay one, with a definite half-life of say one month [Ren, 2014]. This decaying coin-ageing makes new coins accumulating coin age at a much higher rate than old ones and is assumed to incentive PoSV stakeholders to be active in moving their holding, either by mining or transacting with counterparties, as well as staying online and contributing to verifying transactions on the PoSV network [Ren, 2014]. This feature is considered to incentivize money velocity, improve Reddcoin economy's health, and increase the difficulty for 51% attacks [Ren, 2014].

1.3.4 *Hybrid protocols*

There are also hybrid PoW+PoS implementations, in which PoW mining works as both a steady distribution channel for the cryptocurrency and a fall-back network security mechanism. As PoW block rewards decrease over time, the PoS protocol has enough time to migrate into use in a complementary fashion [Ren, 2014].

For example, in King and Nadal's Peercoin[1] design, a new minting process is introduced for PoS blocks in addition to the existing Bitcoin PoW minting, and blocks are separated into two distinct types: PoW blocks and PoS blocks. However, a crucial difference is that the hashing operation is executed over a limited search space (more specifically one hash per unspent wallet-output per second) instead of an unlimited search space as in PoW. Thus, no significant consumption of energy is involved [King and Nadal, 2012]. In Peercoin design, both PoW hash target and PoS hash target are adjusted continuously rather than Bitcoin's two-week adjustment interval, to avoid a sudden jump in the network generation rate [King and Nadal, 2012].

Table 3 exhibits the results of applying this procedure to Reddcoin (PoSV), and a few hybrid cryptocurrencies, using their respective network production rate values on May 12, 2018.

---

[1] http://peercoin.net/.

Table 3. Crutchfield's Statistical Complexity measure C_μ calculated for Reddcoin (PoSV), and a few hybrid cryptocurrencies.

Currency	Reddcoin	Peercoin	BlackCoin	NovaCoin
Block time†	1 min	10 min	60 s	10 min
Hashrate (hash/s)†	$1.30\times10^{+10}$	$3.32\times10^{+16}$	$1.06\times10^{+14}$	$4.42\times10^{+11}$
C_μ	5.26×10-11	3.29×10^{-18}	8.52×10^{-15}	1.86×10^{-13}

† Obtained on May 12, 2018, from https://bitinfocharts.com

1.3.5 *Final comparison*

Figure 4 exhibits a comparison of the calculated complexities according to the consensus protocols. One observes a dramatically higher value of the complexity measure of the Nxt and Qtum PoS protocols in comparison to the other ones.

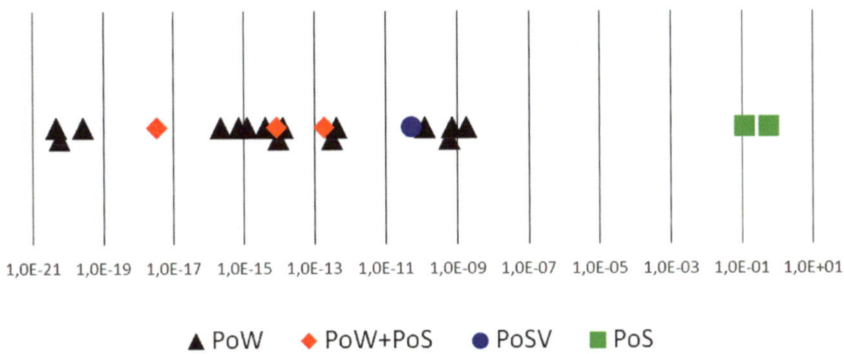

Figure 4. A comparison of the calculated complexities according to the consensus protocols.

The higher difficulty of the other protocols to be selected to mine/forge a block, and consequently the higher required hashrate, leads to their lower complexity value. In contrast, since the time interval between block forging in Nxt is kept around 60 seconds and 2 minutes in Qtum, the probability of any node being selected is substantially higher than in other currencies.

According to Moore, the results above indicate that alternatives to PoW "misunderstand the actual problem and provide a solution to a different problem space" [personal communication, May 23, 2018].

It is not yet clear, however, whether this is a feature of the PoS protocol itself or a characteristic of the Nxt and Qtum implementations. It is conceivable, therefore, that some different implementation of the basic PoS protocol could have a higher competition among 'forgers' and, consequently, a lower complexity.

1.4 Discussion and Future Work

The results obtained here suggest that Crutchfield's Statistical Complexity may be used as an effective analysis tool to evaluate the viability of proposed high-performance network cryptographic methods from the available quantitative data.

1.4.1 *Practical consequences*

A nuance regarding complexity should be distinguished. On the one hand, this chapter argues that economics, financial markets, and systemic risk are domains of complexity, and thus warrant study with complexity methods. On the other hand, the research finding of this analysis is that low complexity is better for blockchains and financial markets.

This study examined various kinds of blockchain consensus algorithms and found that PoW consensus algorithms were generally shown to be remarkably *less* complex, as measured by Crutchfield's Statistical Complexity, and, therefore, are probably safer. Recapitulating simplistically, for blockchains and financial markets, complexity methods are a useful and relevant analysis tool; complexity itself is bad.

The much higher complexity of Nxt and Qtum PoS consensus protocols is undesirable for what should be a simple computational system. Therefore, the proposed PoS methods seem to be too convoluted and complicated to be globally scalable, applicable, and sustainable as a model of decentralized network computing.

Nonetheless, this high complexity does not seem to come from the PoS concept per se but from the implementation. In this case, from the smaller degree of competition among forgers, derived from the tremendously smaller number of trials per second that are made in Nxt and Qtum to select the next forger.

1.4.2 *Future work: Application to next-generation consensus algorithms*

The same principles of Crutchfield's Statistical Complexity could likewise be applied to the assessment of next-generation consensus algorithms as data become available. These include Practical Byzantine Fault Tolerance (PBFT) proposals from projects such as DFINITY, Mimblewimble, HashGraph, and IOTA Tangle, and innovative architectures in the form of directed acyclic graphs (DAGs) and blockless blocks.

1.4.3 *Preventing chaos*

As a final thought, returning to the discussion at the end of previous paper [dos Santos, 2017], while the above results indicate that most blockchain infrastructures present extremely low statistical complexity measures, and in general, would hardly be expected to enter a chaotic regime, unfortunately, the same cannot be said of the ecosystems built upon them. Siddiqi [2014] attributes a likeliness of the emergence of chaos in the Bitcoin market to the non-linearity introduced in it by the presence of capital gains-seekers, hoping to buy tokens cheap and sell them high. Likewise DApps (distributed applications) and cryptoeconomy communities built on top of blockchain platforms such as Ethereum (low complexity) might themselves be subject to higher complexity.

Contrary to the appeal for regulatory policies, Shaffer's study [1991] concluded that regulations alone cannot guarantee freedom from chaos. Perhaps market volume in well-designed cryptocurrencies with low complexity consensus algorithms can accomplish what regulation cannot. One considers the overall financial market effect of the recent surge of blockchain technology-based start-ups, even discounting for ICO scam cases. By launching new venues for functional users (payers and payees) to use cryptocurrencies to save on transaction costs involving the buying and selling of goods and services [Siddiqi, 2014], a helpful side effect is also likely reducing non-linearity and preventing market chaos.

References

Andruiman. (2014). *Nxt forging algorithm: simulating approach.* Retrieved from https://pt.scribd.com/document/243341106/Nxt-forging-algorithm-simulating-approach.

Antonopoulos, A. M. (2014). *Mastering Bitcoin. Unlocking Digital Crypto-Currencies.* Sebastopol, CA: O'Reilly Media.

Belev, E., and Todorov, M. (2015). Volatility. In *Financial Dictionary.* FinancialDictionary.net. Retrieved from http://www.financialdictionary.net/define/Volatility/.

Buterin, V. (2014). *A Next-Generation Smart Contract and Decentralized Application Platform. Ethereum Whitepaper*. Retrieved from www.fintech.academy/wp-content/uploads/2016/06/EthereumWhitePaper.pdf.

Chaitin, G. J. (1969). On the Simplicity and Speed of Programs for Computing Infinite Sets of Natural Numbers. *Journal of the ACM, 16*(3), 407–422. https://doi.org/10.1145/321526.321530.

Crutchfield, J. P. (1994). The calculi of emergence: computation, dynamics and induction. *Physica D: Nonlinear Phenomena, 75*(1-3), 11–54. https://doi.org/10.1016/0167-2789(94)90273-9.

Crutchfield, J. P. (2012). Between order and chaos. *Nature Physics, 8*(1), 17–24. https://doi.org/10.1038/nphys2190.

Dai, P., Mahi, N., Earls, J., and Norta, A. (2017). *Smart-Contract Value-Transfer Protocols on a Distributed Mobile Application Platform.* Singapore: Qtum Foundation. https://doi.org/10.13140/RG.2.2.35140.63365.

dos Santos, R. P. (2017). On the Philosophy of Bitcoin/Blockchain Technology: Is it a Chaotic, Complex System? *Metaphilosophy, 48*(5), 620–633. https://doi.org/10.1111/meta.12266.

Feldman, D. P., and Crutchfield, J. P. (1998). Measures of statistical complexity: Why? *Physics Letters A, 238*(4-5), 244–252. https://doi.org/10.1016/S0375-9601(97)00855-4.

King, S., and Nadal, S. (2012). *PPCoin: Peer-to-Peer Crypto-Currency with Proof-of-Stake. Peercoin Whitepaper.* Retrieved from https://peercoin.net/assets/paper/peercoin-paper.pdf.

Kirman, A. (2010). *Complex Economics: Individual and Collective Rationality*. London, UK: Routledge.

Kolmogorov, A. N. (1959). Entropy per unit time as a metric invariant of automorphisms. *Doklady Akademii Nauk SSSR (Proceedings of the USSR Academy of Sciences)*, *124*(4), 754_755.

Ladyman, J., Lambert, J., and Wiesner, K. (2013). What is a complex system? *European Journal for Philosophy of Science*, *3*(1), 33–67. https://doi.org/10.1007/s13194-012-0056-8.

Lahmiri, S., and Bekiros, S. (2018). Chaos, randomness and multi-fractality in Bitcoin market. *Chaos, Solitons & Fractals*, *106*, 28–34. https://doi.org/10.1016/j.chaos.2017.11.005.

Majdandzic, A., Podobnik, B., Buldyrev, S. V., Kenett, D. Y., Havlin, S., and Eugene Stanley, H. (2013). Spontaneous recovery in dynamical networks. *Nature Physics*, *10*(1), 34–38. https://doi.org/10.1038/nphys2819.

Mandelbrot, B. (1963). The Variation of Certain Speculative Prices. *The Journal of Business*, *36*(4), 394–419. https://doi.org/10.1086/294632.

Moore, C. R. J. (2005). *AU2000030225*. Australia: IP Australia. Retrieved from http://www.ipaustralia.com.au/applicant/moore-charles-rj/patents/AU2000030225/.

Nakamoto, S. (2008). Bitcoin: A Peer-to-Peer Electronic Cash System. *Bitcoin.org*. Retrieved from https://bitcoin.org/bitcoin.pdf.

Nxt community. (2016, February 7). Nxt Whitepaper. Retrieved November 27, 2017, from http://nxtwiki.org/wiki/Whitepaper:Nxt.

Nxt Wiki contributors. (2017, July 24). Forging. In *Nxt Wiki*. Nxt Wiki. Retrieved from https://nxtwiki.org/wiki/Forging.

Popov, S. (2016). A Probabilistic Analysis of the Nxt Forging Algorithm. *Ledger*, *1*(1), 69–83. https://doi.org/10.5195/LEDGER.2016.46.

Ren, L. (2014). *Proof of Stake Velocity: Building the Social Currency of the Digital Age*. Reddcoin. Retrieved from http://reddcoin.com/papers/PoSV.pdf.

Shaffer, S. (1991). Structural shifts and the volatility of chaotic markets. *Journal of Economic Behavior & Organization*, *15*(2), 201–214. https://doi.org/10.1016/0167-2681(91)90029-W.

Shannon, C. E. (1948). A Mathematical Theory of Communication. *Bell System Technical Journal*, *27*(3), 379–423. https://doi.org/10.1002/j.1538-7305.1948.tb01338.x.

Siddiqi, H. (2014). The Routes to Chaos in the Bitcoins Market. *SSRN Electronic Journal*. https://doi.org/10.2139/ssrn.2396997.

Skiadas, C. H., and Skiadas, C. (2008). *Chaotic Modelling and Simulation: Analysis of Chaotic Models, Attractors and Forms*. Boca Raton, FL: Chapman and Hall/CRC. https://doi.org/10.1201/9781420079012.

Swan, M. (2015). Digital Simondon: The collective individuation of man and machine. *Platform: Journal of Media and Communication*, *6*(1 – Special Issue: Gilbert Simondon: Media and technics), 46–58. Retrieved from https://platformjmc.files.wordpress.com/2015/04/v6_swan.pdf.

Taleb, N. N. (2007). *The Black Swan: The Impact of the Highly Improbable*. New York: Random House.

Tsionas, M. G., and Michaelides, P. G. (2017). Neglected chaos in international stock markets: Bayesian analysis of the joint return–volatility dynamical system. *Physica A: Statistical Mechanics and Its Applications*, *482*, 95–107. https://doi.org/10.1016/j.physa.2017.04.060.

Vasin, P. (2014). *BlackCoin's Proof-of-Stake Protocol v2*. Retrieved from https://blackcoin.co/blackcoin-pos-protocol-v2-whitepaper.pdf.

Vuorenmaa, T. A., and Wang, L. (2014). An Agent-Based Model of the Flash Crash of May 6, 2010, with Policy Implications. *SSRN Electronic Journal*. https://doi.org/10.2139/ssrn.2336772.

Chapter 9

Blockchain Theory of Programmable Risk: Black Swan Smart Contracts

Melanie Swan

Purdue University, USA

Abstract

This chapter discusses risk in the context of blockchain technology and proposes a theory of programmable risk that can be implemented with Black Swan Smart Contracts. The theory's foundations are developed from two perspectives: risk theorizing in philosophy, social science, and finance; and black swan financial theory (risk distributions are fat-tailed (Mandelbrotian), not normal (Gaussian)). Event distributions can be formulated as s-curves with convex, linear, and concave segments, such that a desired level of risk may be chosen (convexity equates to lower risk). A blockchain theory of user-selected programmable risk is proposed. Black Swan Smart Contracts instantiate s-curve event distributions such that risk might be more efficiently managed by selecting low-medium-high risk as a standard smart contract parameter. Potential applications of Black Swan Smart Contracts include Insurance as a Digital Service, eBay for Money, Information Markets, and Autonomous Risk Management as a Smart Network property.

1.1 Introduction

Smart contracts are blockchain-based contracts, meaning digitally-instantiated agreements (legally-binding contracts with two or more parties, terms, and consideration) registered to a blockchain, possibly for automated execution [Swan, 2015]. Smart contracts imply optionality (selectable parameters), such as the right to buy or sell an asset at a future moment of time (i.e. the put-call functionality of financial market options). However, this functionality has not yet been widely explored in the context of smart contracts and blockchain-based risk management, and that is the aim of this chapter. The problem addressed is the inability to control risk. The proposed solution is that distributed ledgers might be used to quantize risk and manage future uncertainty more effectively.

One premise is that any form of large-scale activity operated with blockchains could include insurance, automatically priced as a smart contract option. Per the law of large numbers, the required inputs for insurance might be known. To the extent that blockchains encompass a large scale of detailed activity, they could serve as a sort of actuarial table or oracle (validated data service). The overall cost and rate of loss could be determined from the blockchain activity, applying the probability of future loss based on past activity to price an insurance contract. Part of the business model of participating in blockchain-based services could be users receiving micropayments when their (privacy-protected) data is sold, and opting-in to whom to sell it. This is in contrast to the current model in which platform monopolies (Facebook, Google) exclusively reap the economic benefits of user data and community activity.

The goal is not to "insurance-ify" every aspect of life in a domineering algorithmic way that focuses unnecessary psychological attention onto risk and the possibility of loss. The point is rather that blockchain-based models imply the functionality of automatically and unobtrusively including risk management practices in more areas where there could be a risk of unexpected loss (including more robust coverage for situations such as job loss and health issues). Arguably, insurance, risk, loss, and economics are perhaps best experienced as unobtrusive background enablers of life, producing a better quality of life precisely because their presence is recessed.

Following the introduction in Section 1.1, the chapter is structured as follows. Section 1.2 considers classical risk management in the disciplines of philosophy, social science, and finance (both classical financial theory and black swan financial theory). Section 1.3 posits a new risk management paradigm with blockchain-based smart contracts. Section 1.4 considers some potential applications of Black Swan Smart Contracts. Section 1.6 discusses objections and critiques to the proposed solution and Section 1.7 concludes the chapter. Overall, the chapter discusses how smart contracts might reconfigure the management of risk. The conception could shift to seeing risk not as inevitable, but as a computable, controllable parameter of many situations, that might be managed with smart contracts.

1.1.1 *Background*

1.1.1.1 *Definition of risk*

Risk is sometimes desirable and at other times abhorred. The positive possibilities of chance are serendipitous and tantalizing, but the negative surprise of unexpected loss is paralyzing. In both valences, risk is related to the uncertain occurrence of future events. The dictionary focuses on the negative, defining risk as the possibility of loss.[a] However, attitudes toward risk are both risk-loving and risk-averse depending on the situation. On one hand, in fields such as insurance, investment management, and health, the goal is to identify, control, and minimize unwanted risk. On the other hand, in areas such as gambling, lotteries, and speculative investing, the desired outcome is upside gain. Risk is deeply rooted in human psychology and requires the ability to distinguish between reality and possibility [Zinn, 2008]. The thrill of risk-taking may be associated with achievement [Trimpop, 1994], and human triumph over the natural world, including by proxy, one's own mortality [Hall, 2010].

---

[a] Merriam Webster, https://www.merriam-webster.com/dictionary/risk.

1.1.1.2 *A brief history of risk*

Events in the history of risk relevant to the blockchain context are summarized in Table 1. There is evidence of games of chance having been played in ancient civilization, in Greece, Mesopotamia, and China [Bernstein, 1998]. The more formal mathematical foundations of probability theory were developed in 1654 by Pascal and Fermat, while contemplating a gambling problem [Mastin, 2010]. The quantification of risk and return as linked parameters along a continuum of market risk (the efficient frontier) was formulated by Markowitz in Modern Portfolio Theory in 1952 [Markowitz, 1952]. Social science theories start to become prominent in behavioral decision-making related to risk in 1979 [Tversky and Kahneman, 1979]. Black swan financial theory, fat-tailed distributions rather than normal distributions in investment returns, were proposed starting in 1963 [Mandelbrot, 1963]. The data science era has revealed the wider presence of s-curve probability distributions in phenomena ranging from markets to medicine [Davis and Svendsgaard, 1990]. Now with advent of digital network financial tools such as blockchain technology, new possibilities for greater *predictive* risk management may be possible.

Table 1. History of Risk as Related to Blockchain-based Smart Contracts.

	Advance	**Date**
1	Games of chance (Greece, Mesopotamia, and China)	2300 BC
2	Probability Theory (Pascal, Fermat)	1654
3	Modern Portfolio Theory (Markowitz)	1952
4	Social Theories of Risk (Tversky and Kahneman, Gigerenzer, Zinn)	1979-2012
5	Black Swan fat-tailed distributions (Mandelbrot, Taleb)	1963-2007
6	S-curve distributions in medicine (Davis and Svendsgaard, Reynolds)	1990-2015
7	Programmable risk with blockchain-based smart contracts	2018

1.2 Classical Risk Management

1.2.1 *Theorizing risk in philosophy*

In philosophy, risk is primarily considered analytically as the mathematical concept of probability. Scholars analyze the mathematical axioms of probability and their interpretation. One problem is defining a formal theory of probability. The classical view is that Kolmogorov's axioms (1903) are correct. These are a series of axioms which formalize the probability P of some event E, denoted as P(E). Debate ensues as alternative axiom systems are also proposed which extend the basic method, for example, by using game theory instead of measure theory, and stochastic models [Shafer and Vovk, 2018].

Another problem is the interpretation of probability statements [Lyon, 2010]. It is not clear whether probabilities exist as "real" entities in the world (as frequencies, propensities, or other objective features of reality), or only exist mentally (as subjective degrees of belief). These two positions are incorporated as the frequentist/physicalist and the Bayesian/evidentialist interpretations [Eagle, 2009]. On one hand, frequentist or physical probabilities are observable events in real-life associated with physical systems such as rolling dice, gambling games, and lotteries. A given event (e.g. rolling a six) occurs at a certain rate or frequency. On the other hand, Bayesian or evidentialist probabilities are assigned to undeterminable events to represent their subjective plausibility and the degree to which they are supported by available evidence (e.g. climate change) [Hansson, 1999]. Either kind of probabilities may need additional references to convey meaning in practical situations, for example how a probability of 0.2 as opposed to 0.3 translates to human loss in the specific context of oil rig safety, for example [Aven, 2016].

1.2.2 *Theorizing risk in social science*

1.2.2.1 *Prospect theory*

Social theories of risk treat human decision-making in contexts related to risk. This includes individual and collective action in markets, health, military, and corporate R&D situations. An early way of thinking about risk-related decision-making is Expected Value Theory. This is an overall market theory that focuses on the aggregate payout per different event probabilities. Aggregate market theories, however, do not explain empirical results, so more granular models were introduced to incorporate the decision-making of individual agents. One such personal utility model, Expected Utility Theory, was proposed by Bernoulli in 1738.[b] The model comprises the statistical expectation of an individual's valuations of possible outcomes.

However, Expected Utility Theory does not explain the phenomenon of asymmetric loss, so Tversky and Kahneman proposed Prospect Theory in 1979 [Tversky and Kahneman, 1979, 1992]. In Prospect Theory, the *prospect* of positive and negative outcomes is experienced asymmetrically. People tend to find losing $10 agonizing, yet are only mildly happy to have a surprise gain of $10. Prospect Theory thus defines the notion of *loss aversion* as the asymmetry of individuals finding the pain from losing to have a stronger impact than the pleasure from winning. Individuals are risk-averse when it comes to gains, but are risk-takers when it comes to avoiding loss. Risk preference asymmetry and loss aversion can be seen in the *framing effect*, in which people tend to avoid risk when a positive frame is presented, but seek risk when a negative frame is presented [Druckman, 2001].

1.2.2.2 *Other social science theories*

Gigerenzer draws more fundamentally from cognitive psychology to explain and predict judgments related to risk perception [1996]. Risk is distinguished from uncertainty: in risk, the outcome landscape is known

---

[b] https://en.wikipedia.org/wiki/Expected_utility_hypothesis.

(e.g. lottery results), whereas in uncertainty there are open-ended outcomes [Volz and Gigerenzer, 2012]. Since the domains are different, normative strategies used in risk management would not apply to situations of uncertainty, where heuristic methods perform better. A related point is made in Kahneman's *Thinking, Fast and Slow* [2013], delineating immediate fast-thinking based on heuristics (gut reaction) versus longer-term deliberative thinking. Broader societal determinants of risk preferences are also considered. Zinn discusses social theoretic approaches to risk, examining how risk attitudes change with modernization, and the role of power and the formation of groups within society [2008]. Hilgartner hypothesizes that societies construct risk objects, wherein defining and controlling risk objects is a political process [1992]. An example of this is debates about the risk of climate change.

1.2.2.3 *Market wizard practitioners*

From a practitioner perspective, Jack Schwager interviews successful traders about their mindsets and practices in the *Market Wizards* books [Fifield, 2016]. Three key points are first that successful traders are constantly watching for changes in market conditions and staying flexible (today's market is not yesterday's market, or even the same market as a few seconds ago (e.g. a Heraclitian view of markets (it is impossible to step into the same river twice)). Second, successful traders manage risk by deciding exactly when to exit trades ahead of time, often writing it down and calculating the potential win-loss points before entering a trade. Third, successful traders develop their own strategies and do not try to implement the "winning strategies" of others. Traders have a keen sense of what works for their personality, objectives, and risk preferences. The key point is to know oneself as a trader. Schwager could extend the *Market Wizards* franchise with a Crypto Wizards volume detailing the practices and mindsets of successful cryptocurrency traders.

1.2.3 *Theorizing risk in finance: Traditional approach*

1.2.3.1 *Modern portfolio theory*

In finance, a cornerstone of the classical approach to risk management is Modern Portfolio Theory (MPT) [Markowitz, 1952]. MPT involves the hypothetical concept of the *efficient frontier* which denotes an optimal model portfolio with investments plotted along a risk-return curve such that no additional investment could be added to increase return or lower risk. Formally, there is no portfolio with a higher expected return for the same standard deviation. Individuals with varying risk preferences can use the same model to select portfolios with any range of high or low risk along the efficient frontier. Related financial theory developments include Merton's capital asset pricing model (CAPM) [1973] which attempts to describe the relationship between systemic risk (overall market risk) and individual asset risk, and Fabozzi's market-wide risk models that emphasize the role of financial institutions [Fabozzi *et al.*, 2009].

1.2.3.2 *Value at risk*

The modern incarnation of the classical approach to financial risk management is Value at Risk (VaR). VaR is a widely-employed risk management method developed by JP Morgan and other banks in the 1990s [Jorion, 2006]. VaR is a probability-based measure that estimates how much an investment portfolio might lose in a day, given normal market conditions. Firms and regulators use VaR to calculate the amount of assets needed to cover possible short-term losses, and apply it on a daily basis to manage intraday and overnight risk. A normal probability distribution is typically assumed in the application of VaR, which is not always the case in financial markets.

1.2.4 *Theorizing risk in finance: Black swan approach*

1.2.4.1 *Black swan statistical theory*

The term *black swan* refers to the statistical problem of drawing generalized conclusions from a limited number of observations. For example, just because one has not seen a black swan does not mean that black swans do not exist. Thinkers such as David Hume [1748], John Stuart Mill [1843], Karl Popper [1968], and Nassim Taleb [2001] have described the black swan problem [Adams and Thornton, 2013]. Historically, the term meant something rare or non-existent. The expression came closer to its modern use, as a perceived impossibility which might later be disproven, when Dutch explorers actually saw black swans in Western Australia in 1697.

1.2.4.2 *Black swan financial theory*

A black swan event is any outlier event or discontinuity. They occur with greater statistical frequency and effect than is readily apprehended by humans. Black swan events include the advent of the Internet, the personal computer, World War I, the dissolution of the Soviet Union, and the September 11, 2001 terrorist attacks [Taleb, 2001]. In financial markets, black swan outlier events likewise occur with greater statistical frequency than is expected [Mandelbrot, 1999; Taleb, 2007].

Two ways to represent statistical distributions are the event distribution and the probability distribution (Figure 1). The event distribution is the frequency of events (how many times a certain event occurs) and the probability distribution is the likelihood of the occurrence of the event (0-100%). The event distribution of a black swan phenomenon looks like a "squashed Gaussian" or Mandelbrotian curve (fat-tailed). In a normal (Gaussian or Poisson) curve, 68%, 95% and 99% of the values tend to lie neatly in buckets that are within one, two, and three standard deviations of the mean. In a black swan distribution, the center of the distribution curve is lower and the tails are taller (not tapering off as in a normal curve). The interpretation of the fat tails is that outlier events happen more frequently in black swan phenomena than a Gaussian curve would predict.

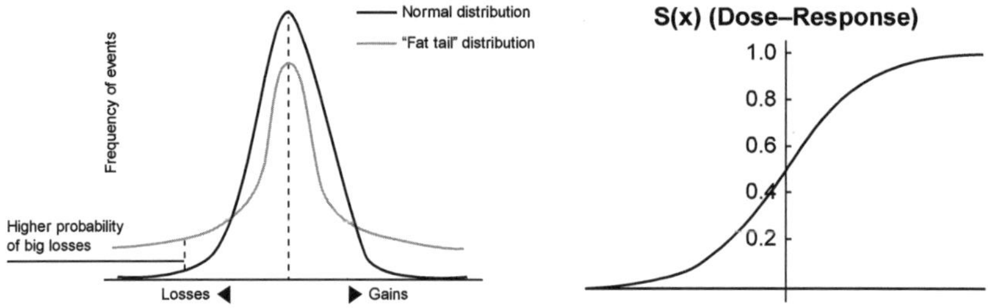

Figure 1. Representing probability: Event distribution and probability distribution.

The second plot in Figure 1 is a probability distribution of the likely occurrence of events, converting the distribution data to a sigmoid or s-curve of probabilities between 0 and 1 (i.e. 0-100%). The standard s-curve formulation starts as convex (facing upward), then becomes linear, and finishes as concave (facing downward). Convexity, the convex portion of the curve, is generally considered optimal since the shape indicates controlled exposure to downside risk and unlimited exposure to upside risk. A practical example would be an investment only being subject to losing the initial funds committed, but having the possibility of unlimited upside gain.

Concavity, in the standard reading, is undesirable, signaling limited exposure to upside gain and unlimited exposure to downside risk. The idea is to "convexify" exposure, risk-managing the position by entering a trade or engaging with a phenomenon only at the convex portion of the curve. This allows investors to "harvest randomness" in the sense of taking advantage of the positive non-linear possibilities of risk while avoiding the negative ones [Taleb, 2012]. The mathematics used to formulate convex functions is inequalities, particularly Jensen's inequality, although Young's inequality or Wagner's inequality might also be used [Dragomir, 2003]. Inequalities describe curvilinear phenomenon, especially strongly-convex functions [Moradi *et al.*, 2016].

1.2.4.3 *Black swan financial theory challenges traditional financial theory*

Classical financial theory was novel and important in 1952 for formalizing the relationship between risk and return. Indeed, the "risk-return trade-off" concept is widely used today in a variety of domains. However, Modern Portfolio Theory (MPT) is a purely theoretical model and its empirical validity has been challenged [Mandelbrot and Hudson, 2006; Taleb, 2007]. Three concerns are cited. First, MPT assumes that market returns congregate around the average expected return more than happens in actuality. Outsized returns (upside and downside) occur more frequently than MPT predicts, and returns are not normally distributed and do not regress to the mean. Second, MPT assumes that returns are independent from one another, but they tend to cluster. Third, MPT assumes that investors are rational actors, which they are not. Investors are driven by diverse risk preferences, and psychological factors such as fear and greed. Since markets are a problem for which no analytic solution exists, different theories explanatory theories are proposed. For example, *reflexivity*, as George Soros theorized, is the idea that agent-modeling feedback loops create market dynamics [Davis and Hands, 2016]. Participants model how other agents might behave, and act accordingly, such that predictions become causal. Overall, given the shortcomings of MPT, alternatives have been suggested, including evaluating the risk of assets and asset classes on an individual rather than portfolio-wide basis, and a more statistically-rigorous analysis of risk through black swan financial theory.

In addition to portfolio analysis, black swan financial theory is also challenging traditional financial theory in the application of Value at Risk (VaR). The Gaussian distribution is typically used in VaR, and although it may be fairly accurate in predicting small daily losses with high probability, it breaks down in forecasting the large catastrophic losses that exist in the fat tail of the distribution (black swan events). When significant deviations occur, the Mandelbrotian distribution can be a better tool for estimating the impact of risk and loss in catastrophic consequences. Thus, advocates of black swan financial theory recommend using both Gaussian and Mandelbrotian distributions when applying VaR [Kolman *et al.*, 1998].

1.2.5 *Black swan risk management: Markets to medicine*

The data science era facilitates the finding that the s-shaped risk curves discovered in finance are present in a variety of other phenomena. The black swan profile is observed in medical interventions such as drug-dosing, pulmonary ventilation, cardiovascular strength in intermittent fasting cycles, and nutrient distribution [Taleb, 2018]. Drug-dosing is known to have a non-linear profile, particularly u-shaped and j-shaped dose-response curves [Davis and Svendsgaard, 1990; Reynolds, 2010]. Further, a biphasic drug-dosing response, *hormesis*, has been noticed along the s-curve function in which a low dose can have a mildly beneficial effect and a high dose can have a toxic effect [Calabrese, 2004]. Drug-dosing techniques thus attempt to find mathematically optimal non-linear profiles for delivery [Swan, 1984]. Notably, an important cause of iatrogenics (harm-producing medical treatments) is the failure to use s-curve risk profiles in treatment specification [Taleb, 2018]. S-curve profiles emerge in other biological phenomena too, for example, neurotransmitter release is inherently random and exhibits Jensen's inequality-type properties (i.e. convexity) [Yang and Xu-Friedman, 2013].

1.3 Risk Management with Blockchain-based Smart Contracts

1.3.1 *Black swan risk management*

The implication of black swan financial theory is that the risk profile of an underlying phenomenon might be mapped into an s-curve format (an event probability distribution from 0-100%), from which risk exposure can be proactively managed. It has been demonstrated in domains from financial markets to medicine that risk exposure can be represented as an s-curve, and risk-managed by selecting the convex portion of the curve. Selecting and managing the desired level of risk exposure for a given context is a method that might be applied to a much wider range of situations, and given its computational nature, lends itself to blockchain-based implementation.

The premise is that s-curve formulations create the possibility of tailoring risk exposure, segmenting the risk-averse, risk-neutral, and risk-loving portions of the curve. Drawing real-life functions as s-curves, with intervals of convexity, linearity, and concavity means that there could be user choice about where to engage the curve for the desired level of risk exposure. The three regions of the s-curve (convex, linear, and concave) would logically correspond to low-medium-high risk.

1.3.2 *Black swan smart contracts*

In financial markets, risk management strategies are often implemented with options. Options are financial instruments that give the owner the right to buy or sell an asset on a certain date at a specific price. Any kind of long or short exposure in financial markets can be manufactured with options. In blockchain environments, risk management strategies might be implemented with smart contracts. Smart contracts are an even more flexible species of options. Smart contracts are programmable contracts that can be used to confer the right to buy or sell any blockchain-based asset or liability at a future moment of time (in either blocktime (the native time regime of blockchains [Swan, 2016]) or "fiat" (regular) time) per certain terms and consideration.

1.3.2.1 *Programmable risk smart contracts*

To implement an active risk management strategy with s-curves, exposure could be formalized and controlled with smart contracts. Black swan s-curve functionality could be automatically instantiated as a selectable feature of smart contracts. *Programmable risk* means the ability to specify the risk parameters of a smart contract. The degree of risk could be a user-selected smart contract parameter. The standard choices could be low-medium-high risk. Just as users need not have a legal background to choose a Creative Commons license for a YouTube Video from a drop-down menu of standard choices (e.g. Attribution, ShareAlike, NonCommercial), likewise users need not have financial expertise in order to select the desired risk level for a smart contract. Low-medium-high risk contracts could be the default, but more complicated programmable risk parameters could be specified (e.g. a dynamically self-adjusting volatility of 12%), particularly if different kinds of financial smart contracts are migrated to blockchain-based execution, for example mortgages and other long-term financing agreements.

1.3.2.2 *Regulation of black swan smart contracts*

The upshot of adding black swan s-curve risk management features to smart contracts is that risk might be effectively and unobtrusively minimized in more domains than had been possible before. Programmable risk smart contracts might be executed both by using existing futures and options products in financial markets (i.e. CBOE and CME cryptocurrency futures and LedgerX options) or by using smart contracts directly. If smart contracts were to be used as financial options to a greater extent, the expectation would be that the CFTC (in the U.S.) would regulate them as financial market options analogous to the way that the SEC brought Initial Coin Offerings (ICOs) under its regulatory purview. Likewise, smart contract betting could fall under gaming and casino laws.

1.4 Black Swan Smart Contracts: Applications

A trader analyzing market volatility or a doctor targeting patient drug-dosing to a certain interval might use the same black swan s-curve tools that an individual could also incorporate into daily decisions such as calculating when to leave for work, whether to wear sunscreen, and accepting a new job. Everyday life has many risk-reward trade-offs, with most decisions being made informally. Automated risk analysis could have a greater presence in daily life, for example, as a standard feature of personal digital assistants. "You have a 10% chance of being late for work if you leave now," Siri advises.

Considering the potential applications of Black Swan Smart Contracts with programmable risk (i.e. selectable levels of risk), there are two tiers. First is replicating existing risk management products and services in the blockchain environment for more efficient execution (the "better horse" implementation of a new technology). Second is greenfield applications that were previously impossible (the "horseless carriage or car" implementation of a new technology).

1.4.1 *Insurance as a digital service*

Blockchain-based insurance is an obvious "better horse" application, given the blockchain properties of large-market liquidity together with the ability to obligate parties with digital contracts [Gatteschi *et al.*, 2018]. Examples of blockchain-based insurance projects include Etherisc (focusing on flight delay and crop insurance) and RiskBazaar (offering peer-to-peer contracts). PrecedentCoin is a project conceptualized for peer-to-peer insurance and peer-adjudicated claims, and is now directed at peer-based legal discovery. Peer-based legal discovery and peer-based claims adjusters (held to standards by reputation) are an interesting "future of work" opportunity for peer labor. Micropayment insurance is another possible market (user-selected and priced per minute of Uber service or day of Airbnb stay, for example).

Insurance could be a digital service that is automatically priced into the purchase of any product or service in large and liquid markets for both individual and enterprise customers. For example, flight insurance is already offered as a standard option with online airline ticket purchases. Since it is straightforward to measure the cost of risk for large-scale phenomena per known probabilities of occurrence and the cost of payout, there could be many classes of automated blockchain-based insurance products. For example, the automobile insurance market might migrate to blockchain implementation (a Geico blockchain can be envisioned). The percent of claims and the cost of repair for any postal code is well-documented. Actuarial tables are already digitized and can serve as an oracle (an independent information provider called programmatically by smart contacts). These metrics could be used to price the cost of insurance in smart contracts. Insurance for any known and quantified situation could be automatically included as a smart contract feature, including in the black swan s-curve tiers of low-medium-high risk. There could be more forms of optional insurance, priced as an easy-to-use smart contract parameter.

Restructuring the insurance market could be a future possibility. Insurance is a highly-regulated industry and the current market structure is comprised by large firms with "large pools of capital." In the U.S., there are a few large companies such as Travelers, Progressive, State Farm, and Allstate, with large pools of otherwise fallow capital kept on hand to support known payout rates (e.g.; annually 4% automobile claims and 12-15% property and casualty claims [Holzberger, 2017]). Instead, the global reach of blockchain technology might enable larger-scale risk-pooling and a more rigorous linking of outcomes to cost. The Interplanetary File System (IPFS) concept (global file-serving) could be extended to insurance in the Interplanetary Risk Pooling (IPRP) concept, in which blockchains could facilitate large and liquid markets for peer-based global risk pooling. The reinsurance market could migrate most quickly to blockchain instantiation since it is already more automated and securitized. Reinsurance is "insurer's insurance," which allows insurance companies to remain solvent after major claims events such as natural disasters. Reinsurance comprises 10% of the insurance market, with $595 billion of capital being available to support claims as of 2016 [Benfield, 2017].

1.4.2 *eBay for money*

Blockchain-based "eBay for money" websites might arise in which long-tail financial services buyers and sellers could meet, based on any variety of assets and liabilities, orchestrated with smart contracts. The demand for long-tail products (i.e. non-mainstream) has been demonstrated in eCommerce marketplaces such as Amazon [Anderson, 2006], where niche books account for 36.7% of Amazon's sales (following a power law, not a Gaussian distribution) [Brynjolfsson *et al.*, 2010]. Therefore, there could be demand for personalized financial products offered through a new kind of blockchain-based eCommerce financial marketplace. These crypto-marketplaces could address the "car" applications of blockchain not covered by existing financial products. For example, some of the biggest areas of unexpected loss are unemployment and uneven income streams, unexpected health situations and medical debt, and unexpected needs to support family members. In an "eBay for financial services," businesses and consumers could solicit counterparties who might be willing to write a smart contract to take on the risk for a mutually-agreed upon price. Standard contracts and automated pricing could help non-specialists (i.e. consumers) price these contracts and avoid exploitation. Another job-of-the-future could be "non-exploitation peer advocates" who review crypto-financial contracts for soundness for a micropayment fee. New kinds of insurance not currently available (flood insurance, peer-to-peer renter's insurance), and hyper-personalized insurance (personalized job loss insurance to supplement government unemployment, and on-demand ride-share, anti-mugging, and other personal security insurance could be some examples.

1.4.3 *Information markets*

Black swan smart contracts might be used in the context of information markets, markets in which information is the commodity of value. For example, a School Admissions Waiting List is a situation in which it is useful for both sides of the market (applicants and administrators) to have information. Smart contracts could help schools manage this process more effectively. Options allow individuals in a marketplace to register their opinion about a situation. Candidates on the waiting list have differing levels of interest ranging from "high demand" to "backup school." Having a secure and anonymous information market could help schools make decisions that better correspond to the demand for their product, and candidates understand their position and chance of being accepted from the waiting list. Smart contract options could facilitate how organizations orchestrate the waiting list, including being federated across multiple schools. Larger systems of preference matching such as medical school acceptances and residency placement[c] could be instantiated with smart contracts and blockchain-based information markets to improve efficiency and transparency.

---

[c] "The Match" https://www.aafp.org/medical-school-residency/residency/match.html.

1.4.4 *myContingencyManager app (analogous to myFitness Manager)*

Insurance products may be best-received when they are unobtrusive and automatic, since like health [Swan, 2012], risk is not typically an area upon which consumers like to dwell. Regarding optional insurance such as flight insurance, an informal survey found that 78% of respondents never purchase trip insurance and 49% did not know what it covers [The Points Guy, 2013]. Consumer risk preferences may be a function of general attitudes about the economy. For example, travelers spent less on travel but more on trip insurance in 2016 than in 2015 [Squaremouth, 2016]. The point is that having standardized insurance products priced into digital services with low-medium-high risk tiers could provide consumers with an easy way to incorporate enhanced risk management practices into everyday lives that does not require a lot of cost, knowledge, and deliberation.

1.4.5 *Autonomous risk management as a smart network property*

Smart networks is the idea of intelligence being programmed directly into network operating software for automated process execution [Swan, 2015]. Next-generation computing platforms such as blockchain financial networks and deep learning systems are indicative of this new and emergent class of global computational infrastructure. The smart network properties of blockchains are automated user authentication, ownership confirmation, value-transfer transactions, and global state updating. The smart network properties of deep learning systems are optimization and being able to classify and predictively identify what objects are, with greater than human-level accuracy [He *et al.*, 2015]. Smart network technologies converge in the idea of Deep Learning Chains that might be used in future-class applications such as autonomous driving, predictive disease analysis, and smart city coordination. Notably, deep learning already operates via s-curve probabilities (mapping problems into logistic regression sigmoidal formats). The black swan s-curves proposed here bring blockchains into a parallel format with deep learning nets from which smart network convergence applications might be further developed.

A property of smart networks could be autonomous risk management. Just as Black Swan Smart Contracts might automatically price risk and offer insurance, so too could smart networks price their own cost of risk management. Risk management is a cost of network operations, similar to the cost of computation, as Ethereum automatically prices in as *gas*, the cost of running computations on the network. Smart networks could calculate the risk associated with any transaction and automatically hedge it by simultaneously entering an offsetting position. Autonomous risk management in smart networks extends the idea of autonomous self-healing networks [Quattrociocchi *et al.*, 2014] and other autonomous network operations. Autonomous risk management is not so far-fetched, as algorithmic trading operations already engage in auto-hedging practices (automatically generating orders to hedge portfolios based on pre-specified risk management parameters).

1.5 Objections and Critiques

There could be several objections to the proposed idea of programmable risk Black Swan Smart Contracts. One of the biggest barriers to smart contracts is enforcement mechanisms to control physical assets by electronic means [Dupont, 2017; Nelson, 2017]. This is a non-trivial issue that is not addressed here, but would be a necessary pre-condition for Black Swan Smart Contracts, to the extent that they are employed in the administration of physical assets.

A second complaint is that blockchain technology is already complicated to understand, and adding insurance products and financial market options just makes this worse. However, it was clarified that the benefit of standardized Black Swan Smart Contracts with low-medium-high risk selection parameters is to package risk in readily understandable and easy-to-deploy offerings in the format of Creative Commons licenses.

A third potential critique is that blockchain finance and black swan smart contracts are indicative of the trend to global marketization and financialization. These are quantitative calculations of market worth that may ignore qualitative factors, and part of what could be perceived as a generally dehumanizing process of technology controlling an increasing portion of human activities. However, as Taleb notes, humans are *fooled by randomness* [2001], and do not think cogently about probability, which suggests that technology tools for facilitating better decision-making might be welcome. The aim of Black Swan Smart Contracts is to background risk management to deliver an improved quality of life.

1.6 Conclusion

The thesis of this chapter is that smart contracts are options, and as such, can be used to control risk (unwanted future uncertainty) in a wider range of areas than has been possible previously, in finance, and in other domains such as medicine and everyday risk-taking. Options as a financial market instrument have long been used to control the amount and timing of risk in specific ways and tailor exposure with granularity. Smart contracts are an even more flexible species of options because they are programmable contracts that can be used to confer the right to buy or sell any blockchain-based asset or liability at a future moment of time per certain terms and consideration. Therefore, smart contracts allow a greater variety in the degree and type of risks that might be brought under improved management.

This chapter proposes programmable risk Black Swan Smart Contracts. Programmable risk is the idea of programmatically selecting levels of risk. Black Swan Smart Contracts instantiate event probability s-curves in user-selectable levels of low-medium-high risk as a smart contract parameter. The potential benefit is that with Black Swan Smart Contracts, individuals and institutions alike might be able to easily execute smart contracts that deploy risk management practices into a wider scope of activity. The impact could be diminishing unwanted risks in more areas of life.

The novel contributions of this chapter are in three areas. First, a multidisciplinary synthesis of the conceptualization and treatment of risk is presented from philosophy, social science, and finance. Second, black swan financial theory is integrated with classical financial theory. Third, a theory of blockchain-based risk management is proposed, arguing that risk is a programmable feature which might be managed with Black Swan Smart Contracts.

Although far from marshalling full control over nature, Black Swan Smart Contracts nevertheless signal a moment of continued progress on the continuum from a reactive to a proactive stance with the world. Black Swan Smart Contracts might allow more aspects of reality to come under the purview of knowability and management. Data science has facilitated a shift in many domains from passivity to action-taking that is predictive, simulated, and constructed (programmable), but economics and finance have not caught up yet. This is because secure-value transfer technologies were not yet available. However, with distributed ledgers, many new applications for modernizing the economy and proactively managing risk could be enabled. The potential impact of having greater control over risk is that Black Swan Smart Contracts might be applied not only in the contemporary context, but also to future situations of high risk and uncertainty such as commercial space flight, climate change and carbon credits, and CRISPR-based genome editing.

References

Adams, A. and Thornton, B. (2013). Black Swans and VAR. *Journal of Finance and Accountancy*. pp. 1-17.

Anderson, C. (2006). *The Long Tail: Why the Future of Business Is Selling Less of More*. New York, NY: Hachette Books.

Aven, T. (2016). Risk assessment and risk management: Review of recent advances on their foundation. *European Journal of Operational Research*. 253:1-13.

Benfield, A. (2017). Reinsurance Market Outlook. *Thought Leadership*.

Bernstein, P.L. (1998). *Against the Gods: The Remarkable Story of Risk*. New York, NY: Wiley.

Brynjolfsson, E., Hu, Y. and Smith, M.D. (2010). The Longer Tail: The Changing Shape of Amazon's Sales Distribution Curve. Available at SSRN: https://ssrn.com/abstract=1679991.

Calabrese, E.J. (2004). Hormesis: a revolution in toxicology, risk assessment and medicine. *Science and Society*. EMBO Rep. 5(Suppl 1): S37-S40.

Davis, J.B. and Hands, D.W. (Eds.) (2016). *Reflexivity and Economics: George Soros's theory of reflexivity and the methodology of economic science*. New York, NY: Routledge.

Davis, J.M. and Svendsgaard, D.J. (1990). U-shaped dose–response curves: their occurrence and implications for risk assessment. *J Toxicol Environ Health.* 30:71-83.

Dragomir, S.S. (2003). A survey of Cauchy-Bunyakovsky-Schwarz type Discrete Inequalities. *Journal of Inequalities in Pure and Applied Mathematics*. 4(3)63: 1-142.

Druckman, J. (2001). Evaluating framing effects. *J Econ Psy*. 22: 96-101.

Dupont, Q. (2017). Blockchain Identities: Notational Technologies for Control and Management of Abstracted Entities. *Metaphilosophy*. 48(5): 634-653.

Eagle, A. Ed. (2009). *Philosophy of Probability: Contemporary Readings*. New York, NY: Routledge.

Fabozzi, F.J., Modigliani, F.P. and Jones, F.J. (2009). *Foundations of Financial Markets & Institutions*, New York, NY: Prentice Hall.

Fifield, A. (2016). 6 Timeless Trading Lessons from Jack Schwager. *Investopedia.*

Gatteschi, V., Lamberti, F., Demartini, C., Pranteda, C., Santamaría, V. (2018). Blockchain and Smart Contracts for Insurance: Is the Technology Mature Enough? *Future Internet*. 10(2)20.

Gigerenzer, G. (1996). On narrow norms and vague heuristics: A reply to Kahneman and Tversky. *Psychological Review*. 103(3):592-596.

Hall, E. (2010). *Greek Tragedy: Suffering under the Sun*. Oxford UK: Oxford University Press.

Hansson, S.E. (1999). A Philosophical Perspective on Risk. *Ambio*. 28:539-542.

He, K., Zhang, X., Ren, S., Sun, J. (2015). Delving Deep into Rectifiers: Surpassing Human-Level Performance on ImageNet Classification. 2015 IEEE International Conference on Computer Vision (ICCV) Santiago Chile. 7-13 Dec. 2015. pp. 1026-1034.

Hilgartner, S. (1992). The Social Construction of Risk Objects: Or, How to Pry Open Networks of Risk. *Organizations, Uncertainties, and Risk*. J.F. Short, Jr., and L. Clarke (Eds.). New York, NY: Routledge. pp. 39:53.

Holzberger, S. (2017). 2017 Insurance Market Briefing. *A.M. Best.*

Jorion, P. (2006). *Value at Risk: The New Benchmark for Managing Financial Risk*. New York: McGraw-Hill.

Kahneman, D. (2013). *Thinking, Fast and Slow*. New York, NY: Farrar, Straus and Giroux.

Kolman, J., Onak, M., Jorion, P., Taleb, N. *et al.* (1998). Roundtable: The Limits of VaR. *Derivatives Strategy.*

Lyon, A. (2010). Philosophy of Probability. *Philosophies of the Sciences: A Guide*. Ed. F. Allhoff, Hoboken NY: Blackwell Publishing Ltd. pp. 92-125.

Mandelbrot, B. (1963). The Variation of Certain Speculative Prices. *The Journal of Business*. 36(4): 394-419.

———. (1999). Renormalization and fixed points in finance, since 1962. *Physica A*. 263: 477-87.

Mandelbrot, B. and Hudson, R.I. (2006). *The Misbehavior of Markets: A Fractal View of Financial Turbulence*. New York, NY: Basic Books.

Markowitz, H.M. (1952). Portfolio Selection. *The Journal of Finance*. 7(1):77-91.

Mastin, L. (2010). 17th Century Mathematics: Pascal. The Story of Mathematics blog. http://www.storyofmathematics.com/17th_pascal.html.

Merton, R.C. (1973). An Intertemporal Capital Asset Pricing Model. *Econometrica.* 41(5):867-887.

Moradi, H.R., Omidvar, M.E., Adil Khan, M. and Nikodem, K. (2016). Around Jensen's inequality for strongly convex functions," arXiv:1611.07780 [math.FA].

Nelson, J.S. *et al.* (2017). Sweetbridge White Paper. https://sweetbridge.com/public/docs/Sweetbridge-Whitepaper.pdf.

Quattrociocchi, W., Caldarelli, G., and Scala, A. (2014). Self-Healing Networks: Redundancy and Structure. *PLoS ONE.* 9(2): e87986.

Reynolds, A.R. (2010). Potential Relevance of Bell-Shaped and U-Shaped Dose-Responses for the Therapeutic Targeting of Angiogenesis in Cancer. *Dose Response.* 8(3):253-284.

Schwager, J. (2014). "Market Wizards" Advice: Doing the Uncomfortable Thing. *American Association of Individual Investors.*

Shafer G. and Vovk, V. (2018). The origins and legacy of Kolmogorov's Grundbegriffe. The Game-Theoretic Probability and Finance Project. Working Paper #4. *Probability and Finance.*

Squaremouth. (2016). 2016 Travel Trends: Squaremouth Report Reveals Changes in Traveler Behavior. Press Release.

Swan, G.W. (1984). *Applications of Optimal Control Theory in Biomedicine.* Chapman & Hall/CRC Pure and Applied Mathematics (Book 81). Boca Raton FL: CRC Press.

Swan, M. (2012). Health 2050: The Realization of Personalized Medicine through Crowdsourcing, the Quantified Self, and the Participatory Biocitizen. *J Pers Med.* 2(3): 93-118.

———. (2015). *Blockchain: Blueprint for a New Economy.* Sebastopol, CA: O'Reilly Media.

———. (2016). Blockchain Temporality: Smart Contract Time Specifiability with Blocktime. *Rule Technologies. Research, Tools, and Applications.* 10th International Symposium, RuleML Stony Brook, NY, USA, July 6-9, 2016. Proceedings. pp. 184-96.

Taleb, N.N. (2001). *Fooled by Randomness: The Hidden Role of Chance in Life and in the Markets.* New York, NY: Random House.

———. (2007). *The Black Swan: The Impact of the Highly Improbable.* New York, NY: Random House.

———. (2012). Understanding is a Poor Substitute for Convexity (Antifragility). *Edge.*

———. (2018, forthcoming). (Anti)Fragility and Convex Responses in Medicine. *Springer Handbook of Complexity in Medicine.*

The Points Guy. (2013). National Travel Insurance Survey Results – Who Buys It and Is It Worth It? The Points Guy blog.

Trimpop, R.M. (1994). How Is Risk Taking Motivated and Emotionally Experienced? *The Psychology of Risk Taking Behavior.* Advances in Psychology. 107: 129-160.

Tversky, T. and Kahneman, D. (1979). Prospect Theory: Analysis of Decision under Risk. *Econometrica.* 47(2):263-292.

———. (1992). Advances in prospect theory: Cumulative representation of uncertainty. *Journal of Risk and Uncertainty.* 5(4):297-323.

Volz, K.G., and Gigerenzer, G. (2012). Cognitive Processes in Decisions Under Risk are not the Same as in Decisions Under Uncertainty. *Front Neurosci.* 6(105):1-6.

Yang, H. and Xu-Friedman, M.A. (2013). Stochastic properties of neurotransmitter release expand the dynamic range of synapses. *J Neurosci*. 33(36):14406-14416.

Zinn, J.O. (2008). A Comparison of Sociological Theorizing on Risk and Uncertainty. *Social Theories of Risk and Uncertainty: An Introduction*. J.O. Zinn. Hoboken, NJ: Blackwell Publishing Ltd. pp. 168-210.

Part 5

Policy, Regulation, and Incentives

Chapter 10

Entrepreneurial Exit: Developing the Cryptoeconomy

Darcy W.E. Allen

Postdoctoral Research Fellow, Blockchain Innovation Hub, RMIT University, Melbourne, Australia
darcy.allen@rmit.edu.au

Abstract

Blockchain technology enables entrepreneurs to develop new decentralized governance structures to coordinate human interaction and exchange. That is, blockchain enables exit from political-socioeconomic systems through new forms of property rights protection and enforcement. This chapter examines the economic problem facing entrepreneurs as they use blockchain to *cryptosecede* and develop the new governance structures of the *cryptoeconomy*. The analysis draws on institutional and new development economics, arguing that blockchain entrepreneurs face a private economic development problem over complementary 'protective-tier' institutional technologies (Leeson and Boettke 2009). This understanding of the parallels between territorial economic development and the cryptoeconomy development helps explain collaboration between blockchain entrepreneurs within governance structures such as hackathons and conferences (Allen 2017). These collaborative governance structures are entrepreneurial efforts of self-governed economic development of the cryptoeconomy.

Keywords: Cryptoeconomics, Blockchain, New Development Economics, Institutional Entrepreneurship.

1. Institutional blockchain entrepreneurship

Blockchain technology enables entrepreneurs to develop new decentralized governance structures for interaction and exchange (e.g. see Atzori, 2015; Swan, 2015; Wright and De Filippi, 2015).[1] The new governance structures that blockchain entrepreneurs create are considered comparatively decentralized because they tend to push the governance of information—that is, the governance of ledgers (Berg *et al.*, 2018)—toward networks rather than hierarchies. As an institutional technology, blockchain applications shift the boundaries of firms, markets and states, thereby reordering social, political and economic activities (Davidson *et al.*, 2016). As an institutional technology, blockchain applications are not constrained to existing political-socioeconomic systems, but can be used as a governance tool to *exit* or *cryptosecede* from those systems, creating new decentralized governance structures (MacDonald, 2015; MacDonald *et al.*, 2016).[2] That is, cryptosecession involves entrepreneurs creating new decentralized governance structures that compete with firms, markets and states as comparatively effective structures of organization. The various applications of blockchain through cryptosecession form the *cryptoeconomy*: a non-territorial collection of governance structures and exchange where interaction is primarily governed through blockchain technology, as compared to firms or governments (Allen, 2017). Before individuals can exit to the cryptoeconomy, however, the governance structures—those institutions that protect property rights and enforce contracts—must be entrepreneurially discovered. Entrepreneurial discovery must *precede* exit and cryptosecession.[3] The evolutionary institutional political economy process of blockchain described in

---

[1] The author thanks two anonymous reviewers for their comments.

[2] Exit in the sense of Hirschman (1970), where individuals have three options to exert power over institutions: exit, voice or loyalty.

[3] This can be viewed within the literature on institutional change (e.g. Denzau and North, 1994) and the evolutionary theory of institutions (e.g. Potts, 2000).

Markey-Towler (2018) rests on top of an entrepreneurial discovery process with similarities to the development of territorial nation states.[4] This chapter explores this entrepreneurial development problem through the lens of development economics (Boettke *et al.*, 2008; Coyne and Boettke, 2006; Leeson and Boettke, 2009), providing insight into the entrepreneurial challenges facing the development of the cryptoeconomy.

In new development economics, Leeson and Boettke (2009) define two-tiers of entrepreneurship necessary for economic development: productive technologies necessary to better support human needs ('productive-tier' entrepreneurship); and institutional governance structures necessary to secure property rights and trade ('protective-tier' entrepreneurship). This analysis is unique and useful because conventional emphasis of entrepreneurship takes the institutional environment as given, constraining entrepreneurs to 'productive-tier' entrepreneurship. In this view, entrepreneurial calculation is shaped by the costs of existing institutions (e.g. Baumol, 1990). By contrast, the study of institutional entrepreneurship—what Leeson and Boettke call protective-tier entrepreneurship—recognizes that the institutional environment must itself by discovered. Here, entrepreneurs undertake protective-tier discovery to solve a higher-order constitutional-level problem (see Kuchař, 2016) of developing institutions that enable trade and exchange through the protection of property rights and the settling of disputes (Boettke and Coyne, 2009; Leca *et al.*, 2008; Leeson and Boettke, 2009).[5] Together, the evolutionary process of productive-tier and protective-tier entrepreneurship enables economic growth, development and prosperity.

This chapter is primarily concerned with protective-tier entrepreneurship using blockchain technology to create and develop the cryptoeconomy. The importance of such institutional entrepreneurship has recently gained prominence within development economics in relation to the institutions within territorial nations that enable trade, growth, and thus

---

[4] Note that the process of institutional evolution within the cryptoeconomy emerges in many ways, including through forking of existing blockchain institutions—that is, deciding to keep some institutions while removing others (Berg and Berg, 2017).

[5] This is a constitutional-level in the sense that "they offer a framework on which diverse ends can be pursued" (Berg and Berg, 2017, p. 3).

development. The central contribution of this chapter is to connect the insights from 'new development economics' to inform the contemporary problem of developing the cryptoeconomy, thereby providing a greater understanding of the entrepreneurial development of blockchain technology. What this reveals is that protective-tier entrepreneurial efforts of cryptosecession to create the cryptoeconomy are analogous to the new development economics understanding of coordinating knowledge to discover complementary institutions. However, while in a developing nation this coordination process can occur hierarchically through government planners, the decentralized nature of the cryptoeconomy means that the process of economic development is governed by coordination between entrepreneurs (whether that governance is on-chain or off-chain). From this perspective, the current widespread collaboration surrounding blockchain technology—in 'innovation commons' such as in Bitcoin Embassies, hackathons and conferences (see Allen, 2017; Allen and Potts, 2016a)—can be identified as a form of privately governed economic development facilitating exit to the cryptoeconomy.

2. Creating the cryptoeconomy

The various applications of blockchains as a governance technology, and the new cryptoeconomy that they form, are different to other techno-economic paradigms such as the peer-to-peer or sharing economy. Applications of blockchain are unique because they enable exit from political-socioeconomic systems toward non-territorial governance structures (Markey-Towler, 2018). While the cryptoeconomy does not have a geographic location, centralized political structure or hierarchical legal system, it enables a spontaneous ordering of exchange. This new decentralized structure of the cryptoeconomy is based on the creation of new native value systems — that is, new economies. This section briefly outlines two categories of blockchain applications based on their differential attempts to exit existing territorial protective-tier institutions, before considering some entrepreneurial costs to that cryptosecession.

Entrepreneurs can apply blockchain technology while maintaining recourse to existing state-based public institutions, such as enforcement of property rights and the settling of disputes through the courts and legal system. In the Leeson and Boettke (2009) distinction outlined above, applying blockchain in this way is entrepreneurship primarily on the 'productive-tier' — operating either directly in, or in the shadow of, existing state-based institutions of enforcement (Mattila, 2016). Blockchain applications within the finance industry, for instance, may achieve efficiency gains and lower costs while maintaining contracts that are resolved through the court system.[6] Indeed, new technologies are generally applied or integrated within the existing institutional architecture, and when disputes arise they are dealt with through gradual integration into the courts or private arbitration.

However, one of the central features of blockchain technology is its potential as a governance technology. That is, as a tool to *exit* existing governance structures. Blockchain entrepreneurs can create institutional enforcement mechanisms to secure property rights and facilitate trade — that is, protective-tier entrepreneurship (Swan and De Filippi, 2017, p. 611) — that competes with other forms of organization, rather than operating in their shadow. This process of *cryptosecession* occurs when entrepreneurs apply blockchain technology to create new decentralized governance structures that replace existing hierarchies such as firms and governments. Over the longer term, individual efforts of cryptosecession may lead to political rupture because blockchain better solves governance issues such as opportunism (MacDonald, 2015).

Where blockchains are comparatively effective at solving economic problems — such as substitutability and complementarities as outlined by Markey-Towler (2018) — individuals may choose to exit from existing enforcement mechanisms and move toward decentralized private blockchain-based governance. This choice for individuals to cryptosecede is a question of their subjective perceptions of the relatively costs of territorial versus non-territorial institutions (see Allen and Berg, 2017). While explaining the political economy of the boundaries of the cryptoeconomy is beyond this chapter, it is useful to briefly ask why

---

[6] The question of whether contracts voluntarily entered into within crypto-economic systems will be mutually recognized in existing legal systems is still an open and important question.

entrepreneurs would choose to crytposecede. This question is closely linked with the motivations of the original cypherpunks who developed the technology.

There was no mention in the original bitcoin white paper of integrating within the governance structures of the existing world (Mougayar, 2016; Nakamoto 2008). Indeed, the aim was to shift governance away from the centralized power of hierarchical firms and states (Popper, 2015). Applications such as smart contracts and decentralized autonomous organizations explicitly aimed to eschew all reliance on legal contracts (Buterin, 2014). This motivation can be stated through the institutional possibility frontier (Djankov *et al.*, 2003) as developing a technology that lowers the costs of disorder from private expropriation and lowers the costs of dictatorship through public expropriation. Furthermore, applying blockchain within the existing political-socioeconomic institutions may face regulatory uncertainty and resistance as incumbents lobby to defend their territory (see Juma, 2016) and draw blockchain technology within existing regulations, potentially suppressing its benefits (e.g. Harwick, 2016; Nair and Sutter, 2018). The decentralized nature of blockchain may increase the transaction costs of organized rent-seeking from others seeking to hold back blockchain technology, thereby reducing the cost of exit.

While on one hand cryptosecession partially overcomes the resistance and tension with existing regulation, this choice is not costless. There is likely to be a combination of both territorial institutions and non-territorial institutions — a combination that will be discovered when their comparative efficacy at governance exchange is tested and trialed. Partly this will be due to the entrepreneurial costs of discovering decentralized governance enforcement mechanisms. Take the example of OpenBazaar, which is a peer-to-peer decentralized marketplace with core governance based on blockchain technology. To be truly decentralized, the team at OpenBazaar therefore had to form trusted governance structures that verify and secure pseudonymous trades without recourse to state-based enforcement or the organization itself. That is, they had to undertake protective-tier entrepreneurship in two directions: a decentralized enforcement mechanism and a decentralized reputation mechanism [7] There is also a growing focus on the use of blockchain technology to facilitate collective decision making over rules themselves — that is, the formation of a cryptodemocracy ordered by blockchain technology (Allen *et al.*, 2017; Berg, 2017). This is also understood as a form of protective-tier entrepreneurship that may ultimately be used to replace some decision making within the territorial economy, raising interesting questions over the dynamics of decision making in groups when votes or stakes can be coordinated in a decentralized way.

Cryptosecession, as we have seen here, must be intimately linked with entrepreneurial discovery of self-enforcing and self-executing institutional mechanisms of governance. Indeed, the notion that the early stages of a new industry or technology face a different set of economic challenges than a completely formed industry is not a novel concept (e.g. see Aldrich and Fiol, 1994). For blockchain entrepreneurs this is intuitively clear: they lack precedent over the institutional structure in which they operate and are seeking to change.

The challenge of cryptoseceding is a coordination problem requiring information about future changes in the state of the world, business models, financing, timing, consumer demand, competitors, failed ventures, and so on. Blockchain entrepreneurs must also must discover, create and test novel institutional structures and mechanisms that act as the core ordering principle of governance. This requires the discovery of self-contained and self-executing mechanisms of blockchain governance that are not embedded in the existing institutional environment. In this way the entrepreneurial process of cryptosecession is best viewed not just through the lens of a new industry, but rather from the perspective of developing the protective-tier of a *new economy*.

In the following section we examine this economic problem using the development economics literature. Therefore, in the following sections we first describe the economics of development before examining how this

[7] The central institutional governance mechanism involves two parties creating a contract which is sent to a third party (the moderator) who witnesses the contract and creates a multisig account. While there are no fees on the system, individuals can decide to pay for dispute resolution, and the third party can receive funds through tips.

literature applies to the cryptoeconomy and cryptosecession. and cryptoeconomy and cryptosecession as outlined in the previous section.

3. Institutions, entrepreneurship and development

The economics of development is primarily concerned with the origin of economic growth, and thus the drivers of prosperity. The various approaches to this problem, however, range from the mid-twentieth century mainstream allocation and efficiency focused 'old development economics' (Chenery and Strout, 1966; Domar, 1946; Harrod, 1939) to the entrepreneur-centered and institution-centered 'new development economics' (Engel, 2010). While the old development economics explained economic growth using allocation, investment and accumulation of capital (e.g. Rostow, 1990; Swan, 1956), the new development economics brought several new foci to the forefront of growth and development: the complexity, stickiness and path dependence of both formal and informal institutions; the epistemological limits of allocating investment through centralized governments; and the importance of bottom-up entrepreneurial discovery for overcoming uncertainty (e.g. Bauer, 1976). These understandings about the growth of developing nations can help us understand the challenges in the development of the new decentralized cryptoeconomy.

Chenery and Strout (1966) argued that one of the core problems facing developing nations was a savings-investment gap. Once identified, this savings gap needed to be filled through either government intervention or aid.[8] In addition to the need for further savings, the 'big push' theory also proposed that economic development required several coordinated investments in different sectors of the economy because the marginal product of investments was higher when made simultaneously (Murphy *et al.*, 1989; Rosenstein-Rodan, 1943, 1961). That is, investments

---

[8] As Chenery and Strout (1966, p. 268) notes in the first paragraph: "For most underdeveloped countries, foreign assistance is already a critical source of development finance and one of the main hopes for accelerated growth in the future."

exhibit complementarity.[9] Because of fundamental uncertainty over those complementarities, a 'big push' of investment required not just foreign aid to meet the minimum level of investment, but also some centralized government *planning* of where those investments should be allocated within the economic system (see Jomo and Reinert, 2005). It is in this context that new development economics emerged and pushed back on this capital-centered and planning-centered approach to economic development.

Throughout the 1980s, a resurgence of institutional economics and entrepreneurial theory, a range of historical failures of centralized planning, and a falling of the neoclassical consensus, led to the realization that investment and centralized planning weren't the standalone key to development (Boettke *et al.*, 2007; Coyne and Boettke, 2006). Many criticisms of the old approach to development focused on the notion that while a minimum quantity of investment may be a necessary condition for development, it is not a sufficient one (e.g. see Rosenstein-Rodan, 1961, p. 2). It became increasingly clear that the study of economic development needed to incorporate institutions and entrepreneurship.[10] Focusing solely on investment and capital accumulation ignores the reality that information is imperfect and economies are complex. Institutional analysis, governance and knowledge coordination were brought to the foreground of the economics of development and growth (e.g. Acemoglu and Robinson, 2010).

Persistent critiques of the role of government in economic development slowly severed the connection between central planning and development. Effective state-led investment requires both an omnipresent state (to overcome the complementarity and allocation of investment problem) and an omniscient state (to know those sectors or investments which are necessary for success). Indeed, Bauer (1976) argued that the central

---

[9] As Murphy *et al.* (1989, p. 1004) note: "spillovers give rise to the possibility that coordination of investments across sectors — which the government can promote—is essential for industrialization."

[10] New development economics emerged on a different set of analytical principles and intellectual traditions (Fine, 2006; Rodrik, 2008), following advances in entrepreneurial theory (e.g. Kirzner, 1978), new institutional economics (e.g. North, 1990; Williamson, 1975), and Austrian economics (e.g. Mises, 1949).

problem with foreign aid was a *knowledge problem*: how could a planner ever hold the necessary information for aid to be successful and effective? Economic development became focused on how distributed and dispersed contextual information can be coordinated through institutions and put to use to meet human needs (Glaeser *et al.*, 2004). Development, then, is a discovery problem — a job for the *entrepreneur* (e.g. see Kasper and Streit, 1998). As we will see in the following section, we can also approach this process of cryptosecession and the emergence of the cryptoeconomy as an economic development problem.

4. Cryptosecession as an economic development problem

The approaches and understandings of new development economics have clear parallels with the economic problem of developing the cryptoeconomy. In part, economic development is driven by entrepreneurial discovery of the complementarity of various combinations of heterogeneous capital (Leeson and Boettke, 2009; Manish and Powell, 2015). For blockchain, this entrepreneurial discovery of the institutions of the cryptoeconomy occurs under fundamental and radical uncertainty, compounded by the quick development of blockchain technology (see Lachmann, 1976; Shackle, 1992). Blockchain entrepreneurs must develop institutions that incentivize individuals to exit the existing state-based political-socioeconomic system. In this way the development of the cryptoeconomy is perhaps the most explicit form of protective-tier entrepreneurship yet, given that there are no existing protective institutions, and that those institutions must be publicly secure and verifiable, as well as trusted. As the brief example OpenBazaar revealed, cryptosecession requires the discovery of institutions necessary to enforce exchanges of information on distributed and secure public ledgers. The understanding aligns with Williamson's hierarchy of institutions and entrepreneurship, as outlined in Bylund and McCaffrey (2017): at deeper levels of institutional entrepreneurship — of shaping public affairs and institutions — entrepreneurs face a higher level of entrepreneurial structural uncertainty. Indeed, to cryptosecede to the cryptoeconomy requires its own knowledge structures, enforcement, and incentive mechanisms built in; the institutional environment cannot be taken as given, it must be created.

What's more, blockchain entrepreneurs not only have to discover the enforcement mechanisms of each blockchain application, but also the most basic institutional structures that connect those applications together. In this way cryptosecession requires the discovery of blockchain complementarities. Capital goods are heterogeneous and exhibit complementarities in the sense that they satisfy different plans for human actors. They also have "multiple specificity" in the sense that capital can be put to use in different plans (Lachmann, 1956). Blockchains not only exhibit complementarity both with existing technologies (e.g. the Internet of things) and institutions (e.g. firms and government), but also with other heterogeneous blockchains within the cryptoeconomy itself. The range of blockchains within the cryptoeconomy exhibits heterogeneity and multiple specificity because blockchain technology can be applied to multiple problems, and they can also be combined and used in multiple plans. The entrepreneurial development task, then, is to make judgements over how these bits of capital will be structured to form the cryptoeconomy. This is an entrepreneurial problem requiring discovery of how each potential application for blockchain will fulfil a need, yet also discover how the other blockchains within the cryptoeconomy will interact with the new institution. Blockchains also exhibit complementarity with other blockchains within the cryptoeconomy because the technology multiplier applies on inter-blockchain interactions (an investment in one application of blockchain will alter the return of a different blockchain). Multiple decentralized processes of blockchains in the cryptoeconomy can interact, which lowers the cost of additional blockchain applications.[11] For instance, the decentralized marketplace OpenBazaar is a complementary application to other cryptocurrencies. The development of platforms such as Ethereum and NEO enable the creation of interacting blockchain applications. The success of a remittance business not only relies on

---

[11] This may lead to a type of multi-level selection as the cryptoeconomy develops — between the decentralized institutions of the cryptoeconomy and state-based political-socioeconomic institutional systems (e.g. see Hamilton, 1964; Wilson *et al.*, 2013).

transferring value between different individuals, yet also requires exchanges in each jurisdiction.

There are two critical differences between the economic development of a territorial economy and the economic development of the non-territorial cryptoeconomy. First, the cryptoeconomy has few existing institutional systems, or even norms. While development economics tends to recognize that the existing indigenous institutions matter (see Coyne and Boettke, 2006) — including for instance skills, culture and conventions — this is unique for the blockchain ecosystem because there are no clear existing institutions. Indeed, cryptosecession could be understood as a private effort to 'shock' and overcome the path dependence of existing sovereign institutions (Boettke *et al.*, 2008).

Second, there is no central planning authority to guide the discovery of institutions. While, as discussed above, the economics of development shifted from a focus on capital and investment toward institutions and change, the question of precisely how those institutions change given issues such as stickiness and path dependence remains unanswered. Recent efforts include the use of private cities (e.g. Rajagopalan and Tabarrok, 2014) and charter cities (Fuller and Romer, 2012), both of which are attempts to push significant shifts in institutional mechanisms through developing special economic zones. However, such territorial special economic zones require state-based political change. Cryptosecession, on the other hand, requires no sovereign permission to change institutions — it is a privately driven entrepreneurial process — but can still be viewed through the same lens of changing existing institutions. In this way cryptosecession and the development of the cryptoeconomy can be viewed as a permissionless non-territorial special economic zone.

The entrepreneurial process of discovering the institutions of the cryptoeconomy does not occur within an institutional vacuum. Blockchain entrepreneurship requires non-price coordination of distributed information about market opportunities (Allen and Potts, 2016a, 2016b). Indeed:

> Economic development is an eternal process of innovation, in which economies make progress as they discover a better combination of activities, or a better system of coordination.

> The discovery of any new system, by its nature, cannot be designed or even anticipated; all we can do is to design a better search mechanism or discovery procedure.—Matsuyama (1997, p. 149)

This raises a question: If not through government planning, what is the search procedure underlying the development of the cryptoeconomy? When Easterly (2006) criticized the old development economics paradigm he shifted attention away from 'planners' toward 'searchers' in driving development. Searchers are necessary because of the inherent epistemological challenges in economic development. The blockchain cryptoeconomy does not have a central planner — it is governed by the consensus of the nodes maintaining the system through various blockchain protocols. Although attempts have been made to create quasi-state off-chain bodies, such as the Bitcoin Foundation, to coordinate some aspects and facilitate debates the cryptoeconomy itself has no centralized sovereign. This is despite the fact regular debates within the blockchain and bitcoin community concern the most effective mechanisms to maintain the robustness and efficiency of the cryptoeconomy (e.g. see van Wildum, 2016).

Because there is no centralized sovereign state within the cryptoeconomy, the entrepreneurial development process must be *privately governed* by 'searchers' rather than *publicly governed* by 'planners'. The implication of having no sovereign state — the cryptoeconomy is more accurately described as having sub-components of economies — is that the development of the cryptoeconomy must be a bottom-up 'searching' entrepreneurial process. Indeed, the new development economics literature has previously examined how the private governance of development may be optimal as compared to poorly performing states (Leeson and Williamson, 2009).

As we have seen here, entrepreneurial coordination within the blockchain ecosystem requires comingled discovery of protective-tier technologies. Blockchain entrepreneurs are not only concerned with their own market opportunity, but are also concerned with how other agents are acting on their opportunities. How are blockchain entrepreneurs solving this problem? Initial evidence suggests that blockchain entrepreneurs are collaborating and coordinating in private polycentric governance mechanisms to share information under collective action rules (Allen, 2017). These blockchain innovation commons — such as Bitcoin Embassies, hackerspaces and conferences — involve entrepreneurs pooling and coordinating non-price information to develop the cryptoeconomy.

In this way, the contemporary collaborative nature of the blockchain ecosystem can be viewed as a robust system of private institutional controls to develop the cryptoeconomy in the absence of a nation state. This suggests there are in fact *two* levels of protective-tier technologies developing the cryptoeconomy, which are not at first clear. The lower level is the collectively developed rules within innovation commons where blockchain entrepreneurs govern non-price information necessary to apply blockchain technology — where entrepreneurs seek to discover opportunities. This level of protective-tier technologies includes, for instance, the reputation mechanisms, signaling and nested hierarchies of rules that constitute Bitcoin Embassies, hackathons, online forums and mailing lists. Each of these involves protective-tier entrepreneurship in the sense that entrepreneurs must overcome the hazards of coordinating non-price entrepreneurial information. The higher level of protective-tier technologies are those that constitute the cryptoeconomy itself, which enable individuals exchanging within the cryptoeconomy to enforce and coordinate their economic activities outside of territorial nation states. Together, these governance mechanisms are entrepreneurial efforts to lower the costs of political-socioeconomic exit, thereby developing the new decentralized cryptoeconomy.

5. Conclusion

This chapter has made theoretical connections between development economics and the entrepreneurial problem of developing the blockchain cryptoeconomy. The process of cryptosecession to the cryptoeconomy is an entrepreneurial process of discovering complementary governance structures that may more effectively govern than existing hierarchical firms and governments. My central proposition is that while in developing territorial nations institutional discovery may be undertaken by centralized governments — that is, through central planning — the non-territorial cryptoeconomy must be developed privately by entrepreneurs. This provides a greater theoretical explanation for the range of collaborative innovation commons where blockchain entrepreneurs are undertaking institutional discovery. By drawing the connection between development economics and the entrepreneurial challenge of the cryptoeconomy, this chapter has provided a better understanding of the institutions necessary for the development of the cryptoeconomy, and provides direction for future fruitful research between development economics and the economics of blockchain.

References

Acemoglu, D and Robinson, J 2010, The role of institutions in growth and development, in D Brady & M Spence (eds), *Leadership and Growth*, The World Bank, Washington, DC, pp. 135-64.

Aldrich, HE and Fiol, CM 1994, Fools rush in? The institutional context of industry creation, *Academy of Management Review*, vol. 19, no. 4, pp. 645-70.

Allen, DWE and Berg, C 2017, Subjective Political Economy, *New Perspectives on Political Economy*, vol. 13, no. 1-2, pp. 19-40.

Allen, DWE 2017, The Private Governance of Entrepreneurship: An Institutional Approach to Entrepreneurial Discovery, Doctoral Thesis, RMIT University, Melbourne.

Allen, DWE, Berg, C, Lane, AM and Potts, J 2017, The economics of crypto-democracy, paper presented to *Linked Democracy: AI for Democratic Innovation, 26th International Joint Conference on Artificial Intelligence*, Melbourne, Australia, 19 August 2017.

Allen, DWE and Potts, J 2016a, How the Innovation Commons Contribute to Discovering and Developing New Technologies, *International Journal of the Commons*, vol. 10, no. 2, pp. 1035-1054.

———. 2016b, The origin of the entrepreneur and the role of the innovation commons, paper presented to *86th Annual Meeting of the Southern Economic Association Conference*, Washington, D.C., 19-21 November 2016.

Atzori, M 2015, *Blockchain Technology and Decentralized Governance: Is the State Still Necessary?*, Available at SSRN.

Bauer, PT 1976, *Dissent on Development*, Harvard University Press.

Baumol, WJ 1990, Entrepreneurship: Productive, Unproductive, and Destructive, *The Journal of Political Economy*, vol. 98, no. 5, pp. 893-921.

Berg, A and Berg, C 2017, Exit, Voice, and Forking, *RMIT University Working Paper.*

Berg, C 2017, Delegation and Unbundling in a Crypto-Democracy, *RMIT University Working Paper.*

Berg, C, Davidson, S and Potts, J 2018, Ledgers, *RMIT University Working Paper*, Available at SSRN 3157421.

Boettke, PJ and Coyne, CJ 2009, *Context matters: Institutions and entrepreneurship*, Now Publishers Inc, Hanover, MA.

Boettke, PJ, Coyne, CJ and Leeson, PT 2007, Saving government failure theory from itself: recasting political economy from an Austrian perspective, *Constitutional Political Economy*, vol. 18, no. 2, pp. 127-143.

———. 2008, Institutional stickiness and the new development economics, *American Journal of Economics and Sociology*, vol. 67, no. 2, pp. 331-358.

Buterin, V 2014, *Ethereum White Paper: A Next Generation Smart Contract & Decentralized Application Platform*, Ethereum.

Bylund, PL and McCaffrey, M 2017, A Theory of Entrepreneurship and Institutional Uncertainty, *Journal of Business Venturing*, vol. 32, no. 5, pp. 461-475.

Chenery, HB and Strout, AM 1966, Foreign assistance and economic development, *The American Economic Review*, pp. 679-733.

Coyne, CJ and Boettke, PJ 2006, The role of the economist in economic development, *Quarterly journal of Austrian economics*, vol. 9, no. 2, pp. 47-68.

Davidson, SR, De Filippi, P and Potts, J 2016, Economics of Blockchain, paper presented to Public Choice, US, March 2016.

Denzau, AT and North, DC 1994, Shared mental models: ideologies and institutions, *Kyklos*, vol. 47, no. 1, pp. 3-31.

Djankov, S, Glaeser, E, La Porta, R, Lopez-de-Silanes, F and Shleifer, A 2003, The new comparative economics, *Journal of comparative economics*, vol. 31, no. 4, pp. 595-619.

Domar, ED 1946, Capital expansion, rate of growth, and employment, *Econometrica, Journal of the Econometric Society*, vol. 14, no. 2, pp. 137-47.

Easterly, W 2006, *The white man's burden: why the West's efforts to aid the rest have done so much ill and so little good*, Penguin.

Engel, SN 2010, Development economics: from classical to critical analysis, in RA Denemark (ed.), *The International Studies Encyclopedia Volume II*, Blackwell Publishing, West Sussex, pp. 874-892.

Fine, B 2006, The New Development Economics, in KS Jomo & B Fine (eds), *The new development economics: post Washington Consensus neoliberal thinking*, Zed Books, London and New York, pp. 1-21.

Fuller, B and Romer, P 2012, *Success and the City: How Charter Cities Could Transform the Developing World*, Macdonald-Laurier Institute for Public Policy.

Glaeser, EL, La Porta, R, Lopez-de-Silanes, F and Shleifer, A 2004, Do institutions cause growth?, *Journal of economic Growth*, vol. 9, no. 3, pp. 271-303.

Hamilton, WD 1964, The genetical evolution of social behaviour, *Journal of Theoretical Biology*, vol. 7, no. 1, pp. 17-52.

Harrod, RF 1939, An Essay in Dynamic Theory, *The economic journal*, vol. 49, no. 193, pp. 14-33.

Harwick, C 2016, Cryptocurrency and the Problem of Intermediation, *The Independent Review*, vol. 20, no. 4, p. 569.

Hirschman, AO 1970, *Exit, voice, and loyalty: Responses to decline in firms, organizations, and states*, vol. 25, Harvard university press.

Jomo, KS and Reinert, ES 2005, *Origins of Development Economics: How Schools of Economic Thought Addressed Development*, Zed Books.

Juma, C 2016, *Innovation and Its Enemies: Why People Resist New Technologies*, Oxford University Press.

Kasper, W and Streit, ME 1998, *Institutional Economics–Cheltenham, Northampton: The Locke Institute*, Edward Elgar.

Kirzner, IM 1978, *Competition and Entrepreneurship*, University of Chicago Press.

Kuchař, P 2016, Entrepreneurship and institutional change, *Journal of Evolutionary Economics*, vol. 26, no. 2, pp. 349-79.

Lachmann, LM 1956, *Capital and its Structure*, Ludwig von Mises Institute.

———. 1976, From Mises to Shackle: an essay on Austrian economics and the kaleidic society, *Journal of economic literature*, vol. 14, no. 1, pp. 54-62.

Leca, B, Battilana, J and Boxenbaum, E 2008, Agency and institutions: A review of institutional entrepreneurship.

Leeson, PT and Boettke, PJ 2009, Two-tiered entrepreneurship and economic development, *International Review of Law and Economics*, vol. 29, no. 3, pp. 252-259.

Leeson, PT and Williamson, CR 2009, Anarchy and development: an application of the theory of second best, *The Law and Development Review*, vol. 2, no. 1, pp. 77-96.

MacDonald, TJ 2015, *Theory of Non-Territorial Internal Exit*, Available at SSRN 2661226.

MacDonald, TJ, Allen, DWE and Potts, J 2016, Blockchains and the Boundaries of Self-Organized Economies: Predictions for the Future of Banking, in P Tasca, T Aste, L Pelizzon & N Perony (eds), *Banking Beyond Banks and Money: A Guide to Banking Services in the Twenty-First Century*, Springer International Publishing, Cham, pp. 279-296.

Manish, GP and Powell, B 2015, From Subsistence to Advanced Material Production: Austrian Development Economics, in *The Oxford Handbook of Austrian Economics*, pp. 698-712.

Markey-Towler, B 2018, Anarchy, Blockchain and Utopia: A Theory of Political-Socioeconomic Systems Organised using Blockchain. *Journal of the British Blockchain Association*, vol. 1, no. 1.

Matsuyama, K 1997, Economic development as coordination problems, *The Role of Government in East Asian Economic Development*, pp. 134-160.

Mattila, J 2016, The Blockchain Phenomenon: The Disruptive Potential of Distributed Consensus Architectures, University of California, Berkley.

Mises, Ludwig von 1949, *Human action*, Ludwig von Mises Institute.

Mougayar, W 2016, *The Business Blockchain: Promise, Practice, and Application of the Next Internet Technology*, 1st edition, Wiley, New Jersey.

Murphy, KM, Shleifer, A and Vishny, RW 1989, Industrialization and the big push, *The Journal of Political Economy*, vol. 97, no. 5, pp. 1003-1026.

Nair, M and Sutter, D 2018, The Blockchain and Increasing Cooperative Efficacy, *The Independent Review*, vol. 22, no. 4, pp. 529-550.

Nakamoto, S 2008, Bitcoin: A peer-to-peer electronic cash system, *Consulted*, vol. 1, no. 2012, p. 28.

North, DC 1990, *Institutions, institutional change and economic performance*, Cambridge University Press.

Popper, N 2015, *Digital Gold: Bitcoin and the Inside Story of the Misfits and Millionaires Trying to Reinvent Money*, Harper.

Potts, J 2000, *The new evolutionary microeconomics*, Edward Elgar.

Rajagopalan, S and Tabarrok, AT 2014, Lessons from Gurgaon, India's Private City, George Mason University, 14-32.

Rodrik, D 2008, The New Development Economics: We Shall Experiment, But How Shall We Learn?, Harvard Kennedy School, RWP08-055.

Rosenstein-Rodan, PN 1943, Problems of industrialisation of eastern and south-eastern Europe, *The economic journal*, vol. 53, no. 210/211, pp. 202-211.

———. 1961, Notes on the theory of the 'big push', in *Economic Development for Latin America*, Springer, pp. 57-81.

Rostow, WW 1990, *The stages of economic growth: A non-communist manifesto*, Cambridge University Press.

Shackle, GLS 1992, *Epistemics and economics*, Transaction Publishers.

Swan, M 2015, *Blockchain: Blueprint for a New Economy*, O'Reilly Media, Inc.

Swan, M and De Filippi, P, 2017. Toward a Philosophy of Blockchain: A Symposium: Introduction. *Metaphilosophy*, vol. 48, no. 5, pp. 603-619.

Swan, TW 1956, Economic growth and capital accumulation, *Economic Record*, vol. 32, no. 2, pp. 334-361.

Williamson, OE 1975, Markets and hierarchies, *New York*, pp. 26-30.

Wilson, DS, Ostrom, E and Cox, ME 2013, Generalizing the core design principles for the efficacy of groups, *Journal of Economic Behavior & Organization*, vol. 90, Supplement, pp. S21-S32.

Wright, A and De Filippi, P 2015, *Decentralized blockchain technology and the rise of lex cryptographia*, Available at SSRN 2580664.

Chapter 11

Towards Crypto-friendly Public Policy

Chris Berg

Senior Research Fellow, Blockchain Innovation Hub, RMIT University, Melbourne, Australia

Sinclair Davidson

Professor of Institutional Economics and Fellow, Blockchain Innovation Hub, RMIT University, Melbourne, Australia

Jason Potts

Director, Blockchain Innovation Hub, RMIT University, Melbourne, Australia

Abstract

Distributed ledgers are institutional technologies that pose complex challenges regarding regulation and inter-jurisdictional competition. This chapter introduces 'crypto-friendly' public policy as a way to understand these challenges. Blockchains are relevant to public policy in at least three ways. First, they can be adopted by governments for the provision of public services. Second, many blockchain applications interact with existing regulatory frameworks and may provide new regulatory challenges. Third, they present the possibility of 'crypto-secession' as a form of privately provided public goods provision. The chapter applies an institutional theory of regulation to assess how blockchains effect relative institutional costs and guide public policy choices. Blockchain applications such as property rights and identity management are also considered. Finally the chapter considers the possibility of crypto-friendliness as a dimension for international regulatory competition.

1.1 Introduction

Distributed ledger technology emerged in 2009 as the protocol behind bitcoin, a cryptocurrency with origins in the 'cypherpunk' community that sought to use cryptography to secede from government control of money [Narayanan and Clark, 2017]. Bitcoin's pseudonymous inventor, Satoshi Nakamoto [2008] said Bitcoin would be "very attractive to the libertarian viewpoint" and many in the crypto-anarchist community saw, and still see, cryptocurrencies as a means to free citizens from the monetary depredations of governments [Popper, 2015]. But from these revolutionary secessionist origins, it has become apparent that not only are there many possible use cases of distributed ledger technology for government [Walport, 2016], but that government action through both regulation, legislation, and public investment might be a key factor in the adoption and development of this technological innovation. Governments can use blockchain technology to exploit the service efficiencies they may bring. But also, and perhaps counter-intuitively given their revolutionary origins, private blockchain applications are likely to need government cooperation to reduce policy uncertainty and facilitate the development of the blockchain economic system. We call this policy stance 'crypto-friendliness'.

Davidson *et al.* [2018] characterize blockchains as an institutional technology rather than a general purpose technology [see also Berg, 2017]. One consequence of this characteristic is that blockchain applications tend to interact with existing regulatory frameworks. A growing number of smaller countries or autonomous regions have moved to position themselves as broadly crypto-friendly. Great Britain [Walport, 2016] and Australia [Data61, 2017a, 2017b] have issued high-level science reports on the prospects of the technology. Other smaller countries (such as Estonia) and city-states (such as Singapore) have folded blockchain into a broad digital and e-government investment strategy. City-states such as Dubai, states or cantons such as Zug and Illinois, and self-governing dependencies such as Gibraltar and the Isle of Man have developed and enacted strategic initiatives to move many aspects of government services to the blockchain, or to create special crypto-economic zones. Singapore and Australia have directed their financial regulators to issue detailed guidance about the regulatory, legislative and tax treatment of crypto-assets, incentivizing the global location of crypto-investment within their jurisdictions. Political leaders in Japan and Russia have made multiple announcements broadly supportive of crypto-investment within their nation.

Most countries still retain a degree of benign neglect, largely due to the relatively small scale of cryptoeconomy presence, or lack of dedicated government interest or capability to deal with these issues (an example is New Zealand). Some regions, however, have adopted a relatively hard line in terms of regulatory compliance (e.g. New York State's bit-license) due to immediate pressures created by growing activity within their jurisdictions and the need to remove regulatory and legislative ambiguity. On the other hand, some countries have gone from neglect to outright hostility to the cryptoeconomy, such as China's ban of initial coin offerings and cryptocurrency exchanges. So, where some countries are already seen as more investment-friendly, other countries are equally emerging as difficult places for crypto-investment.

The global geography of the emerging cryptoeconomy is also significant, and traces to national government differences. Much of the development of the cryptoeconomy is also geographically concentrated, especially around Silicon Valley in California. But the distributed nature of the technology means that the relation between the geographic regions that develop and build the technology, and the regions and places that subsequently adopt it is not as strong as might be expected. Which is to say that the geography of invention is not the same as the geography of innovation.

The US, for instance, is highly successful in inventing blockchain technology. Yet it has been finding it hard to adopt because of regulatory complexity. Regulatory agility, particularly in dealing with local vested interests through deregulation or political buy-out, will therefore be a significant factor determining which nations are able to successfully adopt blockchain technology. This favors city-states and smaller countries

(Singapore, Zug, Estonia, Australia) because of lower coordination costs. However, pilot programs such as the Illinois Blockchain initiative demonstrate that where dedicated efforts are made, positive results can nevertheless be achieved.

The tax treatment of the cryptoeconomy is also a major unresolved issue. Most countries are still struggling with the tax classification of cryptoassets, and specifically whether to treat these as money (untaxed, but rather taxed as spending), debt or equity (in which case it would be treated as income or gains from a capital asset or investment vehicle). Berg *et al.* [2017a] argue that cryptoassets are what Williamson [1988] called 'dequity', and should be taxed as capital assets, not as money. The complexity is that blockchain technology is not just another productivity enhancing technology that can be taxed at the point of adoption. Blockchain adoption (at least at present with cryptocurrencies) is actively associated with tax avoidance or tax shifting owing to the pseudo-anonymous nature of transactions and the difficulty of establishing the correct jurisdiction for taxation.

Interestingly, unlike many new technologies, there are few active programs of government subsidy of blockchain technology development, such as R&D tax credits or industry or research policy. Some exceptions to this do exist. In the past year some governments have started to fund university-based research institutes on blockchain technology. The Australian government has also directed funds to a blockchain energy trading platform, PowerLedger, through its Smart Cities and Suburbs Program [Power Ledger, 2017]. Furthermore, to the extent that government funding of academic mathematicians and cryptographers produced the initial research papers that were subsequently developed into blockchain technology, then the early development of this technology was publically sponsored [see Narayanan and Clark, 2017], but not publically planned.

1.2 Economics of government support for blockchain technology

To what level *should* government support the development of blockchain technology, and to what extent should government seek to adopt and use blockchain technologies? From a public policy perspective, the simple economics of blockchain can be considered using social welfare analysis.

Most new technologies can be analyzed from the perspective of uncertainties and positive externalities in private investment and adoption resulting in market failure [Arrow, 1962]. There is usually therefore an *a priori* case to be made for public support of technology development (or the public creation of artificial monopolies through intellectual property). However, there does not appear to be notable market failure in early investment in blockchain technology, which is instead experiencing a surfeit of private investment flows. This is in considerable part a direct consequence of the design of token sales to incentivize early adoption through built in inflationary mechanisms, such as Bitcoin's periodic halving of mining rewards.

Instead, consider government spending and action to adopt blockchain technologies into its own services. Where blockchain technology is a substitute for an existing technology (such as the provision of money, or property registries), economic analysis of investment and use of substitute technologies should be evaluated by the marginal productivity benefits to the delivery of government services to citizens. This requires identifying specific use cases — such as identity and asset registries, licenses and certification, open government data, reporting and management of government contracts and public assets — and then estimating the marginal cost and benefits of government investment and adoption of this technology. For instance, a Bank of England staff working paper estimates a 3 percent gain in GDP from the issuing of a government crypto-currency owing to transaction and tax efficiencies [Barrdear and Kumhof, 2016].

This method should enable calculation of optimal public investment in blockchain technology by the state in order to maximize social welfare, just as with the calculation of the economic benefits of public adoption of any new technology (such as renewable energy) or public infrastructure (such a communications network).

In these calculations, a key parameter is the utility gain to consumers (citizens), which the planner seeks to account for in their (social choice) objective function. A similar argument is made in respect of efficient (Pigovian) regulation of the cryptoeconomy, such that the costs of regulation (in monitoring compliance and enforcement) and the restricted space of permissible economic activities is more than compensated for by the public benefit that accrues through the effects of the regulation in preventing social bads (such as investment fraud). This same argument also holds for effective tax treatment of cryptoassets, whether the objective is (Ramsey) tax maximization, or (Pigovian) minimization of negative externalities.

There are also public goods problems owing to the need for (especially) digital communications and network infrastructure upon which a cryptoeconomy operates, and also public investment in creating open access data regimes and registries that can be harnessed and used by cryptoeconomy businesses and DApps (decentralized applications) as inputs into smart contracts and DAOs (decentralized autonomous organizations). As mentioned above, countries have made different levels of public investment in this sort of digital communications and data infrastructure.

Similarly, countries have made different public investments in establishing high quality legal institutions (regulators, courts, bureaucracies, democratic systems, etc.) resulting in varying degrees of predictability, efficiency, transparency, accountability, corruptibility and efficacy. These make for systematically different transactions costs in using government institutions. In consequence, there will also be different complementary gains to investment in new institutional technology, or benefits of leap-frogging to blockchain technology. These benefits accrue for internal trade and investment within a region or nation, but also to gains from international trade with nations that have made corresponding investments.

In all such contexts, the economics of blockchain public policy is considered from the social choice perspective of the rational planner seeking to maximize social welfare. To the extent that blockchain technology benefits (lower transactions costs, information costs and coordination costs for society, driving productivity gains in delivering existing services, and the prospect of new services) are greater than adoption costs (public investment), then we expect to observe widespread public investment and adoption.

Why might some countries lag behind in social welfare maximizing investment and adoption? Explanations could be based on constraints, such as bounded rationality or information constraints (governments may not know about the benefits, or misunderstand them), or financial constraints (governments might not be able to afford these investments or effectively be able to raise the capital to make these investments).

An interesting further constraint is trust in government itself. Efficiency gains to a citizenry from moving government registries (identity, property titling, tax, voting, central bank coin) to blockchains require a 'trust-fall' in which only high-trust institutions will be able to make the transition to trustlessness. For example, a country such as Haiti might benefit most from moving its property register on to a secure blockchain, but Haiti may lack the high-trust institutions necessary to ensure that the information being put on the blockchain is accurate. By contrast, Sweden has the high-trust institutions necessary for such an approach, but the benefits from doing so are correspondingly smaller. Sweden has been developing a blockchain land registry since 2016 [see Lantmäteriet, Telia Company, ChromaWay and Kairos Future, 2016].

A further factor constraining government adoption of blockchain technology is its own capabilities to implement cryptoeconomy infrastructure and to create effective regulatory governance. This will be a function of the quality and experience of bureaucrats in the civil service, or the extent to which governments can access outside skills and capabilities through contracting.

However, a further possibility is that governments that are slow to adopt, or are outright hostile to adoption of this new technology do so not out of ignorance or constraint, but are actively and deliberately maximizing their own objective function, not that of their citizens (as in social choice theory). This is the rational actor model of government, or public choice theory.

1.3 The economics of government control of blockchains

In the political economy model of government, governments and citizens have distinct objectives that they seek to maximize. Citizens trade votes for services, and governments seek to create benefits for themselves subject to the budget constraint of getting elected. What citizens want and what governments want will be in conflict, resulting in political exchange. The study of this exchange using economic analysis is called public choice theory, and this is a useful framework through which to analyze the interaction between the citizen benefits of blockchain adoption versus the government benefits (and costs) of that same adoption.

A good example is identity [Berg *et al.*, 2017b, 2018]. Governments want (or benefit from) a single point of identity (centralized). This is because a single identity is useful for identification of citizens for the claims governments make on them, such as for taxation or conscription [Scott, 1998]. Every citizen must have one and only one identity from the perspective of the government's objectives. These centralized identity registrations are co-opted for commercial identity (e.g. to open a bank account, or to rent a car). But from the citizen perspective this is inefficient, because identity is owned and managed by the state (the citizen has no control over their identity, and cannot choose how to permission and share this data), and this creates problems of trust and privacy (for example in health and criminal records). A decentralized identity would be more efficient, facilitating variety of types of identity for specialized uses, and enabling user control. But governments don't want that; hence the trade-offs and conflict.

In a series of papers Andrei Shleifer (and various co-authors) has developed an institutional theory of regulation (Shleifer [2005] refers to this as the 'enforcement theory' of regulation) that examines four broad governance strategies that 'society' can pursue in order to achieve some objective relative to the trade-offs associated with those strategies. These strategies are; 'market discipline', 'private litigation', 'public enforcement through regulation', and 'state ownership'. The societal trade-offs as being the costs of private disorder and the costs of government dictatorship. Disorder relates to the ability of private individuals to inflict harm on others, while dictatorship relates to the ability of government and its bureaucrats to inflict harm on others. The framework has been applied to productivity and red tape [Berg, 2018; Davidson, 2013], the environment [Davidson, 2014], media regulation [Berg and Davidson,

2015], freedom of speech [Berg and Davidson, 2016], innovation [Davidson and Potts, 2015, 2016], education [Lane, 2017], democracy [Allen *et al.*, 2017], and tobacco control [Davidson, 2016]. Allen and Berg [2017] emphasize that the dictatorship and disorder costs are subjective.

In this framework, market discipline should be considered as the regulatory default. Of course, that is not always possible and at this point the control strategy becomes private litigation. The state begins to play a role as the rules of contract and tort law are administered by courts of law staffed by bureaucrats and judges. Courts of law exist, at this level, to enforce private agreements and to adjudicate disputes between private parties.

Chicago school economists have argued that the combination of market discipline and courts of law should suffice for any regulatory framework. Shleifer [2005], however, has argued that courts cannot always resolve disputes cheaply, predictably, or impartially. This is especially the case when the parties to the dispute have vastly different resources that they can deploy to a legal dispute.

Regulation occurs when the state not only provides a dispute resolution mechanism but also writes the rules that govern economic behavior and transactions. There is substantial variation in how government can enforce its regulations. It can, for example, allow bureaucrats to engage in a regime of inspection and verification with fines being issued for non-compliance. Alternatively, the state can provide a set of rules that are privately litigated, or publicly litigated. Public litigation can consist of either civil or criminal charges. Similarly the regulatory agency can initiate litigation itself for breeches of the regulations, or act once a complaint has been received. This notion has been extensively debated in the context of financial regulation.

Finally, state ownership appears to be an efficient response to those situations where the disorder costs are likely to be very high. Shleifer gives the examples of prisons, police force, and military where this is likely to be the case. The costs of disorder resulting from private ownership here are potentially so large that government needs to maintain control over these institutions. While Shleifer does not explicitly include prohibition in this category, it is clear that prohibition should be included at this stage of the analysis as being equivalent to state ownership.

Given the recent emergence of blockchain technology and its experimental nature it is very likely that most crypto-entrepreneurs are of the opinion that their activities are not subject to any regulation. This view is not entirely correct. To the extent that they enter into market exchange (either via the labor market or product markets) they are regulated by existing regulations. The question of interest is whether they should be subject to unique regulations.

That question is best answered by determining whether blockchains and cryptocurrencies are the source of any unique market failure. Economists usually describe market failure as originating from one of three sources: asymmetric information; externality; and market power. The existence of any one of those three factors will lead to a decline in the number of transactions and unrealized gains from trade will persist in the economy. At this point (traditional) economists usually prescribe some or other government intervention to overcome market failure. By contrast, the field of crypto-economics has rapidly evolved and employs incentives, mechanism design, and technology to overcome market failure [Buterin, 2017; Stark, 2017]. Ironically the field of crypto-economics has few economists working within it — most practitioners are computer scientists.

The observation, however, that market failure is not apparent as some might perceive does not distract from the fact that understanding the basics of blockchains and cryptocurrency is a non-trivial task. Consumers do not need to understand the technical details of a technology to enjoy the benefits of that technology. How many people understand how the internal combustion engine works, or how electricity is generated and transmitted? The fact that there are high initial costs to understanding blockchain technology does not mean that it is itself a source of asymmetric information. Indeed blockchains are designed to reduce or overcome asymmetric information and market power problems [Berg *et al.*, 2017c].

Similarly, the disruption to existing industry that a blockchain is likely to achieve (and various platform economy applications have already achieved) is not a source of externality. Externality is best understood as being nuisance — a cost imposed on a third-party to a market transaction. The impact of a blockchain on existing business is not nuisance, it is direct competition. In a market economy a new and superior good or service should displace older and inferior goods and services. Of course, it is not always possible to predict in advance what a 'new' and 'superior' product might be; that depends upon the margins that consumers prefer.

In essence then, our argument is that the blockchain economy is little different from the existing economy in regulatory terms — it imposes no new, unique or additional disorder costs upon the economy. In that respect, it should not be subject to new, unique or additional regulations. It should be regulated *mutatis mutandis* as are existing industries. In the first instance the courts are best placed to enforce those regulations.

The public choice insight is that what citizens want (or would benefit from, and be willing to pay for) is not identical with what governments want. We would therefore expect to observe departures in the levels of public investment and public policy from the social welfare maximum as a function of government self-interest. This helps us to understand why governments might nevertheless be reticent to adopt or support new technologies that their own citizens would value and benefit from.

1.4 International strategy and crypto-secession

Once we recognize that governments have their own interests in promoting or constraining the cryptoeconomy through public investment and public policy, and allowing that cryptoassets, cryptomarkets, and the productive resources involved are in some degree globally mobile, it follows that there will be a strategic (international) dimension to each governments' choices. What a government chooses needs not only to be rationally optimal from the perspective of its own citizens, but also a *best response* to the expected moves of other governments. Further complicating this game is the fact that other players (nations) differ in size, level of economic development, and quality of institutions.

Governments, or at least parts of government such as Treasury, will often have some interest in constraining or controlling the growth of the cryptoeconomy, not least because it makes some of its functions (such as taxation) harder. However, the expected response of citizens (including cryptoeconomy companies) depends upon the moves of other countries, especially those that they might credibly seek to exit. Because the most effective public policy settings are not *ex ante* obvious, there are learning costs involved and governments might rationally decide to delay decision making (as a real option strategy) in order to learn from first-movers who can then be expected to incur costly mistakes in the experimental process of policy settings. (From a global social welfare perspective, it is best that the early experimenter countries are those that are representative, but smaller, minimizing the opportunity costs of experiments but maximizing the potential to import lessons.) We would thus predict that larger countries will be much more cautious in adopting crypto-economic poles that are significantly divergent from other countries that are competitors for crypto-investment or mobile assets.

An alternative to unilateral strategy (Tiebout competition) is bilateral or club-like coalitions of strategic investment and public policy harmonization (as in tax and trade treaties, see Potts [2017]). This would create crypto-economic unions in which internal distributional consequences could be dealt with through club-level Coasian bargaining and transfers.

When governments impose high dictator costs of centralized control, the exit option at some margin becomes valuable. Blockchain technology facilitates the movement of many aspects of an economy (identity, contract, money and payments, organization, data, etc.) to a decentralized protocol, in part evading centralized control. This makes possible a phenomenon that MacDonald [2016] calls *nonterritorial secession*, or *crypto-secession*. With a federal model of local public goods, people move to jurisdictions that meet their needs, and governments competitively provide these at different offering and price points [Tiebout 1958]. If an individual prefers a different bundle of public goods in a federal system, they exit. If a group of individuals collectively prefers a different bundle of pubic goods, they secede. But to secede, they must go somewhere else, which also imposes costs [Berg and Berg 2017]. Non-territorial secession is choosing a different bundle of public goods, but without leaving the territory, just opting out of all or part of the government bundle. Crypto-secession is when the new bundle of local public goods is organized, coordinated and delivered through blockchain technology.

An example of such emergent private governance of local public goods might occur at a local or regional level where a group of citizens create a pooling mechanism of social insurance, energy grid, or asset titling management through smart contracts, DApps and DAOs. This is more likely at the local, regional or city level than that of a nation state because of set up costs and self-selection. We would therefore predict that exit adoption of blockchain technology for governance will be a bottom-up phenomenon beginning with small groups.

1.5 Blockchains and property rights

Blockchain technology may also disrupt the relation between government and property rights. Property rights matter because they reduce uncertainty and entropy in a transactional system. Better property rights improve transactional efficiency and are value-creating institutions.

A fundamental question in the economics of law is whether property rights originate from the state and are then transacted in markets, or whether property rights arise from markets and from economic activity, and is then efficiently enforced by the state? While the former view, called legal centrism, is the most widely held among law and government scholars, public choice and market institutional economists tend to argue for the latter [Alchian and Demsetz, 1972, Cooter, 1993]. Nevertheless, economists do know that property rights interact strongly with governance [Hart and Moore, 1990]. Crypto-currencies and crypto-assets provide an interesting test of these competing views because it is not obvious what role the state plays in either creating or enforcing the property right claims over these assets.

One argument is that crypto-currencies and crypto-assets have emerged entirely outside state jurisdiction and instead occupy a new software-enforced constitutional governance realm. In this strong form view, these are native crypto-property rights from which there is a risk of government predation. An alternative argument is superficially similar, but allows that this parallel crypto-property rights regime has emerged in-the-shadow-of state law and enforcement and remains private law only to the point of irreconcilable dispute, and which point it reverts back to government enforcement and sanctions. It is unclear where we are at this moment in respect of whether crypto-property breaks the covenant with the state (as a kind of 'stationary bandit' [Olson, 1993] model of crypto-property), or whether it is only possible because of the shadow of state law and enforcement power.

This distinction about the origins of property rights matters because while governments can provide benefits in furnishing public goods and supporting property rights institutions, governments also impose costs through the centralization of power and the implications this has for the centralization of other functions such as money, record keeping and registries. Blockchains reduce opportunism and therefore economize on disorder costs.

1.6 Creative destruction

Governments also have a role in addressing the effects of creative destruction, or the economic disruption to jobs, firms, industries and ways of doing things in consequence of new technologies. A key way that governments can facilitate the adoption of a new technology is to support or compensate those negatively affected by the technology and to facilitate their adaptation to a new technological regime by complementary investment (e.g. education and retraining) and redistributing resources, for instance brokering compensation and re-structuring displaced resources. Without such government action, including the work of private coalitions such as industry associations, those who expect to be harmed by the adoption of a new technology may form coalitions to seek political redress, seeking to use legislative means to block or substantially raise the private costs of developing the new technology [Juma, 2016].

Blockchain technologies face substantial hurdles from incumbents and vested interests with powerful economic incentives to invest in political means (lobbying) to slow or outright ban uses of the technology. Governments may find themselves on both sides of creative destruction, seeking to promote the development and adoption of this new technology for social welfare maximizing reasons, while at the same time being captured by protection seeking vested interests.

1.7 Conclusion

Governments have a complex relationship to blockchains. Governments find themselves in both acting in support of blockchain technology — both as potential major users of blockchains for government services, and to encourage private sector crypto-investment — and acting opposed — much blockchain use cases will be highly disruptive to its existing regulatory and taxation frameworks. Blockchains are also a very new technology with substantial uncertainty associated with its future uses, adoption levels, and properties. In consequence, governments around the world have adopted a range of positions, ranging from ignorance to studied indifference to actively engaged, of which those engaged reactions range between outright hostility to active and enthusiastic support.

Yet it seems likely that blockchain technology will have a significant effect on public policy as the technology is adopted for multiple uses in government, and as government makes significant investments in infrastructure, regulation and legislation. Government adoption of blockchain technology should also be considered beyond the aggregate benefit to citizens, and also considered from the strategic perspective of governments themselves, for whom the civilian adoption of blockchain technology imposes costs (as well as benefits). There are strategic conflicts between governments and citizens that will affect the geography, speed and form of blockchain public policy.

In this chapter we have explored some dimensions of crypto-friendly public policy. Determining crypto-friendliness involves a consideration of the levels of policy uncertainty surrounding blockchain regulation and taxation, the willingness of governments to facilitate blockchain adoption and integration into existing regulatory and tax frameworks, the use of blockchains for government service delivery (such as property rights registers or identity management) and the rhetorical support of governments for blockchain industries. We expect a great deal of competition among governments for crypto-investment, the result of which will be partly determined by national and subnational crypto-friendly policy stances. Forward-thinking policymakers should to consider how crypto-friendly their jurisdictions are and act accordingly.

References

Alchian, A., Demsetz, H. (1972) Production, information costs, and economic organization, *American Economic Review*, 62(5): 777-95.

Allen, D. W. E., Berg, C., Lane, A. M. L., Potts, J. (2017) The economics of crypto-democracy. Presented at Linked Democracy: AI for Democratic Innovation, *26th International Joint Conference on Artificial Intelligence*, 19 August 2017. Available at https://ssrn.com/abstract=2973050.

Allen, D. W. E., Berg, C. (2017) Subjective political economy, *New Perspectives on Political Economy*, 13(1-2): 19-40.

Arrow, K. (1962) Economic welfare and the allocation of resources for invention. In *The Rate and Direction of Inventive Activity*, R. R. Nelson (Ed.). Princeton: Princeton University Press. pp. 609-626.

Barrdear, J., Kumhof, M. (2016) The macroeconomics of central bank issued digital currencies, Bank of England Working Paper No. 605, available at https://www.bankofengland.co.uk/working-paper/2016/the-macroeconomics-of-central-bank-issued-digital-currencies.

Berg, C. (2017a) An Institutional Theory of Freedom of Speech, available at https://ssrn.com/abstract=2910563.

Berg, C. (2017b) What Diplomacy in the Ancient Near East Can Tell Us About Blockchain Technology, Ledger 2.

Berg, C. (2018) Red Regulation and Red Tape in a Small Open Economy: An Australian Overview, in D.W.E. Allen and C. Berg (Eds.). Australia's Red Tape Crisis, Connor Court Publishing, Brisbane.

Berg, A., Berg, C. (2017) Exit, Voice and Forking, available at https://ssrn.com/abstract=3081291.

Berg, C., Davidson, S. (2015) Media Regulation: A Critique of Finkelstein and Tiffen, available at SSRN 2669271.

Berg, C., Davison, S., Potts, J. (2017a) What is a token? presented at Cryptoeconomics and Security Conference, Blockchain @ Berkeley, Berkeley, 2 October 2017.

Berg, C., Davison, S., Potts, J. (2017b) The Institutional Economics of Identity, available at https://ssrn.com/abstract=3072823.

Berg, C., Davison, S., Potts, J. (2017c) Blockchains Industrialise Trust, available at https://ssrn.com/abstract=3074070.

Berg, A., Berg, C., Davidson, S., Potts, J. (2018) Identity as an Input to Exchange, available at https://ssrn.com/abstract=3171960.

Buterin, V. (2017) Introduction to Cryptoeconomics, presented at EDCON 2017, Paris, France, 17 February, available at https://www.youtube.com/watch?v=pKqdjaH1dRo.

Catalini, C., Gans, J. (2017) Some simple economics of the blockchain. No. w22952. National Bureau of Economic Research.

Cooter, R. (1993) Against legal centrism, *California Law Review*, 81(1): 417-429.

Data61 (2017a) Distributed Ledgers: Scenarios for the Australian economy over the coming decades.

Data61 (2017b) Risks and opportunities for systems using blockchain and smart contracts.

Davidson, S. R. (2016) Submission to Parliamentary Joint Committee on Law Enforcement Inquiry into Illicit Tobacco.

Davidson, S., de Filippi, P., Potts, J. (2018) Blockchains and the Economics institutions of capitalism, *Journal of Institutional Economics* 14(4): 639-658.

Davidson, S. R. (2013) Productivity enhancing regulatory reform. Australia Adjusting: Optimising national prosperity 66.

Davidson, S. R. (2014) Environmental protest: an economics of regulation approach, *Australian Environment Review* 29: 283-286.

Davidson, S. R., Potts, J. (2015) Social Costs and the Institutions of Innovation Policy, available at https://ssrn.com/abstract=2565574.

Davidson, S. R., Potts, J. (2016) A New Institutional Approach to Innovation Policy, *The Australian Economic Review Policy Forum: Research and Innovation*, 49(2): 200-207.

Djankov, S., Glaeser, E., LaPorta, R., Lopez-de-Silanes, F., Shleifer, A. (2003) The new comparative economics, *Journal of Comparative Economics* 31(4): 595-619.

Hart, O., Moore, J. (1990) Property rights and the nature of the firm, *Journal of Political Economy* 98: 1119-58.

Lane, A. M. L. (2017) Institutions of Public Education, available at https://ssrn.com/abstract=2985318.

Lantmäteriet, Telia Company, ChromaWay and Kairos Future (2016) The Land Registry in the Blockchain, available at http://ica-it.org/pdf/Blockchain_Landregistry_Report.pdf.

MacDonald, T. (2016) Theory of Non-Territorial Internal Exit, available at https://ssrn.com/abstract=2661226.

Nakamoto, S. (2008) re: Bitcoin P2P e-cash paper, Fri Nov 14, 13:55:35 EST, available at http://www.metzdowd.com/pipermail/cryptography/2008-November/014853.html.

Narayanan, A., Clark, J. (2017) Bitcoin's academic pedigree. ACMQueue, 15(4): 1-30.

Olson, M. (1993) Dictatorship, democracy and development, *American Political Science Review* 87(3): 567-76.

Potts, J. (2016) Innovation policy in a global economy, *Journal of Entrepreneurship and Public Policy* 5(3): 308-324.

Power Ledger (2017) Australian Government Awards Grant to $8 Million Project In The City Of Fremantle Using The Power Ledger Platform, Medium, available at https://medium.com/power-ledger/australian-government-awards-grant-to-8-million-project-in-the-city-of-fremantle-using-the-power-2dbadfad50ae.

Scott, J. (1998) Seeing Like a State. Yale University Press.

Shleifer, A. (2005) Understanding Regulation, *European Financial Management*, 11(4): 439-451.

Stark, J. (2017) Making Sense of Cryptoeconomics, Coindesk, 19 August.

Tiebout, C. (1958) A pure theory of local public goods, *Journal of Political Economy* 64(5): 416-424.

Walport, M. (2016) Distributed Ledger Technology: Beyond Blockchain, UK Government Office for Science.

Williamson, O. (1988) Corporate finance and corporate governance, *Journal of Finance*, 43(3): 567-591.

Part 6

Income Inequality and Economic Inclusion

Chapter 12

The Implications of Blockchain for Income Inequality

Mikayla Novak

Postdoctoral Research Fellow, Blockchain Innovation Hub, RMIT University, Melbourne, Australia

mikayla.novak@rmit.edu.au

Abstract

This chapter discusses the implications of blockchain technology for income inequality. Although inequality is identified as a complex and emergent (rather than simple and static) phenomenon, we nonetheless are able to identify channels through which blockchains are likely to affect the distribution of income. Any erosion of economic positions held by third-party intermediaries, charged with maintaining the integrity of conventional ledgers, is likely to reduce inequality. On the other hand job-creation opportunities which emphasize the need for specialist technical skills in the blockchain-enabled economy may increase inequality. The net effect of these two forces alone is ambiguous. There is the alternative possibility that the inequality-reduction potential of blockchain activity could be mitigated by the appropriation of distributed ledger technology by incumbents. To help prevent the possibility of income inequality being reproduced through the blockchain, an open and permissionless environment for blockchain participation should be maintained to the greatest extent possible.

1.1 Introduction

The advent of information and communications technologies, such as the Internet and mobile phones, has had a profound influence upon the lives of most individuals around the world. Arguably the most beneficial effect of these technologies is the enhanced ability for people to communicate with each other, to discover and implement economic, social and political projects, on a global basis. The speed with which individuals, and groups of individuals, can engage one another online — via personal computers or smartphones — helps ease transactions costs and other barriers against social coordination. In very meaningful senses, information and communications technologies have helped draw us ever closer.

Blockchain is seen as the next iteration of technological advancement that is expected to substantially reduce costs of doing business, solicit more effective coordination, and perhaps even to reshape institutional structures [Davidson *et al.*, 2018]. In essence, the blockchain is a ledger protocol arrangement enabling data to be stored and appended in a distributed manner. It is anticipated that the adoption of blockchain technology would unleash an "Internet of value" transcending the existing role of the Internet to propagate information.

Stewardship over blockchain-embedded data in a permissionless public ledger context is not vested in hierarchical, centralized organizational structures — such as firms and governments — that are easily identifiable as targets for data hacking, theft, fraud and misrepresentation. Embracing insights from cryptography, computer science and economics, blockchain technology enables data such as financial transactions, identity records, property ownership titles and other information to become robustly secure in the face of potential threats to data integrity. The heterogeneous participants engaging with the blockchain maintain identical copies of the ledger, providing for a distributed protocol of data maintenance. Furthermore, participants are incentivized to spend time, money and resources to check and approve the addition of data to the blockchain.

An assessment of the consequences of information and communication technologies (ICTs), now accompanied by the blockchain, should not be solely informed by consideration of their economic, social and political benefits. It is necessary to appraise the alternative view that online technologies have brought with them some downsides, or at least reflect upon the idea that benefits have not been evenly shared. In this context research focuses upon varied aspects of the "digital divide," the ability of the state to utilize online technology to repress citizens, and the emergence of data as an asset class facilitating the emergence of market concentration.

In this chapter we focus on the potential impact of blockchain upon income inequality, and accordingly structure the chapter in the following way. First, we undertake a brief outline of the nature and effects of income inequality with specific reference to online technologies. This is followed by an examination of the potential specific impacts of blockchain upon inequality. In this context, we broadly align the inequality implications of blockchain with the broader cryptoeconomic discussion which distinguishes blockchain as either a general purpose technology or an institutional technology. Given the longstanding interest of policymakers in redressing economic inequality (reflected in fiscal and regulatory policies enacted in the name of redistribution) we then discuss the inequality implications of blockchain from a public policy perspective. This discussion is followed by brief concluding remarks.

1.2 Income Inequality and Its Technological Dimensions

Although distributional issues have represented a mainstay of public discourses, the 2007-08 "global financial crisis" (GFC) and the ensuing period of relatively low economic growth in developed countries have revived discussions about the appropriateness of the observed state of income inequality. Income inequality, in short, refers to the extent to which income is distributed non-uniformly amongst those individuals who receive it.

We consider income inequality as something of a "kaleidic" phenomenon. In other words, inequality is the by-product of interactions between individuals and groups spanning economic, social and political activities [Novak, 2018]. Specifically, commingling between and amongst people, in the respective pursuits of various gains and advantages, lead to *emergent* and *complex* structures of *network* connections which underpin the differentiated income flows. Given the variety of institutional technologies, operational procedures and technical standards in existence, and the diversity of human preferences, tastes and capabilities, our claim is that there is no *a priori* expectation that income flows will be uniform across the population.

The provision of the Internet on home and office computers, mobile phone devices and other ICTs have fast become a prevalent means through which relationships are being forged in civil society. With regard to the Internet alone, it has been estimated that about 3.6 billion people are using the Internet globally [ITU, 2018]. Although the rate of Internet penetration in developing countries is still roughly half that found in developed countries, there is evidence of use-convergence; the annual growth rate in Internet use in developing countries since 2009 (about 11.9 percent) has outstripped that found in developed countries (about 3.1 percent). One may identify similar trends with respect to mobile phone adoption.

It is unquestionable that ICTs provide significant benefits for users, and that many of those benefits derived from use are conducive to suppressing income inequality. To some extent, people use ICTs to uncover information enabling them to entrepreneurially pursue new sources of value that enhance their own economic positions, and that of others. There are many anecdotal instances of individuals, families and communities, even in relatively difficult circumstances, being able to access credit online, to receive and send remittances virtually, and to engage in commercial activities electronically. The Internet and mobile phones equip some with the capacity to sidestep hierarchies — which tend to conceal information or restrict access to opportunity — and to collaborate in ways that promote economic mobility. These effects, all else being equal, would tend to compress the skewness in income distribution.

Inasmuch as ICTs are an emancipator of the impoverished or downtrodden, it must also be recognized that ICT, in reshaping factor and product markets on a global scale, is also viewed as a major underlying factor aggravating inequality. At one end of the spectrum, ICTs, and automation more generally, have displaced certain workers with fewer skills and lesser work experiences. At the other, individuals with computer programming skills and other forms of ICT expertise earn significant wage premiums. Occupation-specific concentrations of ICT workers in places such as Silicon Valley have also contributed to what is identified in the literature as the "superstar effect," wherein a relatively small cohort of ICT specialists enjoy substantial relative income growth [Rosen, 1981; Brynjolfsson *et al.*, 2014; Zumbrun, 2017]. More generally, the advent of skills-biased technological change has been identified as an important contributor to income inequality.

The inequality-inducing effects of ICTs are potentially more far-reaching than labor market considerations alone. Countless individuals frequently use Internet search engines such as Google, and participate in social media platforms such as Facebook and Twitter. As a consequence of their online participation, people effectively provide personal data to those companies maintaining the online services, for subsequent marketing and other lucrative purposes. Given the emergence of data as a *bona fide* asset class, this development has been seen by some as problematic: ""digital conglomerates" such as Amazon, Google, Apple, and Facebook — all Internet start-ups at one time — are capturing the treasure troves of data that citizens and institutions generate often in private data silos rather than on the Web" [Tapscott and Tapscott, 2016, p. 13]. Governments also apply ICTs for surveillance purposes, consequently increasing the relative power held by political actors.

At this juncture it seems appropriate to posit the preceding discussion with a broader frame of economic theorizing. It is well known that innovative processes have the potential to create market concentrations, generating inequality favoring those perpetuating the innovations. Such processes reflect generic, disequilibriating phases of micro-level origination and meso-level adoption which happen to pervade any robustly functional economic order, with an extensive degree of interaction amongst participants [Dopfer and Potts, 2008]. The (micro-) entrepreneur originates an economically novel idea which, then, becomes adopted by some (meso-) population of users.

There is a school of thought that innovation can be potentially monopolizing, but only on a temporary basis. Even if the innovation pervades the relevant meso-population, the open and competitive character of the economic process is such that the possibility of monopoly-retention is incessantly threatened by the exercise of entrepreneurial talents propounding new and improved technologies into the future. Flexible education and training systems, and cultural norms which encourage adaptiveness and flexibility in the face of innovation, are more likely to enable people affected by technological unemployment to re-engage within a more innovative economy [Swan, 2017]. Therefore, on each count we observe the evolutionary turnover of income and wealth.

It should also be recognized that Schumpeterian creative destruction of incumbent, high income-generating positions is not the only possibility. Heterogeneous participants within organizational hierarchies, and concentrated network hubs more broadly, congregate about a shared interest in perpetuating their privileged positions. Privilege-seeking can exude a surprisingly robust character, coming in the form of responses which effectively absorb or co-opt innovation within existing operations. In the face of innovative activity potentially threatening the institutionalized structures that have solidified, individuals and groups may also seek to lobby for a politically-induced slowdown of meso-level innovative adoption. Which tendency prevails — openness or closedness — in reaction to technological development will also have an important bearing upon the kind and extent of inequality impacts that follow.

1.3 Potential Impacts of Blockchain Inequality upon Income Inequality

The blockchain represents a new characterization of the age-old technological artefact of the ledger. Introduced in 2009 by that person, or persons, known as "Satoshi Nakamoto," the uniqueness of blockchain is that it ingeniously combines principles from cryptography, computer science and economics to provide a distributed-network, append-only public ledger that also relies upon participant "consensus mechanisms" to verify and record the data appearing on the blockchain. Given the elicitation of incentives for cooperation on the part of blockchain participants to monitor the evolution of the blockchain, and the difficulty of organizing a majority of diverse, decentralized participants to organize fraudulent conduct through the blockchain, it can be said "the distributed ledger of the blockchain as fundamentally creating a new way to generate trust" [Nair and Sutter, 2018, p. 532].

It is reasonable to suggest the blockchain firmly remains in a nascent stage of its development. That said, there have been numerous suggestions regarding how blockchains could be applied to reduce transaction costs and improve economic coordination, enhance the effectiveness of mutual assistance orchestrated by social enterprises and other civic associations, and to improve the quality of public governance [Swan, 2015; Tapscott and Tapscott, 2016; Allen *et al.*, 2017]. Virtually all of these applications involve an element of disintermediation, given that blockchain participants could generate and transfer value inherent in data without the need to rely upon third parties such as financial institutions and other large corporations, and governments.

Should blockchains remains largely open and permissionless in nature — enabling anyone to join the virtual network at minimal cost, participate in consensus mechanism procedures, and to append the blockchain by creating "smart contracts" — the blockchain promises to deconcentrate presently-existing network structures organized about third-party data storage and utilization. MacDonald [2015] and Allen [2017] describe how agents might use the blockchain to "crypto-secede" away from well-established organizations that insufficiently respect the need to maintain privacy and security of data at reasonable cost. One way in which crypto-secession could unfold is through the development of "crypto-firms" within blockchain economic sub-structures, with decentralized autonomous organizations (DAOs) and decentralized collaborative organizations (DCOs) able to self-organize with distributed and decentralized profit margins, management and services [Manski, 2017].

The crypto-secessional erosion of conventional network concentration would be expected, all else being equal, to contribute toward a reduction in income inequality. Individuals and groups would be able to collaborate within a distributed blockchain network environment of global scale to unlock new sources of value inhered in data, in accordance with "crypto-rules" emergently established and agreed between participants. Blockchain participants under this scenario can largely eschew the need to engage, albeit under duress, with highly-entangled firms and states that attempt to leverage data for the purposes of appropriating mark-up revenues, capturing rents and stoking inflation.

It is readily admitted that much of the potential scope for crypto-secession, and the income inequality impacts that would accompany it, has yet to come to fruition. If anything, much of the contemporary interest in blockchain appears to emanate from existing intermediary organizations — including for-profit concerns in highly concentrated markets — seeking to apply distributed ledger technology to achieve their objectives. Whereas the adoption of blockchain may be expected to reduce transaction and other costs for such incumbents, there is little reason to expect that dominant firms would seek to embrace blockchain for its disintermediation or rent-corroding potentials. In such instances, blockchain is largely reduced to a co-opted media for storing and validating data within the context of existing production structures, with minimal effect upon income inequality amelioration.

As mentioned previously, the accretion of specialist skills and work experiences by ICT workers have been seen as contributing to income inequality within society more generally. It is conceivable that the process of acquiring skills to develop blockchains may also create wage premiums for those who engage in such endeavors. According to Sarah Manski, "blockchain applications may differentially reward the technologically adept, in this case those most skilled in coding, contracts, finance, and online applications. … We are seeing an emergence of a blockchain technological elite, in which blockchain users must place their trust" [*Ibid.*, p. 517].

The emergence of superstar effects in blockchain labor markets is likely to reflect a combination of high demand, for blockchain-literate workers, and a low supply of new workers, should education and training systems be slow to respond to blockchain adoption [Goldin and Katz, 2008]. There is some anecdotal evidence that blockchain developers and other specialists in the United States have been attracting salaries well above average, and that blockchain-related work skills are presently in high demand [Mearian, 2017; Shilov, 2018]. To the extent that relatively high demands for blockchain workers persist, and education systems facilitate the teaching of coding and other skills relevant to blockchain developmental activity, any corresponding increase in labor supply over the longer term might eventually erode some of the inflated earnings currently observed in the market.

The most prevalent application of blockchain to date has come in the form of cryptocurrencies, in itself serving as something of a crypto-secessional form of financial engagement beyond central banks and private-sector financial institutions. Generally speaking, cryptocurrency is a blockchain-supported digital asset that may be used as a medium of exchange. The value of a given cryptocurrency — such as Bitcoin, Ethereum, Litecoin, Ripple, NEO and so on — is determined consensually amongst the users of the asset interfacing through blockchains.

Space does not permit a comprehensive appraisal of the impact of all crypto-assets on inequality, and so we restrict our attention to Bitcoin. The Bitcoin cryptocurrency, introduced in the midst of the GFC, is the single largest cryptocurrency with an aggregate value exceeding $US 140 billion in May 2018 (after a previous peak over $US 326 billion in mid-December 2017).

It has been estimated that a large percentage of Bitcoin in circulation is held by a small number of addresses (individuals or exchanges) — according to Credit Suisse [2018], about 97 per cent of Bitcoins are held by four per cent of addresses. Given that blockchain transactions can be undertaken anonymously, the personal profiles of all those with substantial Bitcoin holdings are not known. It is considered that some of the individuals with sizeable holdings of Bitcoin may include founders and early adopters with ideological and other dispositions to largely retain their Bitcoins, even in "bear market" conditions, some of whom were profiled by Doherty [2017]. In early 2018 *Forbes* magazine compiled a "cryptocurrency rich list" of twenty individuals with self-reported cryptocurrency portfolios in excess of $US 350 million, although the list is unlikely to be representative because of the extent to which cryptocurrency wealth is undisclosed.

Notwithstanding the growing interest generated in Bitcoin the adoption rate — as measured by the number of active users of cryptocurrency (Bitcoin and other) wallets — remains low, considering the number of mobile phone and Internet users globally. According to a study by Hileman and Rauchs [2017], it is estimated that there are between 2.9 million and 5.8 million unique users actively using a cryptocurrency wallet. This figure is considered an underestimate, given Hileman and Rauchs did not include users whose crypto-exchange accounts serve as their *de facto* wallet, nor users from payment service providers or other platforms enabling cryptocurrency storage. Others have reported estimates of more than 13 million active users with Coinbase, a US-based exchange exchanging Bitcoin and other cryptocurrencies [Young, 2017], but even with this higher-point estimate about 0.36 percent of Internet users own a cryptocurrency wallet.

The distributional characteristics of Bitcoin holding appears broadly consistent with Hayek's [(1960) 2006] hypothesis that relatively small numbers of early adopters will disproportionately receive benefits by virtue of ownership, such as generating returns as the result of holding Bitcoin. These same early adopters bear immense risks as they involve themselves in a discovery process surrounding the most efficacious use of these crypto-assets (and not to mention risks associated with potentially adverse regulatory changes). Whether any economic discoveries derived from early-onset engagement with cryptocurrencies by small numbers of people will yield benefits with much broader applicability for the remainder of society, including those yet to take up cryptocurrency holdings, largely remains to be seen.

Instead of delegating data validation responsibilities to distant third parties, blockchain applications such as Bitcoin enable participants the opportunity to add blocks of new data to the blockchain. Participants in the blockchain network known as "miners" are accorded economic incentives to compete against each other to validate and add to the public ledger. Under the "proof of work" concept, miners are assigned a cryptographic puzzle to computationally solve if they are to be given the responsibility of appending the blockchain. The miner that successfully solves the puzzle also receives some Bitcoins as well as the right to impose fees against the new transaction.

From a practical standpoint Bitcoin mining is a costly undertaking, requiring time, substantial electricity consumption and resources to validate transactions. Given the absorption of significant computing power involved, most miners now require specialist hardware — such as application-specific integrated circuit chips (ASICs) — to solve and validate Bitcoin blocks. Although the ultimate purpose of mining is to convert energy-intensive computation into economically-valuable trust [Berg *et al.*, 2017], there have been some concerns expressed about the tendency toward concentration in mining activity [Tasca, 2015]. Gencer *et al.* [2018] note that Bitcoin mining has tended to be subject to centralizing processes, and there is also some evidence of geographic clustering of miners (though not exclusively in existing ICT hubs such as California's Silicon Valley). Even if the mining process induces an unequal distribution of income within the Bitcoin network to date, this should be weighed against the social benefits accruing from the validation of data on the immutable, secure blockchain ledger.

1.4 Implications for Public Policy

The blockchain is likely to alter the ways and means through which individuals, enterprises and bureaucracies interact in the pursuit of gains achieved economically, socially or politically. Existing network connections, which already entail the flow of uneven incomes amongst economic actors, could be affected by blockchain adoption as mentioned previously, albeit of a strength and direction which cannot be predicted *ex-ante* in any precise detail. That said, continuing blockchain adoption is highly likely, in any event, to create "winners" and "losers" of opportunity in meso-evolutionary trajectories, and this could translate into political pressure to respond to blockchain impacts.

Distributional concerns have long animated the setting of public policy, and it is not a great stretch to imagine reactionary fiscal and regulatory policies being enacted in an attempt to arrest blockchain's adoption. Governments may attempt to frustrate the organic development of blockchain as a permissionless ledger of a genuinely distributed nature. One way in which they may hypothetically do this is by trying to co-opt blockchain as a "general purpose technology," encouraging the adoption of permissioned, closed ledgers (a.k.a. "spreadsheets") which fit into existing production and operational modes. Public sector agencies may also support the efforts of actually-existing intermediary businesses to pursue similar strategies that head off extensive crypto-secession. More dramatically, political actors might introduce onerous tax regimes or prescriptive regulations discouraging cryptoeconomic participation altogether. In either respect what we observe is the "socialisation of evolutionary failure" reflecting "a legacy of accumulation of legislative redress of the negative consequences of meso trajectories" [Potts, 2005].

In general terms it is possible to conceive a spectrum of fiscal and regulatory responses to further blockchain adoption. These range from policy abstention ("pure crypto-friendliness") and accommodation ("crypto-friendless") to outright policy suppression ("pure crypto-unfriendliness"). This spectrum essentially corresponds with political receptions as to whether the blockchain represents an "opportunity," or "threat," to existing frames of operation and interaction.

The emergence of blockchain is relevant to Adam Thierer's [2016] call for a public policy environment facilitating what is known as "permissionless innovation." Under this model new technologies, products, business models, management styles and other facets of innovation should not be necessarily disallowed, curtailed or pre-empted in any way. The framework of permissionless innovation may reasonably be discerned as being consistent with a policy tilt toward crypto-friendliness.

In practical terms adherence to crypto-friendly permissionless innovation incorporates the adoption of self-restraint and patience on the part of fiscal and regulatory political enterprises, as well as relaxing antiquated rules upon incumbent economic and social actors as new crypto-actors challenge the *status quo* of ledger integrity and management. It also encourages "educate and empower" responses to new challenges, which build upon the inherent capabilities of people to constructively respond to blockchain activity, rather than a reflexive and potentially self-defeating "legislate and regulate" approach.

The maintenance of a crypto-friendly approach also seems an appropriate response toward the inequality implications of blockchain. Given the kaleidic nature of inequality and its determinants — such as the introduction of new technologies, e.g. blockchain — there are considerable economic and other risks associated with governments attempting to redress any undesired inequality outcomes in a highly-targeted, and potentially prescriptive, manner. The multitudinous impacts of innovation, combined with epistemic limitations upon finely-grained political action, appreciably increase the chances of policy failure [Wegner, 1997]. It seems the more effective policy strategy is to set abstract, generic rules enabling crypto-participants to discover their own methods of advancement within open-ended blockchain spaces. Maintaining blockchain openness could enable liberating *and* pro-equality ventures — such as empowering the unbanked in the developing world, and ensuring greater transparency with respect to charitable donations and remittances — to play a crucial role in the emerging cryptoeconomy.

1.5 Conclusion

This chapter contributes to the literature on the impact of ledger innovation upon income inequality, and considers the extent to which blockchain technology may affect the income distribution. In a complex society, typified by networked relations between and amongst people spanning numerous domains of activity, it is difficult to be definitive about the potential impacts of blockchain upon income inequality. This uncertainty partially rests upon the institutional and operational contexts within which technological impacts unfold, and how these affect the ever-shifting patterns of income flows [Bauer, 2017]. We also recognize that blockchain impacts will not occur in isolation from the array of other, non-technological changes affecting local, national and international economies, societies and polities.

From the available, albeit largely anecdotal, evidence gleaned thus far, there is some evidence of wealth concentration and income inequality amongst participants within cryptocurrency applications of blockchain. One may question the durability of such effects, given that exchanges within Bitcoin and other cryptocurrency markets presently coincide with the formation of a dynamic, open-ended virtual network realm presently subject to energetic attention, early adoption and use-discovery processes. Given that "proto-entrepreneurial" activity is also prevalent within the broader blockchain space at this time [Allen and Potts, 2016], it is difficult to make concrete assessments as to whether any given degree of income inequality will persist over the longer term. In this respect, we have identified the cross-cutting effects of blockchain with respect to disintermediation and labor market impacts.

With income inequality elevated as a central policy issue in recent years, there seems little doubt the inequality implications of distributed public ledger technologies will be added to the seemingly lengthy list of inequality-related concerns attracting the attention of governments. We suggest that it is at this relatively early, attention-gathering stage that the potential for policy error is magnified, when policymakers are tempted to prescribe heavy-handed fiscal and regulatory measures in an effort to head off any unequal sing consequences of blockchain, which may or may not eventuate.

The temptation to "impose policy interventions first, and ask questions later," might seem an intuitively obvious approach to some risk-adverse political actors, but we call for a sense of policy cautiousness aptly reflecting the meso-evolutionary adoption stage in which blockchain technology appears largely situated. An emphasis on clear and concise policy rules will be integral to ensuring that blockchains maintain the characteristics of decentralization, openness and widespread participation, leveraging the innate properties of this unique ledger technology to help mitigate the emergence of unwarranted income inequalities.

References

Allen, D. (2018). Discovering and Developing the Blockchain Cryptoeconomy, https://papers.ssrn.com/sol3/papers.cfm?abstract_id=2815255, accessed March 12, 2018.

Allen, D. and Potts, J. (2016). The Origin of the Entrepreneur and the Role of the Innovation Commons, https://papers.ssrn.com/sol3/papers.cfm?abstract_id=2867850, accessed March 12, 2018.

Allen, D., Berg, C., Lane, A. and Potts, J. (2017). The Economics of Crypto-Democracy, https://papers.ssrn.com/sol3/papers.cfm?abstract_id=2973050, accessed March 13, 2018.

Archer, S. (2018). The Winklevoss twins have seen about $600 million wiped off their bitcoin wealth in 2 days. Business Insider, http://markets.businessinsider.com/currencies/news/bitcoin-winklevoss-twins-millions-wiped-out-2018-1-1013164917, accessed March 12, 2018.

Bauer, J. M. (2017). The Internet and income inequality, *Telecommunications Policy*, doi: 10.1016/j.telpol.2017.05.009.

Berg, C., Davidson, S. and Potts, J. (2017). Blockchains Industrialise Trust, https://papers.ssrn.com/sol3/papers.cfm?abstract_id=3074070, accessed March 11, 2018.

Brynjolfsson, E., McAfee, A. and Spence, M. (2014). New World Order: Labor, Capital, and Ideas in the Power Law Economy, *Foreign Affairs*, 93 (4), pp. 44-53.

Credit Suisse (2018). Blockchain 2.0, https://research-doc.credit-suisse.com/docView?language=ENG&format=PDF&sourceid=csplusresearchcp&document_id=1080109971&serialid=pTkp8RFIoVyHegdqM8EllLNi1z%2Fk8mInqoBSQ5KDZG4%3D, accessed March 12, 2018.

Davidson, S., Filippi, P. de and Potts, J. (2018). Blockchains and the economic institutions of capitalism, *Journal of Institutional Economics*, doi: 10.1017/S1744137417000200, pp. 1-20.

Doherty, B. (2018). In Search of the Elusive Bitcoin Billionaire. Reason magazine, https://reason.com/archives/2017/11/28/in-search-of-the-elusive-bitco, accessed March 12, 2018.

Dopfer, K. and Potts, J. (2008). *The General Theory of Economic Evolution*. Routledge, London.

Gencer, A. E., Basu, S., Eyal, I., Renesse, R. v. and Sirer, E. G. (2018). Decentralization in Bitcoin and Ethereum Networks, Financial Cryptography and Data Security Forum, https://fc18.ifca.ai/preproceedings/75.pdf, accessed March 12, 2018.

Goldin, C. and Katz, L. F. (2008). *The Race Between Education and Technology*. Belknap Press of Harvard University Press, Cambridge, MA.

Hayek, F. A. [1960] (2006). *The Constitution of Liberty*, Routledge Classics Edition. Routledge, London, UK.

Hileman, G. and Rauchs, M. (2017). Global Cryptocurrency Benchmarking Study, University of Cambridge, Cambridge Centre for Alternative Finance.

International Telecommunications Union (ITU) (2018). World Telecommunication/ICT Indicators Database, https://www.itu.int/en/ITU-D/Statistics/Documents/statistics/2017/ITU_Key_2005-2017_ICT_data.xls, accessed March 10, 2018.

MacDonald, T. J. (2015). Theory of unbundled and non-territorial governance, RMIT University, Doctoral Thesis.

Manski, S. (2017). Building the blockchain world: Technological commonwealth or just more of the same?, *Strategic Change: Briefings in Entrepreneurial Finance*, 26 (5), pp. 511-522.

Mearian, L. (2017). Blockchain jobs continue to explode, offer salary premiums, https://www.computerworld.com/article/3235972/it-careers/blockchain-jobs-continue-to-explode-offer-salary-premiums.html, accessed March 13, 2017.

Nair, M. and Sutter, D. (2018). The Blockchain and Increasing Cooperative Efficacy, *The Independent Review*, 22 (4), pp. 529-550.

Novak, M. (2018). *Inequality: An Entangled Political Economy Perspective*. Palgrave Macmillan, Cham, Switzerland.

Potts, J. (2005). Politics is just evolutionary failure socialized, Oysterium blog, http://oysterium.blogspot.com.au/2005/12/politics-is-just-evolutionary-failure.html, accessed March 13, 2018.

Rosen, S. (1981). The Economics of Superstars, *The American Economic Review*, 71 (5), pp. 845-858.

Shilov, K. (2018). Blockchain jobs and salaries — 2018 report, https://hackernoon.com/blockchain-jobs-and-salaries-2018-report-45d3e7741c19, accessed March 13, 2018.

Swan, M. (2015). *Blockchain: Blueprint for a New Economy*, (O'Reilly, Sebastpol, CA).

Swan, M. (2017). "Is Technological Unemployment Real? An Assessment and a Plea for Abundance Economics," in *Surviving the Machine Age: Intelligent Technology and the Transformation of Human Work*, Hughes, J. and LaGrandeur, K. (Eds.). London: Palgrave Macmillan. pp. 19-33.

Tapscott, D. and Tapscott, A. (2016). *Blockchain Revolution: How the Technology Behind Bitcoin is Changing Money, Business and the World.* Portfolio/Penguin, London, UK.

Tasca, P. (2015). Digital Currencies: Principles, Trends, Opportunities, and Risks, https://papers.ssrn.com/sol3/Papers.cfm?abstract_id=2657598 accessed March 11, 2018.

Thierer, A. (2016). *Permissionless Innovation: The Continuing Case for Comprehensive Technological Freedom, Revised and Expanded Edition.* Mercatus Center, Arlington, VA.

Wegner, G. (1997). Economic Policy from an Evolutionary Perspective: A New Approach, *Journal of Institutional and Theoretical Economics*, 153 (3), pp. 485-509.

Young, J. (2017). Exponential Growth: Number of Bitcoin Users to Reach 200 Million by 2024, https://www.ccn.com/exponential-growth-number-bitcoin-users-reach-200-million-2024/, accessed March 12, 2018.

Zumbrun, J. (2017). The Best $100,000+ Tech Jobs Are Increasingly Concentrated in Just 8 Cities, The Wall Street Journal, https://blogs.wsj.com/economics/2017/07/26/the-best-100000-tech-jobs-are-increasingly-concentrated-in-just-8-cities/, accessed March 11, 2018.

Chapter 13

The Mesh Economy: How Blockchain and Alternative Networks can Bridge the Digital Divide and Facilitate Economic Inclusion

John B. Hooks, IV

Spectramesh, Inc., USA

Abstract

Mesh networking and blockchain technologies are reshaping the telecommunications industry and bringing the promise of economic empowerment to areas currently not served or underserved by traditional service providers. By combining both, it is possible to provide easy and affordable access to the Internet. Several non-blockchain Alternative Community Networks (ACNs) are now successfully deployed around the world. One such case, Guifi.net, has contributed to building the largest community network, with an annual turnover of millions of euros and the creation of dozens of direct jobs. Nevertheless, there continues to be an ongoing debate on how to make them economically sustainable and scalable. The implementation of a blockchain-enabled mesh network and other tools producing extensive data sets will allow characterization of key parameters in the deployment and operation of these infrastructures. This could economically empower those who do not have Internet connectivity, access to non-traditional financial services, and capital.

1.1 Introduction

According to the Global Financial Development Report[1], financial inclusion is defined as "the proportion of individuals and firms that use financial services." Financial inclusion is important because it is positively correlated with economic growth and enables the poor to improve their lives. The poor do not have access to many fundamental financial services most people take for granted, and they have a desperate need for these services. Access to a transaction account is of special importance for financial inclusion, as it provides a possibility to store money as well as send and receive payments, and it serves as a gateway to other financial services. Without access to financial services, the unbanked and underbanked must find other semi-formal or informal means to facilitate their transactions, such as check cashing or money-order stores that charge high transaction fees and take up the user's time. For example, many billers refuse cash payments and require checks; however, without bank access, the poor must pay a fee to convert their cash to a check. The process leaves them with less money than the actual payment amounts. To make matters worse, financial service access not only costs more for the poor, but also takes more time. In areas like rural India, the commute to access a financial service can be as long as eight hours.[2]

The promise and potential of blockchain lies beyond a technology that verifies and permanently records transactions in a decentralized and distributed ledger. In fact, the democratizing potential of this technology may very well be the catalyst behind a new era of globalism and economic empowerment. A good replacement for access to a transaction account could be access to a universally accepted and secure crypto currency. It would enable payments, offer the possibility to store money and could also provide a gateway to other financial services (blockchain-powered or not). In addition, blockchain technology could revolutionize identity-management systems, thus overcoming an important impediment to financial inclusion.

But can blockchain technology bridge the economic divide for the developing world the same way that the Internet has bridged the information gap?

Central to the economic enrichment of any group is a frictionless system of interactions between parties and their given environment. In this context, a blockchain-enabled economy benefiting people that live in disparate and underserved areas where Alternate Network Deployments (ANDs) exist can be formed through the creation of a “Mesh Network” of devices and communication protocols.

1.2 The Token Economy

The creation of tokens either as cryptocurrencies or for use for a specific purpose such as purchasing bandwidth on a Mesh Network, creates a polyculture, that is one in which people can live and work on their own terms. Traditional Centralized Monetary systems, on the other hand, are strictly monocultural, even if frictionless payment systems are introduced to banked as well as unbanked people. These incumbent fiat money systems create debt that must be returned with interest. These systems lead to both local and international wealth inequality by prioritizing the production of more capital above all other things. Unfortunately, they also drive climate change and dampen ecological sustainability as the endless reproduction of capital causes depletion of natural resources.

A virtual currency, blockchain-enabled economy, on the other hand, will have far reaching effects that are political, economic, social, spiritual, and technological. To fully realize these effects, what is needed are free, open, and neutral communication networks. Their principles may be summarized in this way:

- You have the freedom to use the network for any purpose as long as you do not harm the operation of the network itself, the rights of other users, or the principles of neutrality that allow contents and services to flow without deliberate interference.
- You have the right to understand the network, to know its components, and to spread knowledge of its mechanisms and principles.
- You have the right to offer services and content to the network on your own terms.

- You have the right to join the network, and the responsibility to extend this set of rights to anyone according to these same terms.

1.3 Background: A Communications Ecosystem for Economic Empowerment

Through the creation of a blockchain-enabled communications ecosystem that is both extensible and sustainable, individuals and communities can be empowered to create opportunities and connect beyond their geographical borders without requiring users to sacrifice individual autonomy or privacy. By allowing them to participate in "trusted" and immutable interactions within a verified and self-sovereign network, individuals can own their identities and personal data, and create and exchange value peer-to-peer.

As this blockchain communications ecosystem becomes more widely used, billions of marginalized individuals who currently do not have access to the Internet or are underserved will have a better chance of entering and participating in the global economy through financial inclusion and the establishment of property rights. No longer will the world's poorest be denied wealth creation due to a lack of access to local currency (cash) in a grey economy. Tokens created through coding of Smart Contracts will allow payment, value creation and access to credit without involving third parties such as Banks and currency exchanges.

1.4 Changing Wealth Distribution with Distributed Ledger Technology

Introducing a Token-based Mesh Network economy to provide a means by which economically disadvantaged groups will benefit can be thought of as Universal Basic Income (UBI) 2.0.

UBI is simply basic income, the purpose of which is to prevent or reduce poverty and increase equality among citizens. Tech billionaires Mark Zuckerberg, Sir Richard Branson and Elon Musk, among others are proponents of the idea that all citizens are entitled to a livable income, whether or not they contribute to production and despite the particular circumstances into which they are born.

In an experiment undertaken in 2009 in the small poor desert town of Otjivero, Namibia, the introduction of a UBI drastically reduced the poverty level and improved the societal well-being.[3] When the experiment began, almost all the residents lived in cardboard or plastic houses. Each of the 930 inhabitants were given $100 Namibian (roughly $9 US) a month without condition. A year later, the economic effects included average income growth of 39%, and a marked rise in entrepreneurship. The societal benefits included improved access to HIV treatments, malnutrition dropped from 42% to 10%, school dropout rates fell by 40% and women became more independent.

If this experiment had been conducted today using self-sovereign blockchain-enabled economic empowerment communication networks and smart contracts (Tokens) as an economic stimulus, the results can arguably expected to be more impressive because of the globalization potential a connection to the Internet brings to each individual in the community and to the community itself.

Providing a UBI to marginalized populations or by extension a Mesh Network Economy, therefore, won't just bring prosperity and independence, it will also make them healthier and more productive.

1.5 Analysis: Financial Inclusion without Financial Institutions

There are a number of obstacles to providing financial access to the unbanked and increasing usage of financial services by the underbanked. Below are three specific problems that may be solved using blockchain technology.[4]

1. Problem: Opening an account. It is costly and challenging for those without a bank account to open one. There are travel and opportunity costs in going to a bank branch. Individuals also need to provide identification documents and an initial deposit.

Solution: Individuals do not need to travel to a financial institution to open an account or deposit cash. They are able to open an account on their phone thus avoiding the travel costs to set the account up. They are also able to deposit money into the account via a number of third party agents. This makes it easier to get money into the system.

2. Problem: Usability of an account. The challenge is not just in opening the account but in the everyday usability. Current obstacles for bank accounts are high transactional costs for making payments, minimum payment sizes, and settlement times. Making payments via the national payment system often takes a number of days, and there are fees involved. The recipient of a payment is not likely to release the services/goods until they are satisfied that they have received the funds. In order for digital methods of payment (i.e., non-cash) to be more widely adopted, the value has to transfer in real time or near real time.

Solution: One of the differences between the current payment infrastructure and blockchain is that blockchain can transfer value in a near instantaneous manner. (Transfer takes about 10 minutes, which is slow compared to the payment systems of developed economies but faster than those of developing economies.) Transfer fees are applied as a percentage of the transfer's value rather than a fixed rate, and the transfer requires no minimum payment amounts. Low rates, no minimums, and fast value transfers make blockchain useful for unbanked people to complete payment transactions.

3. Problem: Costs to the Financial Institution (FI) for providing financial services. All FIs will have some fixed and some variable costs. Many existing FIs have branches and are reliant on staff to interact with customers as well as perform back office functions such as compliance (KYC/AML). They also incur costs for using their country's national payment system and corresponding bank accounts for cross-border payments. The fees for using the existing payment system are often charged at a flat rate per individual transaction, thus a large number of small payments will be an increased cost for the financial institution.

Solution: Payments via a blockchain do not need to go through the national payment system, and there is no requirement for physical branches. FIs are able to offer more services digitally and thus will not require as many client-facing staff. Agent networks and alternative methods (i.e., cardless ATM services) can be used to add or withdraw funds. The cost to transfer funds via the blockchain is a percentage of the value transferred and thus makes smaller payments more feasible.

While the above examples highlight potential solutions to pre-existing barriers to entry using traditional banking services, the following improvements brought about through Distributed Ledger Technology further enhance financial inclusion among the unbanked[5]:

1.6 Financial Inclusion through Blockchain-powered Economic Identity

- Blockchain provides digital identity to individuals with enhanced privacy, so that identity is restricted to devices as well as other individuals with access.
- Financial institutions have the ease of reissuing identity documents and data in case the documents are lost or stolen.
- Blockchain provides digital identity to individuals with enhanced privacy, so that identity is restricted to devices as well as other individuals with access.
- Citizens lacking appropriate access to the financial system would gain a higher independence and better chances for welfare by creation of digital identity on blockchain.
- The solution can be built with the purpose of integration with external systems in order to diminish the fraud and error possibilities in the delivery of benefits for the financially excluded.

1.6.1 *Blockchain Brings Speed and Transparency in Payments Systems*

- Blockchain eliminates the need for intermediaries which drastically reduces settlement time, which in turn means that customers will be able to access their capital when they need it.

- Storing transactions in blockchain could eliminate the need for complicated procedures and clearinghouses, saving time, money and the risk of error. The allowance of frictionless savings and investment gives people more control over their financial destiny.
- The use of digital technology to embed business rules into a contract, including automated execution of contract terms and payments will simplify complex procurement, negotiation and verification processes.

1.7 Mesh Networks: Internet Access For Financial Inclusion

The challenge that lies ahead in order to realize the potential of a Token-based Mesh Network Economy is how to make network connectivity, specifically to the Internet, available to everyone, not just a privileged few. Different studies have reported that as much as 60% of the people on our planet do not have Internet connectivity. In addition, those unconnected are unevenly distributed: only 31% of the population in "global south" countries had access in 2014, against 80% in "global north" countries.[6]

Recent years have witnessed several initiatives across the globe on enabling Internet access.[7] Many of these employ alternative network technologies with the aim of bringing Internet connectivity to people and providing a local communication infrastructure to serve various complementary needs and objectives.

The problem of expanding Internet access has also received significant attention from the industry, especially organizations such as Google, Facebook, and Microsoft all touting novel solutions in this space.[8] Facebook has been spearheading innovations in open source cellular networks focused on addressing the rural, small cell markets via the Telecom Infra Project, while also looking at airborne solutions such as drones for providing Internet access in hard to reach areas. Recently Facebook has started express WiFi® projects, mostly collaborating with existing Wireless Internet Providers (WISPs) such as AirJaldi in India. Google has also been exploring airborne solutions such as Google Balloons while Microsoft is pushing TV White Space (TVWS) based Internet access in rural areas.[9] Kenyan startup BRCK has built a waterproof, solar powered WiFi® box supporting several backhaul technologies as well as providing localized content. There are also initiatives such as the FON which uses the concept of crowdsharing Internet access that has been extremely successful with more than 20 million hotspots across the globe.[10]

In addition to the aforementioned novel approaches, a set of network access models have emerged with the aim of providing Internet connections that differ from the so-called "mainstream networks" that deploy an infrastructure connecting users, who then pay a subscription fee to use it. These "alternative network deployments (ANDs)" possess topological, architectural, governance, and business models that do not follow those of mainstream networks and are often found in rural or remote areas that lack wired or cellular infrastructure.[11]

1.8 Benefits of Mesh Networks

Information Security

With Mesh Networks all messaging is point-to-point, thus isolating the risk of third-party information being exposed.

Network Congestion

Whether in the train, subway, plane, outdoor camping or sports stadium, User density congests data traffic and people cannot access the Internet properly. However, with Mesh Networks, the quality of the network improves, and the speed will be faster.

Off-internet Communication

Within one local mesh network, as long as one of the mobile phones or router devices has Internet connectivity, everyone on the Mesh will be able to connect to the world.

Scalability

Mesh Networks have many advantages, with lack of scalability so far being a limiting factor in applicability. With the increase of the number of nodes with the growth of a mesh network, functionality of the network is often compromised. This drag occurs because of both protocol overhead and the inability to offload packet congestion. In some circumstances protocol overhead disproportionately grows relative to the overhead of carrying data itself. Collisions, timeouts and a full halt to all packet routing can occur. These scaling problems are almost impossible to overcome in a standard mesh network because there are no alternative pathways or protocols to relieve the congestion. In particular, a regular stand-alone mesh network operating with a single protocol over a single spot on the radio spectrum will simply not scale well.

1.9 The Mesh Economy in Action

Under many conditions, the use of blockchain technology coupled with an alternative (mesh) network can provide an open and autonomous exchange for trading Internet connectivity using a token as intra network micropayment medium of exchange.

A Blockchain-enabled Mesh Network can be thought of as a last-mile connectivity play, which utilizes blockchain to provide a micro-payments layer within a distributed mesh network.[12] The network is rooted in the use of a Mesh Router, a multi-protocol wireless device that far surpasses the conventional mesh used in many community networks. This Mesh Router is not only a router, but a hardware platform for Edge Computing. A full stack edge computing environment is being developed to provide API driven, and micropayment/blockchain supported ecosystem for developers and operators to build comprehensive edge solutions.

In order to deliver the promise of The Mesh Economy, this device will effectively be a heterogeneous mesh hub device (node) extending connectivity well beyond the common WiFi® range of 150 feet. Using a variable and automatically selectable basket of radio spectrum bands and communications protocols discussed earlier in this chapter, this node will work efficiently over several kilometers, subject to regulations and local conditions. Additionally, optional hardware modules can be mixed and matched to support a multitude of frequency ranges and protocols, dependent upon its operational circumstances.

In order to overcome scalability issues mentioned earlier, the proposed mesh router must operate simultaneously across multiple protocols and frequency bands of the radio spectrum. It must support path as well as link diversity. Multiple paths will potentially be resource pooled to route and forward packets. It can also be used either simultaneously or in a backup configuration, for increased reliability, end-to-end throughput, network efficiency and fault tolerance. Backhaul optimization should be designed to reduce the number of hops to the lowest number possible. This is best achieved by providing a direct high-speed route to the backbone from as many points in the network as possible, which would represent the network's backhaul. The network's backhaul would predominantly be supported by its users connecting, or bridging, their mesh routers to existing home and SoHo broadband routers, satellite or wireless broadband. Alternatively, for larger mesh networks, through interconnecting, or peering, to exchange points. It is also envisioned that several mesh networks would be peering with each other directly, thus localizing network traffic.

If additional bandwidth is required for a specific period of time, users of the mesh network may purchase this through token micropayments. Market forces within the bandwidth market would solve congestion problems by means of the automated setting of higher prices resulting from high demand. High prices in a particular zone would attract node operators seeking higher returns. Analytics will be provided to indicate where infrastructure can be added, as well as the type of infrastructure likely to earn most traffic. As a result, market forces attracting infrastructure deployments where needed would then realize the exponential scaling of the network.

1.10 Conclusion and Implications

In this chapter, we take on the issue of addressing trustworthy economic sustainability by proposing the need for an economic substrate built using blockchain that can keep a record of the transactions related to the contributions (of nodes, links, Internet gateways, maintenance) and consumption of communication network's resources in a decentralized and trusted manner. Considering the massive potential of untapped users, mesh network technology driven by blockchain economics could solve the Internet accessibility problem and foster economic inclusion. The missing ingredient has been the issue of economic sustainability.

Economic stimulus through the use of a blockchain-enabled mesh network of multi-protocol routers can directly address this issue by adopting a shared economy model for network access, providing an economic incentive that allows users to share their unused bandwidth for profit. Monetizing the free exchange of bandwidth, via a secondary market, allows for free market forces to drive network growth where it is most needed. With sufficient incentives to participate, the mesh network can quickly grow to provide share connectivity on a global scale.

References

1. World Bank. 2014. Global Financial Development Report 2014: Financial Inclusion. Washington, DC.
2. Realini, Carol and Karl Mehta. Financial Inclusion at the Bottom of the Pyramid. FriesenPress. 2005, p. 2.
3. Stern, Andy. Moving Towards a Universal Basic Income. http://blogs.worldbank.org/jobs/moving-towards-universal-basic-income.
4. Aggarwal, Rina *et al*. Blockchain and Financial Inclusion: The Role Blockchain Technology Can Play in Financial Inclusion. Georgetown University. 2017, pp. 7-8.
5. Baruri, Pani. Blockchain Powered Financial Inclusion. Cognizant, Inc. 2016, p. 5.
6. Sprague, K., Grijpink, F., Manyika, J., Moodley, L., Chappuis, B., Pattabiraman, K., and J. Bughin, Offline and falling behind: Barriers to Internet adoption, McKinsey and Company, August 2014.

7. Rwanda's Digital Ambassadors are Boosting Computer Literacy, https://www.weforum.org/agenda/2017/02/rwandas-digital-ambassadors-are-boosting-computer-literacy/.
8. World Bank, World Development Report 2016: Digital Dividends, Washington, DC: The World Bank, ISBN 978-1-4648-0672-8, DOI 10.1596/978-1-4648-0671-1, 2016.
9. Satellites, Balloons, Solar Planes & Phones: Innovations in Emerging Market Internet Access? An Industry Overview, DIAL, January 2016.
10. Fon, Fon is the Global WiFi Network, 2014, https://corp.fon.com/en.
11. J. Qadir *et al.*, Resource Pooling for Wireless Networks: Solutions for the Developing World, ACM SIGCOMM CCR, November 2016.
12. A. Sathiaseelan *et al.*, Ammbr Whitepaper, Ammbr Foundation, November 2017.

Glossary

Blockchain (Distributed Ledger) Technology: A blockchain is an immutable, cryptographic (cryptography-based), distributed (peer-based), consensus-driven ledger. Blockchain (distributed ledger) technology is a software protocol for the instantaneous transfer of money and other forms of value (assets, contracts, public records, program states) globally via the Internet. Other topologies of distributed ledger technology may include Directed Acyclic Graphs (DAGs), in projects such as IOTA, Hashgraph, Byteball, and DAGCoin.

Cryptoasset: A cryptoasset is a digital or physical asset registered to a blockchain for the purpose of confirmation, control, and transfer. The implication of cryptoassets is that ownership and provenance is already confirmed (since the assets are blockchain-registered), and therefore they may be transacted instantly, including per smart contract terms, on a global basis.

Cryptoeconomics: Cryptoeconomics is an economic transaction paradigm based on cryptography; more specifically, an economic transaction system implemented in a cryptography-based software network, using cryptographic hashes (computational proof mechanisms) as a means of confirming and transferring monetary balances, assets, smart contracts, or other system states.

Cryptosecession: Cryptosecession is the situation of individuals and organizations choosing to opt out of traditional political-economic systems (such as laws and jurisdictional courts) through new forms of governance and enforcement afforded by blockchain technology.

Deep Learning Chains: Deep learning chains are a class of smart network technologies in which other technologies, blockchain and deep learning, converge as a control technology for other smart network technologies. Deep learning chains have the properties of secure automation, audit-log tracking, and validated transaction execution of blockchain, and the object and pattern recognition technology (IDtech) of deep learning. Deep learning chains might be used to control other fleet-many Internet-connected smart network technologies such as UAVs, autonomous driving fleets, medical nanorobots, and space-based asteroid mining machines.

Deep Learning Neural Networks: Deep learning neural networks are computer programs that can identify what an object is; more technically, deep learning is a branch of machine learning based on a set of algorithms that attempts to model high-level abstractions in data by using artificial neural network architectures, based on learning multiple levels of representation or abstraction, such that predictive guesses can be made about new data.

IDtech: IDtech is identification technology, the functionality of object recognition as an in-built feature in technology. IDtech is similar to FinTech, RegTech, TradeTech, and HealthTech; technologies that digitize, standardize, and automate operations within their respective domains.

Payment Channel: A payment channel is a contractually-obligated payment structure that elapses over time, protecting and obligating two parties who need not know and trust each other. The payment channel operates in three steps. First, Party A opens a payment channel with Party B and posts a pre-paid escrow balance (the escrow deposit is broadcast to the blockchain, and a corresponding refund transaction for the same amount is signed by both parties, but not broadcast). Second, Party A consumes a resource (or provides a service such as programming hours) against the escrow balance, and activity is tracked and updated (in revised refund transactions that both parties sign but do not broadcast). Third, at the end of the period (or at any time), the cumulative activity is booked in one net transaction to close the contract. In addition to the FinTech innovation of parties not knowing each other being able to digitally contract in a protected manner over time, payment channels might also provide scalability to blockchains by only logging net transactions.

Private Blockchain (Enterprise Blockchain): A private blockchain is *permissioned* in the sense that users are known and credentialed for specific access and read-write operations. Private blockchains are used by companies and governments, and are *not* trustless, meaning transactions are validated by enterprise blockchain software mechanisms not a competitive mining process. Examples include Hyperledger, R3 Corda, Ethereum Quorum, and Symbiont.

Public Blockchain: A public blockchain is *permissionless* and open to any user worldwide for transaction execution. Users are pseudonymous (known only through cryptographic addresses) or possibly anonymous (via confidential transactions). Public blockchains are *trustless*, meaning transactions are validated through a competitive mining process. Examples include Bitcoin, Ethereum, Litecoin, Monero, and Zcash.

Smart Contract: A smart contract is a software program registered to a blockchain for confirmation (time-datestamping provenance), and possibly some form of automated execution. To be legally-binding as an eContract, smart contracts need to have the four elements of "regular" contracts: two parties, consideration, and terms.

Smart Networks: Smart networks are intelligent autonomously-operating networks. Exemplar smart network technologies include blockchain economic networks and deep learning pattern recognition neural networks.

Token Economy: The token economy is the situation in which web-based communities issue their own cryptotoken money supplies. The tokens serve as an accounting system for coordinating a local economy between members, a tracking system that can be used to link participative contributions with remuneration (solving the credit assignment problem). In Web 3.0, users expect to participate meaningfully in communities, meaning being remunerated for contributions, accessing resources, and voting on community decisions.

Web 3.0 (Crypto Web): Web 3.0 refers to the idea of cryptoeconomic business models such as data markets and computation markets running on the "Internet's new pipes" of distributed network systems, content-addressable file-serving, and IDtech. Web 1.0 (the Static Web) involved the transfer of static information and Web 2.0 (the Social Web) created the expectation that website users can interact, like, and engage with content and other users. In Web 3.0 (the Crypto Web), users may expect to participate meaningfully in economic communities by being remunerated for contributions (such as software code, digital art, and forum posts), and by being able to vote on decisions and access resources.

Trustless Trust (Algorithmic Trust): Trustless trust is relocating human-based trust to cryptography-based trust. Instead of having to know and trust human and institutional counterparties to transactions, all that is necessary is to trust the automated operation of the software network.

Index